BLACK RELIGIOUS INTELLECTUALS

Crosscurrents in African American History

Graham Russell Hodges and Margaret Washington, Series Editors

Writings on Black Women of the Diaspora: History, Language, and Identity
By Lean'tin L. Bracks

The Slaves of Liberty: Freedom in Amite Country, Mississippi, 1820–1868
By Dale Edwyna Smith

Black Conservatism: Essays in Intellectual and Political History
Edited by Peter Eisenstadt

Moving On: Black Loyalists in the Afro-Atlantic World
Edited by John W. Pulis

Afro-Virginian History and Culture
Edited by John Saillant

Unyielding Spirits: Black Women and Slavery in Early Canada and Jamaica
By Maureen G. Elgersman

Historical Roots of the Urban Crisis: African Americans in the Industrial City, 1900–1950
Edited by Henry Louis Taylor, Jr. and Walter Hill

Gender in the Civil Rights Movement
Edited by Sharon Monteith and Peter J. Ling

Hitler's Black Victims: The Historical Experiences of Afro-Germans, European Blacks, Africans, and African Americans in the Nazi Era
By Clarence Lusane

Contested Terrain: African American Women Migrate from the South to Cincinnati, Ohio, 1900–1950
By Beverly Bunch-Lyons

Black Religious Intellectuals: The Fight for Equality from Jim Crow to the Twenty-first Century
By Clarence Taylor

Rebels, Reformers, and Revolutionaries: Collected Essays and Second Thoughts
By Douglas R. Egerton

Invisible Others/Active Pretences in the U.S. Black Community
Edited by Jean Muteba Rahier and Percy Hintzen

BLACK RELIGIOUS INTELLECTUALS

THE FIGHT FOR EQUALITY
FROM JIM CROW
TO THE
TWENTY-FIRST CENTURY

CLARENCE TAYLOR

Routledge
Taylor & Francis Group

NEW YORK AND LONDON

For Marsha, Jason, Tara, and Amanda

Published in 2002 by
Routledge
29 West 35th Street
New York, New York 10001
www.routledge-ny.com

Published in Great Britain by
Routledge
11 New Fetter Lane
London EC4P 4EE
www.routledge.co.uk

Routledge is an imprint of the Taylor & Francis Group.

10   9   8   7   6   5   4   3   2   1

Library of Congress Cataloging-in-Publication Data

Taylor, Clarence.
   Black religious intellectuals : the fight for equality from Jim Crow
to the 21st century / Clarence Taylor.
       p. cm. — (Crosscurrents in African American history)
Includes bibliographical references and index.
   ISBN 0-415-93326-9 (alk. paper)—ISBN 0-415-93327-7 (pbk. : alk. paper)
   1. African American clergy—Biography. 2. African American
intellectuals—Biography. 3. African American leadership. 4. African
American clergy—Political activity. 5. African Americans—Civil
rights. 6. African Americans—Religion. I. Title. II. Series.
   BR563 .N4 T383 2002
   200' .92'396073—dc21

                                                        2002002622

Contents

Acknowledgments   *vii*

Introduction. Black Intellectuals:
A More Inclusive Perspective   *1*

1   Sticking to the Ship:
Manhood, Fraternity, and the Religious World View
of A. Philip Randolph   *11*

2   Expanding the Boundaries of Politics:
The Various Voices of the Black Religious Community
of Brooklyn, New York, before and during the Cold War   *37*

3   The Pentecostal Preacher as Public Intellectual and Activist:
The Extraordinary Leadership of Bishop Smallwood Williams   *48*

4   The Reverend John Culmer and the Politics
of Black Representation in Miami, Florida   *79*

5   The Reverend Theodore Gibson and the Significance
of Cold War Liberalism in the Fight for Citizenship   *94*

6   "A Natural-Born Leader":
The Politics of the Reverend Al Sharpton   *118*

7   The Evolving Spiritual and Political
Leadership of Louis Farrakhan:
From Allah's Masculine Warrior to Ecumenical Sage   *150*

8   Ella Baker, Pauli Murray, and the Challenge to Male Patriarchy   *181*

Notes   *199*

Bibliography   *217*

Index   *221*

Acknowledgments

Truth be told, I had no intention of writing a book on black religious intellectuals. But due to the inquiry of many of my students at Florida International University on the role of black religious intellectuals, I decided to write this work. This book is due, in large part, to the inquisitive minds and probing questions of my undergraduate and graduate students. I owe a great debt to my close friend Jonathan Birnbaum for his careful editing of the entire text and for discussing many of the ideas of this book. Because of his help this is a much better book. I would also like to thank the School of Arts and Sciences at Florida International University, in particular Dean Art Herriot and Dean Ivelaw Griffith, who served as associate Dean of Arts and Sciences until very recently, for their financial support of this project.

I would like to thank Graham Hodges for his encouragement and his urging that I submit my manuscript to Routledge. I owe many thanks to Richard Gringeri for reading, commenting on several chapters, and helping with their conceptualization. Richard's keen mind and generosity helped me shape this book. I would also like to thank Scott Delany for reading, commenting on chapters, providing me with a lot of material, and spending a great deal of time just talking about the work. I would like to thank my colleague Dan Cohen for his very thoughtful comments and careful editing of chapter 3. I owe a great debt to Devon Wright and Chanelle Rose for assisting me in researching and for sharing their findings on Culmer and Gibson. I would like thank Ralph Ginzburg, Azim Thomas, and Yvonne Williams for allowing me use the wonderful photographs in this book.

My brother, the Reverend Lawrence Taylor, also assisted in discussing and educating me on theology. I owe a thanks to Carol Berkin, Judith Stein, and the wonderful group of graduate students at the City University of New York for allowing me to present my chapter on Smallwood Williams and providing me with a great many helpful comments. Likewise, the comments I received from Felice Lipshitz, James Sweet, Valerie Paterson, and Mary Levitt were extremely helpful.

Last but not least, I would like to thank Marsha for her unconditional love and support. I cannot express in words what she has done to help me with this work.

BLACK RELIGIOUS INTELLECTUALS

Black Intellectuals

A More Inclusive Perspective

Black religious leaders have played a central role in the intellectual life of the United States. The following essays examine representatives of this important tradition which has shaped not only intellectual history, but also the general history of the United States.

The popular image of black religious leadership is usually represented by examples of the charismatic male leader. This book studies well-known examples such as Al Sharpton and Louis Farrakhan and less well-known ministers such as Smallwood Williams and Theodore Gibson. The image of the charismatic male leader raises two important questions. First, what are the tactical limitations and strengths of such leadership? And second, is such a leadership a sufficient definition of what has been or should be black religious leadership? Chapters on A. Philip Randolph, Smallwood Williams, and Ella Baker and Pauli Murray suggest the need for a much wider definition of black religious leadership.

A brief survey of the social science literature demonstrates that black religious leaders are rarely studied for their intellectual contributions. With the exception of Martin Luther King Jr., Malcolm X, and a few icons of the American civil rights and black power movements, there has been a general tendency among scholars writing on black intellectuals in the twentieth century to ignore the black religious community.[1] The people in this important community have had a rich heritage of intellectual discourse and fervent politics throughout its history and have been at the center of the struggle for social equality in America.

Because institutions of higher learning and professional schools excluded American citizens of African origins, the black religious community became one of the few avenues for blacks to gain leadership positions and challenge inequality. Black pastors, ministers, and other religious figures became the most prominent activists and black intellectuals in the country. They became writers and orators, interpreting and debating issues that had a direct impact on people of the African diaspora. Because of the brutal impact of racism, black intellectuals combined political activism with their intellectual work. Hence, through artistic and scientific achievements, theorizing, and cultural criticism black intellectuals have dedicated themselves to being "responsible for the race." This has also been true of black religious intellectuals. Unfortunately, their important role has not been reflected in the academic literature.[2]

The most important work to date on black intellectuals is Harold Cruse's *Crisis of the Negro Intellectual*. Cruse takes aim at black intellectuals for adopting a left-of-center politics, becoming too intellectually dependent on white leftists, and ignoring cultural black nationalism. They have failed, according to Cruse, to offer independent leadership to black America. A major fault with Cruse's work is that, despite its length and the large number of people examined in it, he fails to pay attention to black intellectual religious figures.

More recent publications have also ignored the black religious intellectual. Kevin Gaines's *Uplifting the Race: Black Leadership, Politics, and Culture in the Twentieth Century* critically examines the writings of several black intellectuals in the twentieth century, some of whom adopted various approaches for black equality. Some of the people examined in Gaines's book could be classified as integrationists, black nationalists, black radicals, and conservatives and accommodationists. His otherwise insightful and critical examination of several men and women and their various approaches to leadership and views on race, class, and gender oddly enough does not include any black religious thinkers. The same is true for William D. Wright's *Black Intellectuals, Black Cognition, and a Black Aesthetic*. Adopting what he calls an "Africancentric" approach, Wright questionably argues that, for historical reasons, black Americans have developed unique cognition systems in which their ideational components and organizational logic differ from those of white Americans. Hence, it is the job of black intellectuals to shape a black aesthetic that is in line with black cognition systems. Like Cruse, Wright blames black intellectuals for being confused and dependent on other intellectuals and too inhibited to act on behalf of black people. Like Cruse, Gaines, and others, Wright pays no attention to twentieth-century black religious personalities.[3]

William Banks, Cornel West, Henry J. Young Jr., Randall Burkett and Richard Newman, and Mark Chapman are among a handful of scholars who do pay attention to black religious thinkers. In *Black Intellectuals* Banks notes the contribution black clerical figures, black churches, and other black religious institutions have made to higher education, science, literature, journalism, history, politics, and the black freedom struggle. However, Banks's examination of black thinkers in the twentieth century does not pay attention to religious intellectuals. In his survey of intellectual life in the twentieth century, he discusses W. E. B. Du Bois, Booker T. Washington, James Weldon Johnson, figures of the Harlem Renaissance, including Zora Neale Hurston, Langston Hughes, and Wallace Thurman, and the black left of the 1920s and 1930s, but he does not mention black religious thinkers. The same is true of the later part of the century. Banks explores the writers of the 1950s, the civil rights movement, black power movement, and black thinkers of the 1980s, but he fails to turn his attention to religious intellectuals. In fact, he notes that by the 1960s the "ministry, once an important career for black intellectuals, declined in importance. The eminence of theologians such as Howard Thurman, Gardner Taylor, and later Calvin Butts could not stem the tide of blacks aspiring to secular intellectual careers."[4] In his biographies of 116 black intellectuals who lived in the twentieth century, only two are ordained ministers.[5]

In West's book, *Prophetic Fragments*, the only black religious intellectual who receives any attention is Martin Luther King Jr., whom he labels an "organic intellectual." Although black clerical figures are mentioned in other essays, none are seriously examined. This is also true in West's *Prophesy Deliverance: An Afro-American Revolutionary Christianity*. In chapter 4 of the book, "Prophetic Afro-American Christian Thought and Progressive Marxism," West examines what he calls the "prophetic Christian tradition" and takes the reader on a journey in American history by listing "prophetic Christian leaders" who critiqued slavery from Gabriel Prosser and Nat Turner to proponents of black theology who critiqued "U.S. capitalism." Although it is unlikely that West would not deny the importance of black religious leaders, there is only a cursory examination and no in-depth look at these "prophetic Christian leaders."[6]

But major exceptions to this trend have been Henry J. Young's *Major Black Religious Leaders since 1940* and Randall Burkett and Richard Newman's *Black Apostles: Afro-American Clergy Confront the Twentieth Century*. Young examines the early development, religious philosophies, and contributions of several black scholars to religion and the black freedom struggle. Among the fourteen thinkers are W. E. B. Du Bois, the theologian and scholar Howard Thurman, the leader of the Nation of Islam Elijah Muhammad, Martin Luther King Jr., Jesse Jackson, and advocate of black theology James Cone. Young maps out how these figures connected black liberation to religion. According to Young, "Black religious leaders have integrated the religious and social dimensions of existence into a functional approach to social reform."[7]

Burkett and Newman's edited book consists of chapters from various scholars who scrutinize the thoughts and activities of fifteen black thinkers who helped shape African-American religious thought in the twentieth century. Among the fifteen are Edward Wilmont Blyden and his doctrine of race personality, which stressed that all races are unique and make contributions to humanity; Arnold J. Ford's notion of black Judaism and the redemptive role of people of the African diaspora; Gordon Blaine Hancock's advocacy of moral and social uplift, support of the New Deal welfare state, and interracial cooperation; sociologist George Edmund Haynes's theory of racial harmony, and William J. Seymour's Pentecostalism.[8]

Major Black Religious Leaders since 1940 and *Black Apostles* were published in the late 1970s. Despite their contribution to understanding the role of black religious thinkers, scholars since the publication of these works, almost without exception, have paid little attention to black religious thinkers when writing on black intellectuals in the twentieth century.

One exception that specifically focuses on post–World War II black religious intellectual thinkers is Mark Chapman's *Christianity on Trial: African-American Religious Thought before and after Black Power*. The author has selected five major figures, Benjamin Mays, Elijah Muhammad, Albert Cleage, James Cone, and Delores Williams, all of whom represent a certain movement in the black religious experience that interrogates the relevancy of Christianity to the African-American liberation struggle. The ideological leanings of these men range from Christian integrationist to black theology and black womanist advocates. Unlike other scholars examining black religious thinkers, Chapman turns his attention to sexism. However, sexism is only discussed when the author turns to Williams's womanist views. Gender as a means of identity across sex is never scrutinized in the work. Moreover, the fact that sexism is only mentioned when Williams's womanist views are examined leaves the impression that sexism and gender are the concerns of women alone.[9]

One reason for the dearth of study on black religious intellectuals has to do with the emergence of a class of African Americans, at the end of the twentieth century, who were studying more secular university disciplines and going into fields other than the ministry. These fields included history, literature, sociology, philosophy, the various sciences, and art. For this group of university-trained scholars, intellectuals such as Du Bois, Carter G. Woodson, Rayford Logan, Anna Cooper, Franklin Frazier, Alain Locke, and Mary Church Terrell became (and remain) a major focus. Literary and artistic figures of the Harlem Renaissance and later periods such as Zora Neale Hurston, Langston Hughes, and Paul Robeson have also received a great deal of attention, while the ideas of those outside of the academy and the arts, especially those in the ministry, have received scant attention. For the most part they are seen only as activists, and very little attention is paid to them as intellectuals. Even less attention is given to their religious outlook. One can assert, without embellishment, that when examining the black intellectual tradition, especially in the twentieth century, scholars have, for the most part, secularized this endeavor.

Secular black scholars and activists have also had a long history of criticizing the black church. This represents another reason for the omission of black religious intellectuals in discussions of black intellectuals of the twentieth century. This criticism begins in the 1920s. Critiques offered by those in the Harlem Renaissance, black nationalism, and growing black radical left depicted the black clergy and black churches and religious figures at best as irrelevant and at worst as detrimental in the fight for freedom. Writing during the Harlem Renaissance, sociologist Charles S. Johnson argued that black churches were growing more distant from the New Negro. Johnson contended that "a new type of Negro is evolving—a city Negro":

> In the new environment there are many and varied substitutes which answer more or less directly the myriad desires indiscriminately comprehended by the church. The complaint of the ministers that these "emancipated" souls

"stray away from God" when they reach the city is perhaps warranted on the basis of the fixed status of the church in the South, but it is not an accurate interpretation of what has happened. When the old ties are broken new satisfactions are sought . . . it is not uncommon to find groups who faithfully attend church Sunday evenings and as faithfully seek further stimulation in a cabaret afterwards.[10]

During the civil rights era black churches and certain black ministers played a central role in the freedom struggle, but by the mid-1960s, with the emergence of the black power movement and the birth of black theology, black religious figures again came under attack. Religious figures in the civil rights movement were described as members of a class of Uncle Toms, working for the cultural hegemony of the larger white society. According to proponents of black theology, black churches and black ministers lost their revolutionary fervor by the dawn of the twentieth century and became advocates of accommodation. Those who saw ministers as Uncle Toms have little reason to study them.

Another significant reason for the lack of focus on black religious thinkers is that those writing on black intellectuals find the secular revolutionaries, such as Du Bois, Cyril Briggs, Hubert Harrison, C. L. R. James, and, most recently, Amiri Baraka, much more attractive characters. One explanation for the amount of attention these figures receive could be that in large part they reflect the politics of those writing about these revolutionaries.[11]

It is not only black religious intellectuals who have been neglected by social scientists; religion in general has been slighted by the social sciences. Recently this has begun to change. There is an emerging literature on church history and religion in most disciplines.

The problem with many general works that have examined American religious intellectuals and American intellectual thought is that they exclude African Americans entirely. This nonrecognition of black religious intellectual thought dismisses the intellectual capital and activities of African Americans. The scarcity of information about black religious figures as intellectuals presents an incomplete picture of black intellectual traditions. The near nonappearance of black religious thinkers in the literature on black intellectuals and American religion forges the view that few if any religious figures were among this group. It also leaves the racist impression that African Americans stress intuition and not analytical thought.

W. D. Wright contends that black intellectuals have always considered "themselves the voices of black people . . . and have assigned themselves a role to help Blacks develop and to achieve full freedom in America."[12] This is also true of black religious intellectuals. People of the African diaspora have consistently contested the low socioeconomic and political position assigned to them by the larger white society. Just as important, they confronted the racist images employed by white America to justify black subjugation, vigilante and state terror, and the continual project of denying them social citizenship and a sense of belonging. In order to understand and confront these challenges many turned to various forms of religion. Hence, African-American religious figures have been fiercely engaged in attempts to improve the lives of blacks in America. African-American religion should be treated as a significant part of the American religious, intellectual, and political traditions.

African-American religions are not fixed categories but always under construction. Thus, people of African origins have been consistently constructing religious notions useful for black liberation. The categories of race, gender, and citizenship have been tied to the quest for equality and freedom. African-American religious thought has been a crucial tool in understanding and confronting these struggles.

For many in the black religious community in the United States and some outside of it, connecting religion to political struggle has remained an important element of analysis and the freedom struggle. Black men and women who combined politics with a religious worldview were able to motivate numerous people at the same time that a black secular left was being silenced by right-wing and moderate forces outside and within the black communities. The messages and reasons why some politically active religious figures were successful in attracting attention is the major focus of this work.

A variety of leadership styles and models as well as ideologies have been evident in the black religious communities. These ideas have blurred secular and sacred, combining church and state, religious beliefs and secular doctrines. Some religious figures examined in this book combined religious tenets with modern views, such as socialism and the welfare state, and liberal theology advocating a discourse of universal equality, social justice, and equality under the law. Others adopted premodern notions, challenging present modes of inquiry and knowledge based on science and instead relying on earlier forms of knowledge that were more religiously grounded. All these active figures carved out a political space proving that religion was not the sole property of conservative forces but belonged to liberal, left, and other religious people who do not fall into specific political categories.

Black religious intellectuals have adopted a universal approach because of their argument that they are responsible for the well-being of the race and nation. The religious figures in this book have adopted what philosopher Antonio Gramsci described as "organic intellectuals." They are not ivory tower intellectuals divorced from their constituents. They came from and represent the interests of the social group they represent. These religious figures struggle for what philosopher Michel Foucault called the "exemplary" and the " just-and-true-for-all." All of these figures are subjects who defy being defined simply as the other by those having power. The figures in the book attempt to expand the meaning of citizenship in the United States to include people of African origin. Their argument has rested on the premise that inclusion benefits not only them but also the entire nation. They instead labored at defining themselves and the social group they represent.[13]

This book is not limited to a specific region but examines religious personalities in various parts of the nation from the second decade of the twentieth century to the start of the new millennium. At the beginning of this period migration led to massive growth of black urban centers. As black communities grew, churches and other religious entities were formed, and existing ones experienced congregational growth. The development of urban black communities and religious institutions helped spur the expansion and activities of civil rights organizations and grassroots movements. Historians and other scholars have documented the role church people have played in the black freedom struggle. What is less evident in the literature is the way black religious intellectuals interpreted and conveyed the black freedom struggle by using religion, gender, citizenship, and other markers of identity to frame it. One important objective of this work is to do just that. Examining how some of these black religious thinkers constructed blackness and black manhood is an important theme in several of the chapters. For these leaders denomination and church affiliation are less important than how they situated their struggles in a specific religious or secular context. The figures examined range from Pentecostals to atheist.

Chapter 1 takes a look at the religious world of A. Philip Randolph. One may ask why Randolph is included in a volume that focuses on black religious intellectuals. Because, like the other figures in this work, the leader of the Brotherhood of Sleeping Car Porters (BSCP), although a socialist, did not rely on Marxist or socialist discourse to interpret and explain the struggle of the BSCP against the Pullman Company; instead, he relied on biblical and religious ideas to construe and elucidate to porters and the nation the contest for recognition of the union as the sole collective bargaining agent for the porters.

Most scholars writing on Randolph have argued that the labor organizer and civil rights leader was a nonreligious figure who was critical of black ministers and churches. They assume that because Randolph declared himself an atheist and on occasion voiced disdain for black preachers and religion, he either had little to do with the black religious world or, at best, manipulated it in his fight against the Pullman Company. However, few historians and scholars have examined how he used religion and religious symbolism in the struggle to win recognition of the Brotherhood from the Pullman Company. The records of the Brotherhood demonstrate that Randolph used religious language and symbols when communicating with individuals and the membership of the union. His reliance on religious symbolism was more than manipulation. It reflected the impact the African-American religious world had had on him. Because he was an atheist does not mean that Afro-Christianity did not have an impact on his ethical views. This chapter examines the impact black religious cultures had on Randolph and how he relied on the black religious community. When identifying black religious intellectuals this book goes beyond boundaries constricted by denominations and even proclamations of religious faith. By including Randolph in a book on black religious thinkers it focuses on how religion became central to their interpretation of the social, political, and economic conditions faced by people of the African diaspora in the United States.

Chapter 2 turns to Brooklyn, New York, for a close examination of competing religious ideologies during the cold war. Despite the attempt by the anti-Communist network to silence left voices during the cold war, liberal and radical religious voices were heard. The chapter explores three major religious voices among the black clergy of Brooklyn both before and during the cold war. Despite the marginalization of such prominent left figures as W. E. B. Du Bois, Paul Robeson, and others who were associated with secular radical forces, Brooklyn's African-American Christian clergy grounded their progressive politics in Christian doctrine, and they were quite vocal.

The three major voices that were apparent during this period were Afro-Christian liberalism, black Christian radicalism, and black Pentecostalism. All three voices challenged racial inequality, and, to a certain extent, class inequality. Afro-Christian liberalism and black Christian radicalism blurred the lines between the sacred text and secular political dogma while black Pentecostalism adhered to what it saw as a "pure" Christianity to address those social, political, and economic problems confronting the black Brooklynites. Central to all three movements was identity. Closely connected to their ideological views was the presentation of blackness by these three groups. While challenging racial inequality, Afro-Christian liberalism virtually never turned its attention to gender and sexuality. The insider, power broker, connected to those with power was strategy and image presented by Afro-Christian liberals. While certain black Christian radicals challenged patriarchy, that was not central to their religious-political critique. The "defiant man" and revolutionary were central to their form of identity politics. Their critique of black church cultures emphasized the issues of class and race. Black Pentecostalism also emphasized a class and race view that criticized a society that denied blacks access to material comforts. They instead offered a spiritual alternative that could result in changing the world.

One of the most dynamic religious leaders of the post–World War II period was Bishop Smallwood Williams, founder of the Bible Way Church of Our Lord Jesus Christ World Wide, Inc. Because of his interpretation of the scriptures, he became an advocate of an individualist approach to struggle rather than a collective one. He presented an important brand of black Pentecostalism and leadership style. He embraced Afro-Christian liberalism and called on the state to intervene in the fight for racial and economic justice. Unlike other Pentecostal pastors of his day, his sermons and writings combined the secular and the sacred. He argued that black pastors must be politically active by being advocates for social justice. However, he was not just a religious and political theorist but also an activist who struggled to end segregation in Washington, D.C. But Williams's style of leadership was just as important as his activities. The bishop took part in a gendered form of politics by advocating patriarchal and masculine ideology. Thus, he became an advocate of essentialist gender roles in the public sphere. Because of his interpretation of the Scriptures, he became an advocate of an individualist approach to struggle rather than a collective one.

Chapters 4 and 5 move from the North to the South and turn attention to two of the most prominent black leaders of Miami in the twentieth century, both of them of Bahamian origins. John Culmer, considered the city's leading black voice during the 1930s and 1940s, adopted a method of accommodation in a period when there was little militant civil rights activism. Culmer indirectly challenged Jim Crow by adopting what historian Neil McMillen calls "feasible limits." He maneuvered around the Jim Crow system by stressing harmonious race relations. His objective was to win concessions for African Americans in Miami within a white supremacist structure. For Culmer, the best means to an end was not to count on a liberal state or the use of coercion but to rely on the good will of the white elite. Culmer contended that the white elite was more interested in developing harmonious race relations than racial terror.

On the other hand, Rev. Theodore Gibson emerged at the height of the civil rights era as a leading proponent of integration in Miami, Florida. His objective was to win equality for African Americans by legally dismantling Jim Crow. However, despite their differences in approach, both Culmer and Gibson took part in cultural politics by attempting to reshape the black image. They used the signifiers of class, race, and nation as a means in the incessant black liberation struggle. In a period of Jim Crow, Culmer relied on a class-based politics that portrayed the black elite as guardians of a black bourgeois culture. He portrayed himself and others of his class as abiding, congenial, and hardworking, as embracing middle-class values, and as advocates of law and order. A politics of respectability was evident in his approach to politics. Gibson embraced cold war liberalism and reliance on the state. The Episcopalian rector, like Culmer, constructed a black image that was not subversive of the state but loyal and anti-Communist and deserving of full citizenship.

Chapter 6 critically examines the career of the Rev. Al Sharpton and his later attempt to reconstruct his image and situate himself in the struggle for social and racial justice. No other black religious figure has drawn so much attention in New York City since the days of Adam Clayton Powell Jr. and Milton A. Galamison as he. Considered a "natural born leader" by some of his followers and a charlatan by some of his adversaries, this leader and intellectual in a postmodern world has managed to evolve into a cultural icon and major player in city and national politics. He has offered a flamboyant leadership style that continues to stress a nationalist approach. But as his popularity grows, he has attempted to reach an audience across race, class, and gender categories.

By the 1980s, Minister Louis Farrakhan, head of the black nationalist messianic sect, the Nation of Islam, became the most controversial black ministerial figure in the United States. Biographies and numerous articles have been written on the dynamic and controversial Muslim leader. His

Million Man March in October 1995 attracted hundreds of thousands of black men across the nation to Washington, D.C., and proved that despite the attempt by the media, politicians, and others to demonize him and the relatively small membership of his organization, he remains one of the most popular figures among African Americans. Chapter 7 explains the reasons for Farrakhan's popularity by tracing the history of the Nation of Islam (NOI), Farrakhan's and the NOI's construction of black victimization and triumph, and their strong reliance on patriarchy. Unlike other figures examined in this book who have fought for legal and cultural citizenship, Farrakhan in his early leadership fought against belonging to the American nation-state and today remains ambiguous about it at best. To be sure, Farrakhan has attempted to reconstruct his image and that of the NOI by moving away from its racial essentialist position to one of religious ecumenicalism. He has even claimed to abandon his goal of creating a racially exclusive nation with black men as the central force in it. He has even dedicated himself to bridging and healing the rift between blacks and Jews.

The work concludes by focusing on the activities of Ella Jo Baker and Pauli Murray. While some of the men examined in this work relied on patriarchal models of leadership and did not challenge sexism at the same time that they fought racism, Baker and Murray were two leading opponents of the patriarchal mission of male ministers and Christian institutions. They directly confronted a male leadership that refused to accept a more inclusive definition of equality. Baker and Murray were involved in two systematic struggles. On one level they confronted the racism of the broader society, and on a more immediate front they were forced to deal with the chauvinism of their own ranks. Their efforts should now cause scholars and activists alike to reconsider the utility of relying so centrally on a model of charismatic black male leadership. Their efforts demonstrate that black religious leadership has always been much broader than simply a black male model. Finally, the concept of leadership itself needs to be reconsidered. While all of the figures in this work have used this approach, I contend that in a time of turbo-capitalism, the movement of production by those who control capital, the weakening of the institutions of labor, the destruction of the welfare state, and the ecological and crimes committed by multinational corporations, the charismatic or prophetic leadership championed today by black religious intellectuals and leaders is quite problematic. In the absence of strong and coherent social movements for social justice, charismatic leadership has led to, at best, power-broker politics.

Black Religious Intellectuals: The Fight for Equality from Jim Crow to the Twenty-First Century is not a comprehensive examination of black religious leadership but argues that more attention needs to be paid to the thoughts and ideas of black religious figures because they have greatly contributed to the black intellectual and American political tradition.

CHAPTER I

Sticking to the Ship

Manhood, Fraternity, and the Religious Worldview of A. Philip Randolph

On July 16, 1926, the African-American socialist, president of the Brotherhood of Sleeping Car Porters, and avowed atheist, A. Philip Randolph, issued a letter to the Organizing Committees, Organizers, Secretaries and Treasurers of the Brotherhood of Sleeping Car Porters (BSCP), declaring: "We are now in the high tide of our struggle. Let us rejoice and be glad, for the God of Justice and freedom is our captain and salvation." Randolph gave instructions to the recipients of the letter that his statement should be read at meetings of the Brotherhood. For a person who described himself as an atheist and antireligious this language seems odd, because he invoked the very entity that scholars have noted he rejected.[1] Even the term *rejoice*, a biblical term, seems out of place for a person who has been accused of rejecting the religious world of his father.

Indeed, many Randolph scholars have noted his views on religion and concluded that the union leader and civil rights activist was hostile to religion and in particular to the black clergy. Biographer Jervis Anderson argued that although Randolph was the son of an AME preacher and attended Methodist and Baptists churches when he moved to Harlem at the age of twenty-two, he stopped being a "son of the church." His interest in black churches was "more intellectual than religious" (as though the two are diametrically opposed). In fact, Anderson contended that Randolph started having doubts about religion before he left Jacksonville, Florida, and that "after being drawn into the world of politics and protest, Randolph had stopped going to church altogether." Anderson asserted that Randolph did not brush off black churches but made a distinction of the social, political, and economic value compared to their spiritual dimension. Anderson writes that during interviews Randolph told him that the black church was "the most powerful and cohesive institution in Negro life." Anderson concluded that Randolph "had ceased to believe it had value as a religious institution." He believed there were too many black clergy who were selling heaven to the people.[2]

Anderson placed Randolph in the militant political camp of W. E. B. Du Bois. "It was [Randolph] who rallied the most militantly around the Du Bois banner [as opposed to Booker T. Washington's]. He had found *The Souls of Black Folk* to be the 'most influential book' he ever read."[3] Thus, Du Bois's politics shaped Randolph. Anderson makes no mention of religion having any impact on Randolph's worldview. Biographer Paula Pfeffer has also made the claim that Randolph had divorced himself from a religious worldview. According to Pfeffer, Randolph believed "that the black church was a reactionary institution because it bowed to the money power in the community." Randolph and his associate, socialist Chandler Owen, "also criticized black preachers for failing to educate the people and rouse them against the evils of disfranchisement and lynching. The editors of the *Messenger* [Randolph and Owen] thought the churches would be performing a higher function if they served as places to house cooperative stores."[4]

In her portrayal of Randolph's atheism, Pfeffer notes he believed the black churches were inadequate. "Not only did emphasis upon the next world dilute pressure for change in this one, but black preachers failed to encourage their flocks to protest racial oppression because of the financial support they received from white capitalist philanthropists. As these benefactors were also opposed to labor organizations, whether black or white, black churchmen were antagonistic toward the BSCP, giving Randolph no cause to change his opinion of the clergy." However, Pfeffer contends that Randolph recognized the social significance of black churches, and so attempted to manipulate black church culture. "Despite his opposition to the church, Randolph now realized, as he had not earlier, the dependence of his followers on the institution. He therefore submerged his own disbelief and appealed to the porters in biblical terms and with evangelistic zeal on behalf of the cause, never hesitating to remind his listeners that he was a preacher's son." She notes that he selected black churches to hold meetings and that the meetings began with prayer. The problem with her assertion is that it is too sweeping and mechanical. Pfeffer presents Randolph as much too calculating, manipulative, and divorced from religion, but nevertheless able to scheme and fool his followers into believing he was one of them. Moreover, there is no mention in her biography of the agency of the black religious community in the struggle to obtain collective bargaining rights for the porters. The head of the Brotherhood held meetings in black churches because he was aware of the connection of black religious institutions and because the members of the clergy were willing to ally themselves with Randolph's efforts. Consequently, it is important not just to see Randolph and the Brotherhood as the only active agents but also to view people from the black religious community as playing a pivotal role in the struggle.[5]

Like Pfeffer, historian Benjamin Quarles declared in his essay "A. Philip Randolph, Labor Leader at Large" that Randolph had an adversarial relationship with black ministers. "Opposition also came from the black clergy, particularly from those black congregations that depended upon white financial support. Reflecting their religious rationality more evangelical denominations were either antiunion or indifferent ('the greater the religiosity, the less the militancy,' writes Preston Valien). He could not rely on the black clergy. Not able to count on black churches, Randolph sought assistance in other black quarters."[6]

Daniel Davis's *Mr. Black Labor: The Story of A. Philip Randolph, Father of the Civil Rights Movement* mentions Randolph's father and his activities as an AME preacher but does not discuss the impact of black religious culture on Randolph. The author admits that as a child Randolph read each chapter of the Bible several times under his father's supervision. According to Davis, Randolph spent hours reading the Bible, Shakespeare, and other classics. In fact, Davis points out that Randolph's favorite hero was the Apostle Paul. However, despite his studying the Bible, there is no mention in the text of the impact the Book had on how he saw the world or on his association with the black religious community.[7]

The problem with the construction of Randolph by Anderson, Pfeffer, and others is that it presents Randolph's politics as strictly secular, arguing that his relationship with the churches was a manipulative one. It was a fact that for all of his childhood and teen years he was immersed in a community where black religious church culture played a central role. By viewing Randolph as an antireligious person who was hostile to the black clergy his biographers assume that one who rejects the existence of God has managed to become free of any religious influence at all.

A closer examination of Randolph's writings and activities during the early part of the struggle for recognition of the Brotherhood of Sleeping Car Porters as the collective agent for porters reveals that Randolph had a more complicated relationship with black churches, ministers, and African-American religion. This son of an AME preacher did not turn away from black ministers but sought alliances with them and relied on the black church community. Randolph did not view the black religious community as homogeneous but saw a divided one, especially when it came to support of the Brotherhood. Despite the opposition of many clergy to the Brotherhood, there were religious activists who committed themselves to the union.

Just as significant to the alliance between the Brotherhood and certain progressive ministers was Randolph's reliance on biblical phraseology rather than on a secular language; when interpreting the battle for recognition of the BSCP, he displayed a familiarity with black religious culture. This reliance on religious language throws into question the construction of a Randolph who completely divorced himself from or was completely immune to religious influences. Randolph's use of religion cannot be explained as pure manipulation or exploitation devoid of any religious influence. Despite his professed atheism, his language demonstrated he was shaped in part by the black church and African-American religious culture. While rejecting the existence of God, Randolph still embraced a religious ethos espousing religious themes such as hope and salvation, faith and deliverance, and the triumph of good over evil. He clearly depicted a moral order to the universe in tune with the world of black church cultures and the religious thinking of the larger society.

Gender, race, class, and sexuality are important categories when trying to understand identity, but these categories cannot be viewed in a vacuum, isolated from one another, when one is examining identity formation. People have several identities, and these identities interlock, playing on one another. The language of manhood was unifying because it was an idea that was shared by many Americans. American society was viewed in gendered terms. The public sphere of politics and work outside the home was viewed as the male realm. The private world of home and family was viewed as the female realm. This view of divided gender spheres survived well into the twentieth century, and was held by many people across racial and ethnic lines. In forging a collective identity for the BSCP, Randolph and members of the Brotherhood engaged in the rhetoric of proper spheres for black men and women.

Like gender, race and religion played an important role in the construction of black manhood. In the case of A. Philip Randolph and the Brotherhood of Sleeping Car Porters, they became important identity markers in the definition of the union man. In fact, being a good member of the union was described as being a good "union man." Even the name of the union, "the Brotherhood," also reflects this male emphasis. Standing up for the race was being a "race man." Randolph challenged the view of manhood that had become synonymous with white men in a racist society by defining black manhood as masculine, intelligent, dedicated to the family and race, fraternal, and religious and moral. Thus, African-American religious cultures played an important role in defining black manhood, and race played a role in contesting the definition of manhood.

While proclaiming a disbelief in a deity, Randolph did not completely divorce himself from black religious culture or community. In fact, he embraced various aspects of Afro-Christianity, including interpreting the struggle in religious terms rather than relying on a discourse of class struggle.

Randolph's model of unionism was similar to what historian Susan Curtis calls the New Protestantism that emerged in the late nineteenth century. With the advent of rapid industrialization, urbanization, and immigration, working-class people faced a host of problems in the workplace and at home in urban centers. The Victorian morality of self-reliance and the belief in the Horatio Alger myth gave way to a greater stress on the social gospel and greater emphasis on an activist government state. Preachers and others reformulated the old Victorian morality and instead argued that growing societal problems caused by industrialization had to be handled, not by individuals but by society as a whole. Advocates of the New Protestantism moved away from individual initiative to cooperation. They became advocates of the social gospel. Like the old Victorian Protestantism, stress was on marriage and family and improving the material and spiritual conditions of the working class. Under the New Protestantism people had two obligations: one was to improve oneself, the other was to improve society. Improvement would be brought about through collaboration and societal help. This New Protestantism laid the groundwork for reform movements to eradicate poverty and disease as well as to change immoral behavior. Curtis writes that the "social gospelers launched a campaign to attract the working class by supporting their class interests for fairer working conditions, by easing the discomfort of their lives with material and medical assistance and by living among them, sharing their burdens and speaking to them as brothers and sisters with a message of hope." By the early twentieth century, proponents of the social gospel had created the institutionalized church, a body that offered a number of social services to its parishioners and the community.[8]

Curtis argues that through a shift in religious thinking, proponents of the social gospel created new meanings of God, Jesus, and manhood in the late nineteenth and early twentieth centuries. The New Protestantism moved away from the "angry Jehovah" of the eighteenth century to a God who was a "kind parent" and befriended people. Government was expected to follow a similar role. The New Protestantism also depicted a more masculine Jesus who possessed the traits of rugged individualism and at the same time possessed a reform spirit. In books and novels Jesus was reconstructed as a friend who was approachable and civic minded and had a "passion for justice." His attributes—service to people, sacrifice and love, and devotion to humanity—were turned into traits of manhood. Curtis asserted that "Jesus affirmed the social ideal, he relieved the unrealistic burdens of individual success and salvation; but he was not effeminate. The young men who had struggled unsuccessfully to live up to the ideals of the parents in the 1880s helped to create and endorse a new set of masculine ideals that were more appropriate in the larger scale workplaces of turn-of-the-century America."[9]

In his attempt to force the Pullman Company to recognize the BSCP as the collective bargaining agent of the porters, Randolph reached out to the black religious community. Just as important, he employed the New Protestant social gospel in his struggle. Randolph's presentation of manhood stressed several of the traits associated with the New Protestantism, especially masculinity, as essential to cooperation, service, sacrifice, love of Brotherhood, family, and race. But in Randolph's view of the social gospel the alleviation of suffering was not going to be brought about by the state, as many of the proponents of the New Protestantism advocated, but by union activity.

This chapter examines the early period of the struggle as the BSCP sought to become the collective bargaining representative for the Pullman porters. More important, it explores how Randolph constructed an identity of black manhood analogous to the New Protestantism and how this manhood construction became a central component of the BSCP to win support. It also pays close attention to the relationship Randolph forged with the black religious community. This relationship was more than one of convenience. The black religious community that participated in the porters' struggle should not be seen as people being manipulated by Randolph but as agents dedicated to racial and economic equality. Finally, this chapter explores Randolph's language and how this reflected his religious worldview.

This chapter is not an attempt to tell the full story of the battle of the BSCP for recognition but to examine the impact of religion on A. Philip Randolph.

Race Men and "He-Men"

In *Marching Together*, her book on women involved in the Brotherhood of Sleeping Car Porters, historian Melinda Chateauvert contends that early on in the struggle between the BSCP and the Pullman Company, A. Philip Randolph defined the contest as a struggle for manhood. According to Chateauvert: "When a black man could provide a decent standard of living for his family, just as a white union man did, political, civil, and social equality followed. . . . In the early years Randolph's rhetoric stressed the Brotherhood's goal of 'Building Black Manhood.' The BSCP was the vanguard in a new manhood movement, Randolph claimed, for 'only white men are supposed to organize for power, for justice and freedom.' The old porter, the former slave, had passed the way of the wooden Pullman car, and the new porter has come into being." Influenced by the African-American philosopher Alain Locke's concept of the "New Negro," Randolph declared as early as 1919 in a *Messenger* article entitled "The New Negro, the New Crowd," that the new leaders must be made up of "young men" who are radical, educated and unafraid. "Young Negro radicals must control the press, church, schools, politics and labor."[10]

Randolph connected unionism with manhood because he associated the right to bargain collectively with what he and the broader society saw as manhood traits—liberation, economic independence, respect, power, and self-determination. He consistently described the struggle for recognition by the Pullman Company in terms of winning respect for black manhood. In a letter to Milton P. Webster, the vice president of the BSCP, Randolph criticized a conference in which the Pullman Company met with some influential black leaders. Accusing the company of "propaganda" against him, he contended that those "big Negroes" did not speak for African Americans. They were simply selected by whites to do their bidding. In true fashion of attacking the "Old Negro Crowd" and proclaiming the authenticity of the New Negro that was rooted in opposition and defiance, Randolph declared, "One thing I would stress, very fundamentally, never again will Negroes permit white people to select their leaders for them. I would make it very emphatic that upon that principle we shall not compromise, not only with respect to the Pullman porters but [also] with any Negro movement. Negroes will no more permit white people to select their leaders than will white people permit Negroes to select theirs. I would emphasize the fact too, that the Pullman porters organization is a Negro movement, and that it stands for the self-expression and interest of Negroes, for Negroes. I would also indicate to them that it would not matter what the opposition would be, that the question of right of Negroes to change their own leaders is as fundamental as the right of life itself."[11]

Randolph was proclaiming that the Brotherhood was more than a union, representing the interest of the black working class; it was an organization of, for, and by blacks who were struggling for freedom. To support that struggle he used his position as coeditor of the *Messenger*, a monthly magazine of economic and political ideas created by Randolph and his black socialist colleague Chandler Owen. Declaring black independence from white control, the union leader claimed that the *Messenger* was a "new publication which would not permit anybody to dictate what should go into it" and that the Brotherhood "represents a new spirit among Negroes."[12]

He proclaimed the defiance and militancy of the New Negro. He and members of the Brotherhood were "race men" who were the leaders of the African-American community. The New Negro could be classified as an attitude, whereas the race man concept, as seen by Randolph, was a rightful duty of black men. Like the New Protestantism, race men were people who were willing to forgo an individual quest for fame and fortune and define their ambition as a mission to defend themselves, their family, and their race. Randolph's goal was to instill in every porter the notion of "race man." "The Brotherhood expects every man to do his duty. For once, black men are seriously preparing to write their own economic contracts which will benefit their children and their children's children." Like the New Protestantism, the emphasis was placed on helping the downtrodden. According to Randolph, "We stand for service, not servitude. Let us fight and not lose the faith, work and not grow weary. Forward to Victory!"[13]

Randolph even placed the act of paying dues in a context of manhood and race men.

> It will not only be a beautiful and attractive thing [paying dues and receiving a union card], but it will represent the most significant and epochal resolution you could make for the benefit of yourself, your family and your race. Therefore, let me urge you to begin the New Year with a union card, a genuine certificate of manhood. Be able to hold your head erect and look all the world square in the face and say: I am a man, for I am doing the things red-blooded men do; namely, fighting for justice.... Thus, dear brother, now is the time for Brotherhood men to be men—men who have the guts and courage to go after what they want, to stick until they get it; men who are self-reliant and confident; men who are determined to earn their own self-respect, the respect of the Company, of the public, the respect and love of their wives, children, and friends.[14]

Randolph did not talk about race men in the abstract; he gave concrete examples. In a February 28, 1927, letter to Webster, Randolph praised the vice president of the BSCP for possessing the characteristics of a race man. "Permit me to congratulate you on the fine work you are doing. May I say that the Negro race has been greatly enriched by the personality of men of your type as a result of the great work of the Brotherhood which has brought the New Spirit into the first economic freedom for our group."[15]

Bennie Smith, the Brotherhood organizer in Jacksonville, Florida, was also used by Randolph as a model for the race man concept. In the spring of 1927 Smith had notified Webster and Randolph that he was being harassed and threatened by Jacksonville officials and by black men working for the Pullman Company. They accused him of stirring up racial tension. When Randolph urged Smith to leave or stop selling the *Messenger*, the Jacksonville organizer sent Randolph a note refusing to leave. "Conscientiously, feel Brotherhood cause is so righteously important that a firm stand should be taken. Have fully decided to remain and meet the consequences. This means that I am willing to make the supreme sacrifice. Have sacredly dedicated my all to the promotion of Brotherhood's noble cause." But when lynching was mentioned, Smith eventually left.[16]

Not one to miss an opportunity, Randolph portrayed Smith in the *Messenger* as the model of a race man. He argued that the entire African-American population should thank him for what he had done for the race. Smith's importance was reflected in an event sponsored by the Brotherhood that listed him as a speaker with Randolph and other dignitaries of the BSCP.[17]

Another person promoted by Randolph and Webster as a race man was Morris Moore. Moore, nicknamed "Dad," was a retired Pullman porter who was for a while the key organizer of the union on the West Coast, until the arrival of C. L. Dellums in 1928. Dellums became the secretary of the Oakland branch. The exchanges between Moore, Webster, and Randolph about the elderly Oakland organizer reveal terms of endearment, trust, and respect for a male elder. Moore was held up as a man willing to sacrifice his life for the union and his race. Webster wrote to Moore reminding him of his importance to the cause. "The Brotherhood cannot get along without you very long.... Chicago has the highest respect and utmost confidence in Dad Moore, and we are all looking forward to the time when we can have *One Grand Jubilee*." Moore in turn assured Webster that "I am going to do my part as long as I am living, tell all the porters of your division that I am the same old Dad Moore and I will die fighting for them, all from your old faithful servant."[18]

In several letters to Webster, Moore consistently pointed out his hardship in Oakland. "I wanted to answer before now, but being unable I could not. But I refuse to give up.... We have a hard fight but we will run at any price. If I had someone to stand with me and fight it would not be so hard, but I am in the firing line by myself. But even then I have faith that we will win." In another letter to Webster, dated February 16, 1928, Moore declared that he was down to his last five cents and had had to borrow money to pay his rent for the month and that by March he would be forced out of his house. Despite his difficulties, he displayed the attitude of the self-sacrificing race man. "I will be a man at that.... I will die before I will stop fighting for the Brotherhood." For Moore, who was on the brink of personal disaster, being a race man took priority.[19]

In a plea to Webster, the Oakland organizer asked for $40 to pay his rent because he was broke. Webster reassured Moore that the "Brotherhood will not let you fall as it is your spirit that is largely responsible for the success of the movement in Oakland and on the Pacific Coast." After informing Randolph of Moore's financial situation, the president of the BSCP agreed that the union must help the loyal member "because of his spirit and work in developing the BSCP on the West Coast."[20]

Historian William H. Harris declares, "Dad Moore jeopardized both the odd jobs which Pullman made available for him around the yards and his meager pension when he made a public declaration in favor of the union. His selfless action stimulated reluctant younger parties."[21] Indeed, Moore symbolized the ideal version of race man because he seemed to sacrifice all for the Brotherhood and the race and possessed an unshakable faith. Hence, he became an important public figure to the BSCP and larger community. Randolph and Webster presented Moore as an exemplary union man and a fine role model for the ideal black man.

It would be a mistake to see Dad Moore as a tool of the Brotherhood or as a man whose suffering was used to the benefit of the Brotherhood. It is clear from the exchange between Randolph and Webster that there was genuine respect and concern for the well-being of Moore. Just as important, Dad Moore should not be seen as a passive participant in his construction of his image of the suffering and all-giving union member. His letters emphasized his sworn allegiance to the BSCP, thus helping to shape his image as the ideal union member.

Randolph presented himself, Webster, Moore, and other Brotherhood officials as leaders carving out new territory for black people in the American landscape. Unlike those he despised as the "big Negroes," leaders of the NAACP, the Urban League, and proponents of national organizations who proposed a separatist solution, Randolph and the Brotherhood depicted the struggle for recognition as a model for the vast majority of blacks who were members of the working class. However, the contest went beyond economic empowerment. The fight for manhood became synonymous with the struggle for freedom of the race. The Pullman Company was challenging them as race men because, as Randolph noted, the company was attacking the race. It was natural, Randolph argued, for an authentic man to meet challenges to attempts to rob him of his birthright, his manhood. Hence, the call for action was also to stand up as real men and defenders of black humanity. Like advocates of the New Protestantism, who stressed sacrificing one's individual desires for group needs and improving the larger community, race men were willing to make the "supreme sacrifice" to help improve conditions for the race. Randolph emphasized the race men concept to the Brotherhood in a November 17, 1926, letter to Webster. "The whole race will go forward or backward according as the Brotherhood goes forward or backward. More hinges upon our success than any other single movement Negroes have ever attempted. Thus, our obligation to black boys and girls unborn is to stand by the ship, sink or swim, live or die, survive or perish."[22]

The decision by the Interstate Commerce Commission that it did not have the authority to do away with the company's policy that counted tipping as a means of wage compensation led Webster and Randolph to prepare the BSCP to launch a strike. The strike would be used to force the company to recognize the Brotherhood as the sole collective bargaining agent of the porters. Randolph first called for a conference in January 1928 to discuss strike plans, and at the event attendees decided to create a strike committee to make all final decisions. However, the president of the BSCP did not commit fully to a strike; instead, he used the threat of a strike as a means of forcing the company to acquiesce.[23]

The strike vote was an opportunity to display to Pullman, the entire labor movement, and America the manly character and militancy of the Brotherhood. It was a way of bringing to the fore what they saw as the manly nature of African-American society. In a letter to the BSCP Randolph wrote: "Our program must be to stiffen the back-bone of the men so that they will stand up in the supreme struggle just now facing us. The Pullman Company's attitude is a challenge to the manhood of every Pullman porter with any red-blood in his veins, it is also a challenge to every Negro with any pride of race; for while it refused to arbitrate with Pullman porters it is arbitrating with Pullman conductors," who were white.[24]

In order to win support for the strike vote, Randolph issued a letter to the membership arguing the significance of the vote. The purpose was to get the U.S. Mediation Board to enter and settle the dispute between the company and the union. The decision of the Mediation Board, he wrote, depended "entirely upon the power of the Brotherhood and the power of the Brotherhood depends upon nothing but the large majority of porters and maids who are organized, who are paying dues and who are determined to stick and go all the way with the fight to the finish." Maids, who were union members, were only mentioned once in the letter; it was addressed to the "Brethren" and the emphasis was placed on organizing the "men." Randolph affirmed "that our strike vote must be large, at least ninety percent of the men must sign the strike ballot." Striking an optimistic note, he claimed that "ninety percent of the men and more will sign the strike ballot."[25]

In a tone that seemed to call the men to combat, Randolph declared, "Men, we must take our strike vote in double quick time. The times demand ACTION, MORE ACTION AND STILL MORE ACTION!" While assuring the members that it was safe to sign the strike ballot and that they should not worry about retaliation by the company, he also described what he saw as the very essence of manhood by juxtaposing manly qualities to unmanly ones, "However, if you FEAR, DOUBT, or HESITATE, you have lost before you begin. But if you have COURAGE, FAITH, and CONFIDENCE in the justice of our cause and your power to win, you are just as sure to WIN as it is certain that night will follow the day." The reverse of black manhood is one who lacks courage and is not willing to stand up.[26]

The authentic black men, according to the devout socialist, were "red-blooded he-men'" who "realized that we have gone too far to think about STANDING STILL, TURNING BACK, or RUNNING AWAY under FIRE." In this essentialist presentation of masculinities, real men stand up and do not turn their backs. By gendering the fight for the BSCP to become the collective bargaining agency for the porters, he depicted this contest not in class terms or as one fighting for class interest but interpreted it as a battle for the recognition of the manhood of porters because the company was robbing them of their God-given rights as men.[27]

Randolph's use of gender was also a means of unifying the men. Throughout its history, the black freedom fight has been identified with the fight for manhood. From *David Walker's Appeal*, written in 1829 and addressed to the "Colored Citizens," who equated with Randolph's "men of color" and "brethren," to the black men in uniform fighting for the Union in the Civil War, Spanish-American War, and World War I, to the Niagara Movement and its principles calling for "manhood rights," and beyond, manhood has been linked to freedom and independence of people of African origins. Randolph tapped into the language of black manhood.

Randolph embraced this concept along with the New Protestantism's definition of manhood. To win the battle for union recognition, Randolph appealed to the familiar, socially understood language of manhood. Randolph consistently argued that porters were more than willing to defend themselves. "Remember, we have proven that Negroes could build an organization MONEY COULDN'T BUY. They said we could not do that. We did. Now they say you have a YELLOW STREAK, that you won't stand firm. We shall hurl defiance in their teeth and prove them a demagogic liar and hold our ground. . . ."[28]

The almost complete exclusion of women revealed Randolph's view that not only were they less significant in the labor movement, but they had no leadership role to play in the battle for economic and political rights. Work outside of the home in pursuit of wages was identified as a race-man activity. In 1928 Randolph spoke to 1,500 women of the Women's Club in Los Angles a week before the Negro Labor Conference met in that city. Randolph spoke of the necessity of improving conditions for the black worker, "indicating with graphic force the social and economic advantage that must accrue if the industrial conditions of the black man [are] considered and pointing to the dangers that are inevitable if he is deliberately neglected." In his speech, which was reported in the *Flash*, a monthly magazine published in Los Angles, Randolph equated union membership with manhood. Although he was speaking to women, the magazine did not note that women were mentioned in the speech. When he addressed the founding convention of the Ladies Auxiliary of the Brotherhood in 1938, Randolph said that, by their nature, women were only concerned with the security of their children and the well-being of the family. Work outside of the home was the business and concern of men, whereas women should concentrate on the domestic sphere.[29]

Undoubtedly, his major concern was instilling a sense of manhood in the porters. When the union was first founded, its name was the Brotherhood of Sleeping Car Porters and Maids. The decision to remove Maids from the union's name in 1930 was clearly a strategic move to genderize the union. Employing Maids in the union's name would have put severe limitations on Randolph's use of gender as a unifying force. How could one speak of he-men, race men, and other gendered notions if the union had Maids in its title? To take advantage of this language, Randolph's public rhetoric became gender exclusive.[30]

The removal of Maids, coupled with a masculine discourse, strongly suggests that Randolph and union officials would not have tolerated what today some might call the feminization of their organization. In fact, the head of the Brotherhood portrayed the struggle with the Pullman Company by relying on the hypermasculine language used in warfare. "We have forced the Pullman Company into a dilemma where they are now about to recognize [the Brotherhood as the collective bargaining unit for porters]." He went on to say he felt that the company's "surrender" was very close. In November 1927 Randolph told Webster: "Our program now is to fight harder than ever before and create all of the noise and discontent and enthusiasm possible among men. We must demonstrate that the Pullman Company cannot destroy the Brotherhood and that dealing with it is inevitable."[31] Clearly, the company was out to destroy the BSCP and the union was in a fight for its very existence. The terms *surrender, destroy,* and *fight* characterize this labor and management battle in military terms. Randolph couched the strategies and tactics of the Brotherhood in martial vernacular, preparing for a great showdown with the company. "We are in the final stages of our great, intense and noble struggle for economic freedom. Signs are apparent everywhere that the enemy has weakened and [is] ready to surrender. We scored another victory in securing the National Association for the Advancement of Colored People, the Negro's most powerful organization, to endorse the Brotherhood of Sleeping Car Porters. Many and various attempts were made to defeat us in this purpose, but they failed."[32] When Randolph received word that the Interstate Commerce Commission had decided it had jurisdiction to hear the BSCP case, he declared, "We are making rapid progress. The outlook is that the Pullman Company will be compelled to bow before the Brotherhood."[33]

Randolph prepared for a great showdown with the company. When he learned that the Pullman Company was organizing a wage conference for May 1929 as a way to bypass the BSCP when negotiating wages with porters, Randolph told Webster, "I am unqualifiedly committed to the policy of opposing this election with all of the spirit and fire the organization can muster. We should wage a relentless 'Don't Vote' campaign.... We want to throw the whole weight of the organization against any plan of the company to write another contract with the company union.... Therefore, our program now is to mercilessly attack and assail the plan of electing delegates to a wage conference. Therefore, we should mobilize our forces to throw them against the wage conference idea with all the power that is in us and carry the program with fever heat on until we wreck the machinery." Randolph's terminology does not just attempt to organize the workers but to "mobilize our forces" to "wreck the machinery."[34]

For Randolph, the battle lines were drawn. "We have driven the Pullman Company into a dilemma where it must either destroy the Brotherhood or deal with it." There was no doubt that the strategy of the company was to eradicate the BSCP. According to Randolph the company was "making its last stand now with the hope that it will by giving the porters a little increase through a wage conference 'wreck the Brotherhood.'" Sounding the call to battle, he declared the union must "redouble our efforts, fight and work more strenuously so as to show that the Brotherhood is growing by leaps and bounds, that the fighting spirit of the men is more determined than ever...." He concluded his letter with the salutation, "Greetings to the stalwart fighters. Forward to Victory."[35]

In addition to using the language of war Randolph used the language of fraternalism. The mission of fraternities was to protect their members against hardships in what many saw as a cruel and unjust world. They presented themselves as an extended family, and members were bound not by blood but by having a common enemy and sharing common values and objectives. They even reinforced their bonding by referring to members in family terms such as *brother*. The fraternal spirit was evident in the union's effort to provide death benefits for their membership.[36]

Central to fraternities are rituals. One of the few times that God was directly mentioned by the Brotherhood was in its oath. The secret pledge began with the words "I do hereby in the presence of God and my brothers solemnly swear ... " The last sentence also ended by calling on the Deity for strength when carrying out the manly duties of the union members. "I therefore, of my own volition, upon my honor as a man, worker and as a Negro who has pride of race, pledge in the interest of generations of Negro boys and girls yet unborn, my undying fealty to the letter and spirit of the Brotherhood, so help me God." The pledge echoed all of the themes stressed by Randolph in his effort to construct a collective black manhood; the New Negro and race men who were fiercely dedicated to people of African origins and the theme of the moral man were used to forge an identity for the Brotherhood. It was clearly a gender and race-specific identity by which black men had to be accountable to the race and to God. Similarly, by referring to the biblical patriarchs who were responsible for the well-being of their people, the oath attempted to position the porters as leaders of the race. Aware of the Masonic Oath and realizing the importance of the Bible,

Randolph claimed, "I would advise that we make it quite impressive and ceremonious, using the Bible to solemnize it."[37]

Undoubtedly, a major purpose of the secret pledge was to identify members who would remain loyal and those who could not be trusted. "If a man won't take this Oath, we can't trust him very far. I feel we had just as well know who is who now, and this oath will bring it out." More important, the pledge defines fraternity as a central element in being a union man. Borrowing the idea of an oath from the Freemasons, this ritual of secrecy was designed to initiate in its communicants high principles, virtues, brotherhood, morality, and religious values. Rituals have been modified to satisfy the need of the fraternity. Clearly, some of those needs were to feel safe and secure and accepted in their organization. Randolph and BSCP officials were aware that the porters were unlikely to remain members in the organization if they were made to feel insecure, unsafe, and incompetent. According to M. W. Frater and Claude Brodeur, people "need to be identified with others who have interests, problems and values in common." People need a community in which the ingredients of cooperation, companionship, tolerance, thoughtfulness, and generosity are displayed. "The readiness to serve and to share is the essence of community." An important goal of Randolph's was to get the men to loyally serve the Brotherhood. In order to reach this goal, the organization had to be seen as more than a union. It had to be a fraternity.[38]

Onward, Christian Soldiers

In attempting to build the BSCP, Randolph reached out to the religious community. There is no doubt that there were black clerical figures opposed to Randolph and the effort to win the right of the BSCP to be the collective bargaining agency for porters. In fact, the vast majority of clerical figures in Chicago had nothing to do with the Brotherhood, and some even spoke out against its efforts. Despite the clerical opposition, Randolph forged an alliance with some black clergy, and their relationship went far beyond a superficial one or one in which Randolph manipulated some black ministers. On the contrary, the ministers who became close to the BSCP were recognized as progressive leaders fighting for social and racial justice. It was logical that they would enter into alliance with the BSCP.

The Brotherhood's most prominent supporter in Chicago was Dr. William Cook, a left-of-center African Methodist Episcopal pastor who for a while had the largest AME congregation in Chicago. Webster described him as an "outlawed preacher." Because of Cook's left-wing politics, the AME bishop A. J. Carey, who was appointed to his position in 1920, attempted to banish him from the city and remove him as pastor of Bethel AME Church. The AME preacher responded by forming the People's Community Church and Metropolitan Community Center. These structures were independent of the AME, and the pastor was able to dedicate his ministry to working for social uplift outside of the authority of the AME hierarchy. Cook, who managed to attract over 2,000 people to his church, led a campaign to get other black churches in the city to address the social needs of black Chicagoans. Cook's own church became involved with juvenile courts, conducted seminars in industrial relations, and worked with the Communist-led Negro Labor Congress. He even hosted a meeting of American Negro Labor Conference led by Communist member Lovett Fort-Whitman.[39]

Cook openly allied himself with the Brotherhood and allowed the group to meet in his church. Weekly meetings were held in the lecture room at Metropolitan Center until Cook's death in 1930. In fact, on several occasions when the BSCP desired space for a special event, it turned to Cook. In a case in point Randolph asked Webster to arrange with Cook to allow George Schuyler, managing editor of the *Messenger,* to talk about his new article "Our White Folks" in the lecture room of Metropolitan. On another occasion Webster informed Randolph that he was unable to get a big name to speak for a mass meeting. So he had decided to postpone the planned large event and hold a "smaller meeting over at Cook's and get some of the lesser lights to talk." The fact that he could at a moment's notice arrange a meeting at Cook's church demonstrated the pastor's willingness to assist the union. On February 3, 1929, a public mass meeting opening the second Annual Negro Labor Conference was held at Metropolitan. Randolph and Burton were listed as speakers at the event. To help attract a large turnout, admission was free. In addition to granting space to the BSCP for mass rallies and meetings, Cook spoke at many of their meetings. On August 4, 1929, another public meeting was held at Metropolitan and Cook was listed as one of the featured speakers, along with William Green, president of the American Federation of Labor, and Webster.[40]

There was another reason why the Metropolitan Community Center became so identified with the Brotherhood. It was selected over other venues, according to Webster, because Cook only charged a nominal fee. This was not a financial decision by the pastor; it was a political one. The pastor wanted to make the church available at a cost that the Brotherhood could afford. At Metropolitan, admission to mass meetings was free, indicating that Cook was not out to make a profit by renting space but was dedicated to helping the union. Because of the popularity of Cook and Metropolitan, the venue was an ideal place for union officials and members to bring their case directly to the people.[41]

Despite the Pullman Company's authority and the opposition to the union by a large segment of the black religious community, Cook was willing to stand up and give the Brotherhood space. There black men were able to speak their minds without fear of retaliation. Moreover, Cook allowed his church to be used as a way of physically connecting the union to the black community. With the exception of a few, black newspapers usually criticized Randolph and the BSCP's effort. But Cook gave the union officials and members the opportunity to express their side of the story to the black community.[42] In fact, the militant pastor was so closely allied and dedicated to the BSCP that he encouraged Webster to consider setting up the union's headquarters in his community center. "We have not definitely selected a new place for headquarters," Webster told Randolph in January 1927. "Rev. Cook wants us to come over with him to his new community center. But we have another place in view."[43]

Cook was not the only minister to develop a close relationship with Randolph and the Brotherhood. Dr. Charles Wesley Burton, the Yale-educated Congregational minister and attorney, and the Reverend J. C. Austin, pastor of Pilgrim Baptist Church and one of the most noted black clergy in Chicago, were also ardent supporters of the BSCP. Burton was a minister at Lincoln Memorial Congressional Church until he began practicing law in 1926. Cook and Burton proved more reliable than others when it came to supporting BSCP events. When several community and labor leaders had not given confirmation to appear at the first annual Negro Labor Conference in Chicago organized by the Brotherhood, Webster was able to tell Randolph that at least two pastors, Cook and Burton, had committed to the event. The BSCP vice president wrote of Burton that he was "a minister here in Chicago who has been identified with the NAACP, a very brilliant man, Yale graduate and a man who has a world of experience in the various social problems that concern the Negro." Webster had so much trust and confidence in Burton's ability he even suggested that he might help take the place of one of the learned invited guests. "In the event you are not able to get one of those professors, he could make a good talk on the Negro Worker and education." Burton also was listed as the chairman of the First Negro Conference held in Chicago. Scholar Greg LeRoy contends that it was due in part to the BSCP's close relationship with Burton and David Johnson, president of the Men's Club at Lincoln Congregational Church, that the Congregational ministers in Chicago heard the Brotherhood's case, not once but on at least two occasions.[44]

Dr. Junius C. Austin was also strongly allied with the BSCP. According to historian Beth Tompkins Bates, Austin did not rely on patronage and so remained independent of forces that attempted to control the black clergy, such as the Pullman Company. Indeed, like Cook, Austin committed himself to improving conditions for black Chicagoans by creating outreach programs in his church, assisting and advising workers and opening its doors to the Brotherhood for mass meetings soon after he came to Chicago in 1926.[45] The Baptist preacher allowed his church, Pilgrim Baptist, to be used for mass meetings of the Brotherhood. On October 23, 1926, Pilgrim Baptist Church hosted a mass meeting of the Brotherhood. According to Webster, Austin had "promised to render us every possible assistance to make the meeting a success." Randolph agreed with Webster in September 1926 that the venue for a planned meeting be changed from Wendell Phillips High School to a church "where a collection may be taken." He even suggested Austin's church as a possible choice.[46]

Bates also notes that the Reverend Harold M. Kingsley, pastor of the Church of the Good Shepherd became a supporter of the BSCP by speaking at mass meetings sponsored by the Brotherhood, and Greg LeRoy points out that after Cook's death in 1930, his successor Dr. Joseph Evans, continued to open the church's doors for meetings of the Brotherhood.[47]

At the urging of Randolph, Webster established a Citizens Committee in Chicago. Randolph, who said his objective was to organize several citizens committees throughout the nation, claimed that the goal of the committees was to mobilize public opinion in support of the BSCP. In particular, the general organizer of the BSCP wanted to win public support against the Pullman policy of reprisals against porters who joined the union. Webster managed to get several leading Chicagoans to serve on the Chicago committee, including Cook, Burton, and Austin, who told him that the vice president of the BSCP has his "wholehearted support." Burton even served as president of the committee. Webster also extended an invitation to a Rev. Redmond, who Webster claimed was a "staunch supporter of this movement."[48]

The relationship between the Brotherhood and Cook, Burton, and Austin was more than a casual rapport or an association of convenience; it was a strong indication that a bond and trust existed between these ministers and union officials. Despite the difficulties the Brotherhood faced from many black ministers, the union could rely on the support of these black clerical figures. Randolph's and Webster's attitude toward them was respect and not disrespect. These black clergymen demonstrated their devotion to the BSCP by providing public space that was safe from the clutches of the Pullman Company and where both the "lesser lights" and the most prominent in the union and the community could express their views on the struggle. The churches were used as a means of communicating with the community, a way of fellowship between the union and the community, and a means of raising financial assistance. This particular group of progressive clergy supported the Brotherhood by speaking at its events. Mass meetings were, in part, religious events. Scholar Greg LeRoy notes that, for "forty years, Milton Webster was A. Philip Randolph's emcee; he would rough up the crowd, make people uneasy and agitated. Then came Randolph with the eloquent oratorical style he had honed as a Shakespearean actor: something otherworldly. It was like a hell-fire Baptist preacher bringing on the Pope."[49]

While he developed a strong alliance with Austin, Burton, and Cook, Randolph also attempted to win the support of Congregational ministers. Greg LeRoy contends that the "Congregational ministers were the only group of black clerics who would hear the union out." Moreover, on January 29, 1928, the Lincoln Community Men's Club gave a concert on behalf of the BSCP at Lincoln Memorial Congregational Church. The event was clearly religious in structure, with an opening hymn followed by an invocation by the pastor of Lincoln Memorial, Rev. Albert L. Scott. The high-church culture was evident in the selection of songs performed at the event. Only one song was a black spiritual, "Nobody Knows the Trouble I've Seen." Other songs performed included Bach's Solfeggietto in C Minor, Beethoven's "Für Elise," Low's "Brave Little Soldier," Godard's "Berceuse," and Durand and Moszhowski's "Spanish Dance." The conductor that evening was Dr. William D. Giles of Lincoln Memorial. What is important here is that the concert confirms that support for the BSCP extended beyond the predominantly black denominations such as the Baptist and AME. At least one black congregation in a predominantly white denomination backed Randolph's efforts.[50]

The alliance between the Brotherhood of Sleeping Car Porters and the black clergy extended beyond the city of Chicago; other ministers supported the union's cause in various ways. For instance, Central Baptist Church in St. Louis, Missouri, became the place where the sixth annual Negro Labor Conference was held. The conference was billed as one that would attract labor, white liberals, and people from the black community. According to the BSCP, the conference at Central Baptist had the potential of being "the epochal economic conference yet held by Negroes in this community." A mass rally was planned the day before the event at Central Baptist, and at least four of the thirty-two people who signed the call identified themselves as "reverends." One topic listed for discussion by the conference was "The Negro Worker and the Church." The Rev. George E. Stevens was the discussant.[51]

Some pastors in the New York City black religious community also gave their support to Randolph's efforts. Abyssinian Baptist Church, one of the most prestigious institutions in the city, was led by one of the country's most prominent clerical figures, Adam Clayton Powell Sr. It became the scene of what Randolph argued was "undoubtedly one of the most important speeches ever made by a white leader of a great American movement to Colored Americans." William Green, president of the American Federation of Labor, spoke to an overflow crowd on June 30, 1929, supporting the efforts of the Brotherhood to become the collective bargaining agent for porters. According to Randolph, the address by Green did not only "concern Pullman porters, but all members of our race."[52]

On March 14 nine leading black clergymen in New York City held a meeting at the YMCA on West 137th Street and endorsed the Brotherhood. They included Adam Clayton Powell of Abyssinian Baptist, George H. Sims of Union Baptist, William P. Hayes of Mt. Olivet Baptist, John W. Robinson of St. Marks Methodist Episcopal, William Lloyd Ames of St. James Presbyterian, F. A. Cullen of Salem Methodist Episcopal, A. C. Garner of Grace Congregational, J. W. Brown of Mother Zion AME Zion, and Abner Brown of Metropolitan Baptist. The BSCP claimed that the black ministers represented 100,000 parishioners, or 80 percent of "churchgoers in Harlem." Besides endorsing the BSCP the nine ministers "signified their intention to preach alternately a Brotherhood sermon" from their pulpits.[53]

Not all of the clergy who acted on behalf of porters were strongly allied with the union. Some acted out of concern for the harsh treatment the porters received from the Pullman Company. In a letter to Webster, E. J. Bradley, organizer, secretary, and treasurer of the BSCP in St. Louis, was critical of black clergy of the city for not acting sooner to stop the company from dismissing porters, some of them members of the churches the clergy led. Nevertheless, he gave a list of porters who were fired to a Rev. Jackson who was forming "a committee to go to the Pullman office and try to get [company officials] to put all or some of the men back to work."[54]

The Brotherhood's work with religious bodies was not limited to black churches. The BSCP also cooperated with faith-based organizations outside of the black community. One such group was the Congregational Educational Society. It had been founded in 1815 as a joint project of Presbyterians and Congregationalists, and was originally named the American Education Society. (It changed its name in 1894.) Its objective was to aid "indigent young men of talents and hopeful piety in acquiring a learned and competent education for the gospel ministry." By 1894 it had taken over the Society for the Promotion of Collegiate and Theological Education.[55]

The Congregational Education Society provided financial support for theological students, private elementary and secondary schools throughout the country, and state-supported universities and colleges. Webster was invited to speak at an "interracial conference" sponsored by the society. The vice president confessed to Randolph that he did not know about the organization but he was willing to speak anywhere in order to advance the cause of the Brotherhood.[56] What is important here is that the CES, instead of staying clear of the BSCP and its officials, provided a forum where one of its most prominent leaders could present the side of the union.

While Webster declared he knew little about the CES, Randolph was fully aware of the group and the great opportunity given to Webster and the BSCP. "I am glad to know that you will speak at the Interracial Conference for the Congregational Education Society. That is a group which is very broad and can be of great service to us. You might reach some of the other church organizations through them." He also suggested to Webster that he make a special appeal to the "Congregational ministers to preach a sermon on the Pullman porter and the tipping evil." He was very optimistic that the ministers would cooperate with Webster and even suggested that he ask some of the white ministers who attended the event to allow him to speak at their churches.[57]

The Reverend Edmund Chaffee, director of the Labor Temple in New York, and Randolph cooperated with one another for a number of years. As early as 1923, before Randolph became involved in the struggle of the porters, the civil rights leader agreed to Chaffee's request that he speak at the Community Church in New York on the Ku Klux Klan. Chaffee demonstrated his support for Randolph and the BSCP by consistently purchasing tickets to the fund-raising events sponsored by the union and sent words of encouragement, as in a December 5, 1927, letter: "Wishing you great success in this task of organizing sleeping car porters."[58]

Randolph also noted that the Federal Council of Churches of Christ had completed a survey of the Brotherhood and the Pullman Company. Although the results had not been released, the head of the BSCP expressed confidence in the religious body because of its moral integrity. He trusted the Federal Council because its beliefs were grounded in Christian ethics. He was able to appreciate the council as a morally sound institution. In fact, his confidence in the organization was so great that he expressed the hope that the Council could actually help create a conference between the Brotherhood and the Pullman Company after the survey was released.[59] In its February 9, 1929, weekly newsletter, "Information Service," the Federal Council of the Churches of Christ in America reported on the struggle between the BSCP and the Pullman Company. Although the "Information Service" claimed that it was not "passing judgment upon the issues" of the contest, the newsletter nevertheless gave the union positive press. According to the weekly, the BSCP "constitute[s], one of the most conspicuous examples of the large group of workers employed in personal service whose compensation is paid in considerable part by gratuities instead of entirely by wages." From the 1860s, when blacks were first hired by Pullman, to the end of World War I, black employees had to bargain individually with the company. The Information Service raised the question asked by the porters: "if other workers can deal collectively with their employers through organizations and representatives of their own choosing, [why] should they not do the same?"[60]

While not commenting on the grievances presented by the porters, the Information Service gave the union a venue for airing their complaints against the company. The grievances expressed dissatisfaction with the Pullman Company Employee Representation Plan, accusing the company of maintaining a system of espionage and firing and intimidating porters for working for the Brotherhood, and demanded recognition of the union and an end to the reliance on the tipping system.[61]

Although Randolph worked with some elite religious institutions toward his goal of winning union recognition, he did not neglect the religious institutions of the working class. When Webster informed Randolph that he was setting up a Citizens Committee, the president of the BSCP suggested that such a committee "work the churches in the form of having one of the members appear in one of the services of the church on Sunday and make" a brief presentation and "then request the minister to raise a special collection for the organization following the talk." Webster and Randolph were attempting to set up a church-union network that would forge an alliance whereby information could be disseminated and the community could be directly involved in the struggle.

What is also interesting in Randolph's letter is his respect for these working-class churches. He writes that a "large number of the smaller churches that have no high-brow pretensions will be glad to cooperate." Randolph's understanding of black church cultures outmatched that of the Pullman Company. While the company attempted to buy off the prominent ministerial leadership and pastors of the "leading" black religious institutions, smaller churches remained invisible or insignificant to them. The company turned to the churches it thought had influence. Randolph, on the other hand, recognized the significance of the smaller churches, most likely Holiness Pentecostal and other charismatic institutions. The labor leader was aware of the class division in the black communities He knew that the smaller churches were not high-brow and would have congregations made up mostly of working-class people.

Scholar Robert Lee Sutherland has reported that in the 1920s there were close to 100 Baptist churches and 24 African Methodist Episcopal churches in Chicago. He also pointed out that there were 56 Holiness institutions in the city, including 24 Church of God in Christ churches. Sutherland wrote: "When all the Holiness sects are placed together they total more than any other group except the Baptists." Just as significant as the number of Holiness churches were indications of their class status. Most of the Baptist and Holiness churches were lodged in storefronts and houses, which indicated that many of these congregations were poor. Sutherland further notes that 85 percent of the Holiness churches were located in the "disorganized districts" of Chicago. Sociologists Benjamin E. Mays and Joseph W. Nicholson noted in their 1933 work, *The Negro's Church*, that there were 344 churches in Chicago. The Baptists had the lion's share of churches in the city, with 144. However, Mays and Nicholson found that there were 86 "Holiness" churches.[62]

In a 1945 study of black churches, social scientists St. Clair Drake and Horace R. Cayton found in the predominantly black area of Chicago some 500 churches. According to the authors, 300 of the churches were "located in definitely lower-class neighborhoods." The authors discovered that half of the 30,000 "lower-class people were affiliated with churches. At least a sixth of the 30,000 were members of one of the three large congregations, and another sixth were attending one of the many "medium sized lower class churches." Approximately one-third of the working class in Bronzeville (a black community in Chicago) was worshiping in "remodeled stores, garages, theaters, houses, and halls" and yet another third was attending "high brow institutions." "Lower class theology," according to Drake and Cayton, was "Fundamentalist." The preachers of the institutions made up mostly of the black working class relied heavily on "prophesy," and the parishioners became emotional during the service by getting "happy" or by letting out a shout and "flailing their arms about, crying, running up and down the aisles, yelling Amen and Hallelujah! In fact, many churches have special attendants, dressed in white uniforms, to fan and calm the shouters. Shouting may be set off by a prayer or testimony, by singing or a sermon."[63]

A major question is why Randolph would turn to the black working-class religious institutions for support? One explanation is that, as working-class institutions, they most likely attracted people who were more sympathetic to the cause of the BSCP. Just as important, these institutions probably had no ties to the Pullman Company, and so ministers and parishioners had both the independence and the opportunity to provide support. Randolph knew better than the Pullman Company that class divisions manifested themselves in the religious life of the community. His direction to Webster that he target the smaller churches strongly suggests that the Brotherhood attempted to develop a link not only with prominent clergy like Cook, Austin, and Burton but also with those belonging to the working-class religious institutions.

Randolph sought support even among religious leaders who he was aware were hostile to the Brotherhood. On March 26, 1927, Webster informed Randolph that with the exception of one or two members of the Ministers Alliance of Chicago the group had not been kind to the BSCP. Nevertheless, "we may be able to break the ice." He had written to the president of the Alliance and he was going to address each member. Randolph was in full agreement with Webster's actions and declared that he would be "glad" to meet the ministers if the vice president was able to arrange such a meeting. Randolph and Webster attempted to get the support of the National Baptist Convention even though its president, L. K. Williams, was described by the general organizer as a "hard-boiled reactionary."[64]

The Impact of Religion on Randolph's World View

Scholars writing about Randolph have not seriously scrutinized the impact black religious culture had on his worldview. A close examination of Randolph's words reveals that the connection with the black religious community went far beyond an alliance with ministers. There is no doubt Randolph used language carefully to gain support for the porters. He was conscious of the power of words and selected them to appeal to the membership. A case in point was his criticism of a flyer issued by Webster made for a mass meeting to be held at the Pilgrim Baptist Church. Randolph claimed that the phrase "economic mass meeting" used in the flyer was "too high-brow." He advised Webster that he would have a greater impact if he adopted simpler language such as "Victory Dash Rally etc."[65]

Despite his strategic use of a popular discourse to win the support of the porters, it is apparent from his language and his writing that this son of an AME preacher was quite familiar with the Bible, possessed a sense of important Christian motifs, and had a gift for interpreting and describing ordinary events in biblical language. His use of biblical phraseology to explain the successes and defeats, the good and hard times, of the BSCP strongly indicated that his views were shaped by a religious ethos. Without a doubt, Randolph was cynical about clergy and church members who divorced God and religion from social justice.[66]

Randolph's familiarity with the Bible reveals that he was more than someone who was far removed from religion or who remained outside of the black religious community. A closer look at his language reveals that Randolph stressed the important Christian motifs of hope, salvation, faith and deliverance, and triumph over evil.

The hope and salvation theme was evident in a telegram, dated August 25, 1926, marking the first anniversary of the BSCP. Randolph sent greetings to "our stalwart and militant Chicago Division." "Truth and Justice,"

Randolph declared, "are the captains of our salvation and with the spirits and firm determination [to] fight on we cannot fail.... " A month earlier, as already noted, he declared "the God of Justice and freedom is our captain and salvation."[67] Even when the Brotherhood suffered setbacks, he managed to interpret them as victories. When the ICC essentially ruled against the union, Randolph encouraged Webster: "Be Not Dismayed ... Prepare to create Emergency and Finish the fight. Forward to Victory!" The line "Be Not Dismayed" is from a celebrated hymn, "God Will Take Care of You." Written by Civilla D. Martin in 1904 when she was confined to a sickbed in a Bible school in Lestershire, New York, the song was a way of expressing one's faith and hope in a brighter tomorrow in the face of impossible odds or difficult or circumstances.

> Be not dismayed whatever betide,
> God will take care of you;
> Beneath his wings of love abide,
> God will take care of you
> God will take care of you,
> Through every day, over all the way;
> He will take care of you,
> God will take care of you.[68]

Like the song, Randolph was declaring hope and faith at a time when the BSCP faced a major defeat. Interrelated with the hope idea was one of the most important themes of Christianity, the Gospel, or "Good News." The Gospel provides good news for people who have been transformed from an unsaved life to a saved one. The "saved" are assured eternal life with God. Therefore, the faith of Christians in eternal life led to optimism. The hope and salvation theme was transposed into this struggle against the Pullman Company. In many of his letters, the president of the BSCP employed the good news theme by expressing optimism and hope. In one such letter to the membership, after the Mediation Board decided that it had jurisdiction to hear the union's case, which called on the Board to mediate the dispute between the Brotherhood and the Pullman Company, Randolph claimed: "We have won again. The Board realizes that our case must be adequately heard.... Rejoice and be glad at the signal of victory."[69]

Closely related to hope and salvation theme was the motif of faith and deliverance: If one has faith in God, He will deliver you from suffering. This notion became an important component of Afro-Christianity during slavery. Randolph tapped into this language.

The fact that Randolph emphasized the faith and deliverance theme strongly indicated his awareness of its significance in African-American religion. He emphasized it on several occasions. In one letter he told Webster and the members of the Brotherhood to keep the faith and in the end they would be delivered. At the same time that he called on the concept of faith in deliverance, he also used the Book of James by stressing the theme "Faith without works is dead." "May I urge you to keep ever before the men," he advised Webster, "the necessity of fighting with their might and their money for victory. We cannot lose if we remain organized and keep the faith."[70] Randolph was contending that the combination of faith and works would lead to deliverance from the oppression of the Pullman Company.

In a number of letters Randolph summarized these in a slogan: "Keep the Faith." In one such letter to Webster he declared: "Permit me to assure you again that if we fight and not lose the faith, work and not grow weary, it is impossible for us to fail. Long Live the Brotherhood, Forward to Victory!"[71]

He also used religious metaphors to help accentuate the faith and deliverance theme. A letter to Webster on July 5, 1927, is a case in point. "If we stick by the ship with the spirit that sink or swim, live or die, survive or perish, no power under the sun can halt the onward stride of the Brotherhood. . . . The Brotherhood is as firm as the Rock of Gibraltar, and though the winds may blow and the storms rage, the Brotherhood will stand."[72] The religious symbolism is quite evident in this passage. He was attempting to reinforce the importance of keeping the faith. "Sticking to the ship" was known in religious circles to mean those who had faith would not abandon the cause. The ship, used here by Randolph, symbolized the struggle for union recognition amid the raging sea or troubled times. In this case, those who stuck with the ship or kept the faith during troubled times were exhibiting a great faith and would be delivered.

Sink or swim, live or die, survive or perish—according to the president of the BSCP, members should be willing to pay the ultimate price for the cause of the Brotherhood. It does not matter whether one survives or perishes, one should be willing to give up his life for the cause because the recognition of the union is larger than one's personal safety. Even without the belief in God such language reflects deep spiritual sentiments.

The phrase "no power under the sun" also has religious connotations. "Under the sun" means "anything of this earth"; thus, Randolph implies that the company lacks the power to halt the inevitable victory of the union. Likewise, Randolph's reference to the Rock of Gibraltar also invokes a religious message. In both the Old and New Testaments the rock symbolizes God, one's faith, strength, and fortitude. In 2 Samuel, chapter 22, verses 2 and 3, it reads, "And he said, The Lord is my rock, and my fortress, and my deliverer. The God of my rock; in him will I trust." Again, in Psalms, chapter 71, verse 3, it reads, "Be thou my strong habitation, whereunto I may continually resort. Thou has given commandment to save me; for thou art my rock and my fortress." In Matthew 16, verse 18, Jesus says to his disciple Peter, "And I say unto thee, that thou art Peter, and upon this rock I will build my church; and the gates of hell shall not prevail against it." As a symbol of the strong foundation of the Brotherhood the rock signified the strength of the Brotherhood as like that of Jesus' church. Union members would all have recognized these religious references.

This is not the language of scientific socialism but the language of Randolph's father's world. It is the language of someone who was familiar with that religious world and who was able to couch the struggle against the Pullman Company in a biblical framework.

At the same time that he was emphasizing faith and deliverance idea, Randolph conveyed the theme of triumph in his message to the porters. He consistently presented the theme of good and evil to the porters. There was a moral order to the universe. In the struggle between the forces of good and evil the porters were the righteous ones. It was they who were launching a holy crusade, not for themselves but their families and the race. In a May 5, 1927, letter to Webster, Randolph presented the themes of faith and deliverance and the inevitability of victory of the porters' moral crusade. "We are now in the midst of our great case at last [to gain union recognition], and our outlook is bright for the future. In the nature of things, it is impossible to fail to reap our just reward in due season if we will only first fight and keep the faith, work and not grow weary and realize that a winner never quits and a quitter never wins. We have routed the 'doubting Thomases' and put the skeptics to flight. The opposition is crumbling everywhere."[73] Even the reference to "due season" is a religious reference to Ecclesiastes (to everything there is a season).

When praising Webster for his courage and loyalty, Randolph declared: "Therefore, we need not have any doubts about the ultimate outcome of the struggle. We have only to get the men to stand firm and realize that it is a fight to the finish." Again, he told the vice president of the union and leader of the Chicago division of the BSCP, "Let us realize that though victory be delayed, victory is certain and sure if we pursue vigorously our [program] of organization, education and agitation."[74]

Randolph selected biblical metaphors and slogans that were associated with Christianity because that was the language of those who lived in Afro-Christian communities and most communities in the United States at that time. The use of these metaphors and slogans shows Randolph's familiarity with the Bible and black religious cultures. As the use of the concept of manhood reflected the impact of a patriarchal society on his thinking, so the use of biblical language and religious metaphors reflected other aspects of his thinking and his means of communicating.

Conclusion

The story of the struggle of A. Philip Randolph and the Brotherhood of Sleeping Car Porters against the Pullman Company is important because it was a contest for civil rights and the right of a neglected segment of the American working class to gain the power to bargain collectively. Thus it connected civil rights with labor rights. However, historians and other scholars writing on Randolph and the BSCP have for too long ignored the pivotal role some in the black religious community played in that struggle. Scholars are correct to point out that most black clergy in Chicago and elsewhere did not support the efforts of the porters. Indeed, many opposed their effort to organize and bargain collectively with the company. Similarly, most black churches did not take part in the civil rights movement. In fact, the largest black church body, the National Baptist Convention, and its president, Joseph H. Jackson, were in opposition to the efforts of Martin Luther King Jr. and others in the civil rights struggles of the 1950s and 1960s. But it would be utterly absurd to assume that because most black churches sat on the sidelines during the civil rights struggles religion played no important role in the movement. This is the same case with the Brotherhood struggle. Union members were deeply steeped in the religious traditions and language of late-nineteenth- and early-twentieth-century America. The evidence demonstrates that even an avowed atheist such as A. Philip Randolph was also part of this tradition.

Randolph's writings suggest a complicated relationship with Afro-Christianity. Just because he declared himself an avowed atheist and criticized black ministers for preaching too much heaven and not paying enough attention to the worldly needs of their parishioners, one should not paint him as having lost all connections with religion. On the contrary, his interpretation of the struggle, laden with Christian narratives and themes, indicates that his worldview was strongly shaped by the black church community. The story of Randolph and the BSCP's struggle for recognition point to a need for a close examination of the role religion has had in liberation struggles, even those struggles that seem on the surface to be devoid of such an influence. Too many scholars who write on black liberation struggles and other struggles for social justice ignore the part religion plays in them.

CHAPTER 2

Expanding the Boundaries of Politics

The Various Voices of the Black Religious Community of Brooklyn, New York, before and during the Cold War

Students of African-American history and politics have argued that cold war hysteria and political repression of left forces marginalized the black left. The result was the removal of a serious progressive force that had the potential to steer black America to a left-of-center politics. Instead, black America, according to these historians, moved to the right with little dissent. Noted scholar Gerald Horne, for example, argues in the *American Historical Review* that the attack on black radicals silenced important progressive voices during the cold war. Because radicals were too weak and received little support from mainstream organizations, narrow black nationalism rose to fill the void.[1]

Thomas J. Sugrue argues in *The Origins of the Urban Crisis* that anti-Communism during the cold war "silenced some of the most powerful critics of the postwar economic and social order. Red-baiting discredited and weakened progressive reform efforts. By the 1950s, unions had purged their leftist members and marginalized a powerful critique of postwar capitalism. McCarthyism also put constraints on liberal critics of capitalism. In the enforced consensus of the postwar era, it became un-American to criticize business decisions or to interfere with managerial prerogative or to focus on lingering class inequalities in the United States."[2]

Historian Manning Marable also argues in *Race, Reform and Rebellion* that as the "Cold War intensified the repression of black progressives increased." As an example of the growing suppression, Marable notes that the writings of W. E. B. Du Bois were removed from libraries and institutions of higher learning. The result of such politically oppressive acts, according to Marable, was that "black public opinion moved even further to the right." Although Marable notes that black ministers and black churches were not monolithic when it came to political ideology, the black church was nevertheless ambivalent when it came to dealing with black liberation.[3]

These historians have greatly contributed to our understanding of post–World War II black America. They have shed light on the cold war period and its relationship to African Americans. Sugrue has presented a complex account of the reason for deteriorating inner city conditions, challenging earlier works on the underclass that only look at one variable. In particular, Horne and Marable have given a credible explanation of why some black Americans joined America's cold war effort to stamp out the left. These historians have challenged an earlier historiography that either ignored the significance of black radicals or simply labeled them as tools of the white left.[4]

This chapter examines an important dimension of the black left that has received little attention. African-American religious leaders formulated religious beliefs in an attempt to address the concerns of black people in the United States and elsewhere. In Brooklyn, New York, at least three forms of left religious notions operated, before and during the cold war.

For the most part Afro-Christianity has not been a focus of scholars when searching for alternative left voices during World War II and the cold war period. A closer look at Brooklyn, for example, strongly suggests that political ideological debate was not absent in the black community. In fact, there were at least three ideological positions among the black religious community of Brooklyn. Afro-Christian liberalism, closely associated with New Deal liberalism, was one of the most popular ideological positions among the black clergy of Brooklyn. Pastors of some of the largest black churches in the borough embraced Afro-Christian liberalism. A small but significant contingent of black Christian radicals made up another ideological group. A third group consisted of black Pentecostals. Until recently, scholars examining black Pentecostalism have, for the most part, ignored its political leanings before and after World War II. However, the ministers, joined by their parishioners, were quite visible in the political and ideological debate of the cold war.

Afro-Christian Liberalism

The most prominent ideological group among the black clergy of Brooklyn comprised Afro-Christian liberals. This group crossed denominational lines and was made up of some of the most celebrated ministers in the country. It included the Reverends Gardner C. Taylor, of Concord Baptist Church, Sandy F. Ray, of Cornerstone Baptist Church, John Coleman, of Saint Philip's Protestant Episcopal Church, William Orlando Carrington, of the First African Methodist Episcopal Zion Church, and George Thomas of Brown, of Memorial Baptist Church.[5]

In order to legitimize their positions this group of pastors closely allied itself to the white power structure. The *Amsterdam News*, one of the country's largest black weeklies, called Gardner Taylor the "unofficial Democratic chieftain in Bedford-Stuyvesant." In a display of his political influence the pastor of Concord, a church that reported more than ten thousand members, informed the black weekly in 1953 that he would "field" a candidate for a civil court judge in Bedford-Stuyvesant. Taylor's political allies included such notables as Brooklyn borough president John Cashmere and New York mayor Robert Wagner. In 1952 Cashmere appointed Taylor a member of School Board No. 27 in Bedford-Stuyvesant. Wagner appointed him to an advisory board to improve city services, and in 1958 the mayor named Taylor to the New York City Board of Education. In 1962 Taylor was one of three men selected by Mayor Wagner to replace Joseph Starkey as Democratic leader of Brooklyn.[6]

While Taylor was arguably the most politically influential black pastor of Brooklyn, other ministers had their political connections. In 1941 the mayor of New York appointed the Reverend John Coleman to the Board of Higher Education. In 1949 the Reverend Boise Dent, pastor of Tabernacle Baptist Church in Brownsville Brooklyn, was selected to head Republican politician Abe Stark's campaign for Brooklyn borough president. The Reverend Benjamin Lowery, of Zion Baptist Church, headed a ministers and citizens committee to reelect New York Republican governor Thomas Dewey, and the Reverend George Thomas, of Brown Memorial Baptist Church, was selected by the Republican Party to run for Congress.

The Reverend Sandy Ray, of Cornerstone Baptist Church, was so closely allied with the Republican Party that he was referred to as "Mr. Republican." Serving in the Ohio state legislature before he came to Brooklyn, Ray campaigned for Republican candidates and even developed a close friendship with Nelson Rockefeller, who served as governor of New York from 1958 to 1974. Besides working for the election of Republican candidates, Ray even considered running for office as a Republican.[7]

These prominent black pastors, who had close ties to the politically powerful, were not just seeking political accommodation. Instead, they saw themselves as ambassadors of their race. They believed that their mission was to use their influence to better the black community. They became close to local and state officials and politicians not to gain personal advantage but to win concessions for the community. As power brokers, these men did not call for an alliance with the black working class, but attempted to win favor with the Democratic and Republican parties because the parties controlled and decided how resources and services would be distributed.

The tactic of ambassadorship for the race was not new, and it was not limited to the black ministerial class of Brooklyn. Many historians have noted that the black elite in various black communities at the turn of the century adopted this approach.[8] Although the New Deal had assisted in giving a political voice to those on the margins, including African Americans, the politics of ambassadorship did not disappear by the 1930s and 1940s. In fact, the New Deal helped foster this tactic.

Although most Afro-Christian liberals in Brooklyn were affiliated with the Republican Party, they nevertheless embraced New Deal liberalism, because they were concerned about the poor and were believers in the New Deal State. Their affiliation with Republicans on a local and state level never diminished their faith that the role of government was to assist the disadvantaged, many of whom were members of the churches they led. The New

Deal had expanded the government's role in the lives of its citizens. Its attempt to relieve suffering from poverty by providing aid and employment was embraced by Afro-Christian liberals. Despite the Republican affiliation of most of African Americans they were advocates of the social gospel. Some had received degrees from liberal institutions, and most were active members in the NAACP and the Urban League. Their brand of Republicanism was a moderate to liberal version. They identified with the Republicans because they believed that the party offered them access to power in order to win concessions for the black community. These men headed churches that had thousands of members. Zion Baptist had over twenty-five hundred members. Sandy Ray claimed that Cornerstone had five thousand members in 1952, while the First AME Zion reported over nine thousand members. Because the ministers were in a position to influence voting behavior, politicians, Republicans as well as Democrats, were willing to associate with them. In fact, it was not unusual to see prominent Republican politicians on a Sunday morning at Cornerstone Baptist or other black churches in Brooklyn.[9]

While Afro-Christian liberal ministers viewed the New Deal state as the best avenue to address black grievances, they did not just rely on the government to help the poor. They, along with their parishioners, tried to reconstruct a civic-oriented black community that stressed moral and social uplift. Since the formation of African-American communities, black elites have pushed for moral and social uplift. They advocated that blacks be instilled with Victorian virtues, good moral character, and a strong work ethic in order to be successful citizens. They emphasized strict gender roles, attempting to reinforce traditional roles for women such as mother and home provider.

This notion did not disappear with World War II and the cold war. The black middle class, including members of the black clergy, attempted to shape the behavior of the poor and turn them into "respectable human beings." Hence, the home and family remained an important focus.

One of the most popular family events was scouting. By the 1940s, dozens of Brooklyn's black churches had established scouting programs. Scouting was not just a children's affair, but reinforced bonds among family members. Parents became scoutmasters and den mothers and they adopted other important positions within the scouting community. These activities emphasized the importance of the family and attempted to instill in their children the notion of responsible citizenship and independence. They provided adult role models and helped reinforce traditional family values by creating social space where adults and children could interact in a congenial atmosphere. This type of voluntarism, in particular, attempted to address problems that plagued the black community, including juvenile delinquency.[10]

Because Afro-Christian liberal ministers adopted an ambassadorship type of politics and became advocates of a civic culture, they distrusted militant protest and radical politics. In fact, some members of this Brooklyn group, like other black clergy in other parts of the country, adhered to cold war liberalism. Like other cold war liberals, they were quite critical of red scare tactics used by the anti-Communist network. For example, in the summer of 1953 eight AME ministers issued a statement denouncing Senator Joseph McCarthy's remarks claiming that Protestants were the largest body supporting American Communist fronts. The AME ministers asserted that the Wisconsin senator's accusation followed the method of fascists and Communists: "Such political onslaught is the same process used by the leaders of Communism to rid the nation of God and to destroy the faith of the humble believers." They argued that the true friends of democracy were those fighting for equality. The eight declared that McCarthy's statement was a vile attack on "religion and the faith upon which this nation is founded."[11]

Sandy Ray adopted the approach of identifying their cause with God and country. At a National Baptist Conventions Ray claimed: "Our approach is from the Christian point of view. We have not, and shall not commit our convention to any foreign or subversive ideology. The justification for our fight is within the framework of our constitution and our accepted Christian principles. We are calling for a practical application of the principles of Democracy for all citizens of the United States." Ray also defended Protestant ministers against McCarthy's attack by denying any links between the clergy and Communism. "Neither the Negro Protestant clergy nor laymen have given any support to Communism."[12]

However, cold war liberal ministers were no allies of more left-leaning forces. One strong indication of the distrust that Afro-Christian liberals had of radicals was their refusal to lend support to militant grassroots action. In fact, some black militant pastors complained that their fellow prominent clergy refused to join them in working with the grass roots. The Reverend Milton Galamison, a radical black Presbyterian minister, accused his fellow prominent black clergy of red-baiting and staying away from the Bedford-Stuyvesant Health Council. Although this group, consisting of community activists, struggled to obtain a city hospital in Bedford-Stuyvesant, Galamison claimed that the ministers were staying away from the organization because they believed that it was Communist controlled. When he was president of the Brooklyn branch of the NAACP, Galamison also complained that some distinguished black clergy red-baited the more militant members of the civil rights group.[13]

It should be noted that although many prominent black pastors decided to help lead demonstrations at the Downstate Medical Center construction site in July 1963 to protest the fact that few blacks and Puerto Ricans were hired as construction workers, they attempted to rely more on their political contacts than on the ordinary men and women taking part in the protest. Years after the protests Taylor bragged about his close association with Mayor Robert Wagner. He noted that when a police captain mistreated him, he contacted City Hall and had him removed from his precinct. During the two-week protest against the building trades union and the state of New York, which was building the medical center, Sandy Ray, Gardner Taylor, Benjamin Lowery, and other well-known ministers contacted Gov. Nelson

Rockefeller to work out an agreement to end the demonstrations; they did not to invite the militant Brooklyn chapter of the Congress of Racial Equality, which had initiated the protest. The agreement reached between the governor and ministers essentially gave only promises that the state would enforce already existing antidiscrimination laws and set up hiring halls in black and Puerto Rican areas.[14]

Black Christian Radicals

To the left of Afro-Christian liberals were black Christian radicals. This group consisted of just a few pastors, but they were extremely vocal and gained citywide notoriety. The most noted were the Reverends George Frazier Miller of Saint Augustine Protestant Episcopal Church, Theophilus J. Alcantara of Saint Simon African Orthodox Church, Thomas Harten of Holy Trinity Baptist Church, and the Reverend Milton A. Galamison. Common beliefs united this group. Unlike Afro-Christian liberals who embraced nego-tiation, the black Christian radicals identified with the grass roots and partici-pated in militant action. These pastors linked the issues of race and class and did not hold the faith that the state would address these concerns on its own. They believed that people and powerful institutions that decided on the allo-cation of resources and services had to be coerced into taking action for the working class. Black Christian radicals were not afraid to associate with left forces and even publicly advocated such alliances. Their rhetoric and action placed them in the camp of political radicals. Like Afro-Christian liberals they called for an intrusive role of government in eradicating poverty. However, while Afro-Christian liberals viewed the New Deal state as ideal, black Christian radicals called for greater economic and structural changes. Their vision of the ideal state went beyond just an entity that would assist the poor. At least two of these ministers were critical of capitalism and called for drastic changes in the distribution of wealth.

The Reverend George Frazier Miller was a member of the Socialist Party. Although the Socialist Party officially welcomed blacks into its ranks during its founding convention in 1901, very few joined. One possible explanation for the lack of black members is that, though the party debated the issue of race, it made no special effort to address the concerns of African Americans. The party's main concern was the issue of class. Moreover, southern social-ists were hostile to blacks.

Despite the fact that the Socialist Party did not attract a large number of blacks, the party did have a cadre of black activists during the early part of the twentieth century, including Miller, A. Philip Randolph, Hubert Harrison, and Chandler Owen. These early-twentieth-century black radicals joined the party during its heyday because they believed that the race problem in America would be solved by addressing the class problem. These black socialists were joined by tens of thousands of Americans who gave their sup-port to Socialist candidates. For example, Eugene Debs, the leader of the Socialist Party ran for president in 1912 and attracted nearly one million votes. The party also grew during the early part of the twentieth century. Its membership jumped from 10,000 in 1901 to 120,000 twelve years later.

George Frazier Miller was also active in the Women's Suffrage Movement. He attacked sexism by referring to those who oppose suffrage and equality for women as "he-men." Frazier claimed that because of his involvement in the suffrage movement, he became interested in socialism and joined the party.

Unwilling to associate with the mainstream political parties, Miller ran for Congress as a Socialist candidate. His activities also included writing and editing A. Phillip Randolph's socialist journal, the *Messenger*. He opposed war and refused to fly the American flag outside Saint Augustine Church during World War I. Miller blamed the Great Depression on the greed of capitalists and warned that if a fairer distribution of wealth did not take place, a great upheaval would erupt. "Revolution is in the air" and "if the masters of industry are not wise enough to share profits with the workers, they may themselves be responsible for the impending dangers, and they might as well expect any kind of outbreak." Miller, who died in 1943, never renounced the left or his belief in socialism.[15]

Like Miller, Theophilus Alcantara participated in left politics He was a founding member of the left-wing American Labor Party and ran for a New York State assembly seat in the 1930s and 1940s. He became very critical of the black clergy who accepted patronage and went along with the status quo by supporting his mainstream opponent for the assembly. Although he would later renounce his membership in the American Labor Party, he did not move away from his militant leanings. He joined the campaign to free members of the American Communist Party who were jailed under the Smith Act, and he became a central figure in the fight for better housing for the poor and worked with grass-roots organizations to get it.[16]

The Reverend Thomas Harten was unique among Baptist ministers of Brooklyn. On several occasions he participated in militant street protests against police brutality. He was head of the local chapter of the National Equal Rights League, organized by William Monroe Trotter, editor of the Boston newspaper, *The Guardian*, and a leading opponent of Booker T. Washington. He also became head of a group called the Afro-Protective League, which protested police brutality and lynching. Harten was able to draw thousands of people to his church to protest injustice. He denounced FDR, claiming that the president did not have the best interests of blacks at heart. He was an early supporter of the Scottsboro Nine and called for an alliance with the American Communist Party. Although Harten would later curtail his militant activity and concentrate on church matters, he remained critical of the Democratic and Republican parties and he called for a black independent candidate to be elected to the New York Assembly. "We must endorse our own man that will prevent the political leaders from endorsing one of us who would be a Negro handkerchief head Uncle Tom political pigeon." Like Alcantara, Harten also supported the struggle to free jailed Communists in the 1950s.[17]

Unlike some of the radicals, whose activities had waned by the late 1940s, Milton Galamison was just beginning his career as the cold war began. Born in 1923, he was twenty-five when he became pastor of Siloam Presbyterian Church in 1948. By the 1950s, he had become the most radical black minister in Brooklyn. In his sermons he offered a race and class analysis, blaming imperialism, class exploitation, and racism for the underdevelopment of blacks in the United States and the peoples of Africa, Asia, and Latin America, and linking capitalist greed to militarism. The Presbyterian pastor condemned capitalism for its failure to end hunger. He felt politically connected to radicals and defended Communists and other leftists against red-baiting. In one sermon he argued that Marxism stressed human dignity and that socialism and "Russian Communism" were attempts at winning respect for humanity. Soon after the Cuban Revolution, Galamison visited the island nation and praised the revolution.[18]

More than any other Brooklyn pastor, Galamison worked with left forces and ordinary people. In the 1950s he became allies with Annie Stein, a member of the Communist Party, and other militants active in the Brooklyn NAACP. Galamison, Stein, and others helped develop the NAACP School Workshop, which struggled to integrate New York City schools. The workshop was made up of hundreds of parents whose children attended the public schools of New York.[19]

Complaining that the NAACP was too moderate in the fight for desegregation, Galamison organized an independent grass-roots organization to work for school integration. The Parents Workshop for Equality in New York City Schools became the most militant advocate of school integration. It led numerous demonstrations and boycotts in an attempt to force the New York City Board of Education to integrate the entire school system. In February 1964 the Parents Workshop helped organize a citywide boycott for integration. Over 460,000 students stayed home in an attempt to coerce the board into producing a plan and timetable for integration. Although Galamison and the movement failed to win their demands of the board, he later became involved in the struggle for community control of schools.[20]

Black Christian radicals argued that the Bible was a book dealing with social justice. They blurred the premodern text with modern ideology, taking the narratives of the Old and New Testaments to address the problems of class exploitation, racism, and other social evils. Although they were not contemporaries, George Frazier Miller and Milton Galamison blended Enlightenment western doctrines with the Bible. Miller once asserted, "I look upon the whole teaching of Christ as Socialist." He declared that "Christ was fundamentally a revolutionist, revolutionizing society from one in which the powerful suppressed the poor for their own enrichment to one where all could live abundantly." "The Saviour," the Socialist pastor declared, "was not only interested in moral righteousness but also in social and economic righteousness."[21]

Galamison praised Marxism and the Russian and Cuban revolutions. However, he was not an advocate of a workers' state. Instead, he argued for a harmonious community based on Christian principles. He connected his social activism to his religion and maintained that it was the duty of Christians to address the social sins of society. According to the Presbyterian pastor, the Bible was a blueprint for Christians. True Christians struggled to rid the world of social injustice.[22]

It is not surprising that both Miller and Galamison had turned to ideas that grew out of the modern period. Both had been educated in prominent universities where they were exposed to western thought. Miller had received a bachelor's degree from Howard University and had studied philosophy at New York University. Galamison received his bachelor's degree from Lincoln University, where he was exposed to Kant, Marx, Betrand Russell and other western thinkers. Both also belonged to predominantly white denominations.[23]

More than the other black Christian radicals, Alcantara's religious radicalism was shaped by black nationalism. The African Orthodox Church, founded in 1921 by George Alexander McGuire, a follower of Marcus Garvey, was born out of protest against white Christian domination. McGuire believed that blacks should reject the whiteness in Christianity and envision God in their own image. It is not surprising that Alcantara found the AOC attractive. He was born in Guyana in the early part of the century, under British rule, and experienced colonialism firsthand. However, besides adopting a black nationalist approach, followers of the AOC also embraced an Anglican worldview. Its hierarchical structure and liturgy is modeled on the Anglican Church and the religion adheres to the Niceo-Constantinopolitan Creed. Unlike believers in an African sacred cosmos, where one reaches God through experience, AOC followers reach God through the Enlightenment principles of reason and the written word. Hence, Alcantara came out of a western as well as a black nationalist tradition.[24]

Little is known about Thomas Harten's early life and education. However, descriptions of his sermons note that he relied on an Afro-American folk religious tradition. His sermons were described as ecstatic, and the black press reported that the pastor's delivery was so emotional that on any given Sunday one could witness men and women fainting at Holy Trinity Church. What is certain is that Harten came out of an African-American religious tradition that had at its core a sense of social justice. Author David Howard-Pitney has labeled this sense of social justice the Afro-American jeremiad. It is a rhetoric that offers a religious critique of America's racial practices but also declares that the nation has the potential to climb out of its quagmire of racial hatred. Harten, like other black ministers, drew upon this tradition. In his sermons and activities he condemned American racism while insisting that radical social change could take place.[25]

Black Pentecostals

While Afro-Christian liberals put their faith in the liberal state with its mixed economy and black Christian radicals advocated an alternative society in which all forms of social injustice would be eradicated, black Pentecostals relied on premodern notions for a critique of present conditions and for solutions that would end black oppression. They put their faith in a fundamentalist political vision. Unlike the radicals who attempted to modernize biblical narratives, the Pentecostals stressed a strict interpretation of the Bible. They did not extend the boundaries of Christian doctrine and link it to modernity or even draw on Enlightenment ideals. Thus, socialism, liberalism, and rationality were not relevant for survival. The ideal society predated modernity and was based on biblical social relations. The Pentecostals relied on an "unadulterated" form of "pure Christianity." Their assertion that "you are in the world and not of the world" meant that believers had to be concerned only with their spiritual well-being.

For Pentecostals, the narratives of the Bible became paradigmatic acts that one attempted to relive. By reenacting them the narratives were brought to life. As in biblical times believers claimed that they received "gifts" from God in order to demonstrate his power, including the gifts of "speaking in tongues," "interpreting tongues," and "healing the sick." By turning to the text and reenacting the narratives one found the perfect model for harmony. The Bible spelled out the correct behavior for Christians and their relationship with God. One had to be in constant communion with the divinity. All of the believer's time had to be sacred time, and he had to spend as much of it as possible among other followers of the faith. Pentecostals noted that it was not unusual for followers to attend church four or more times a week or for services to last well into the night.[26]

Early explorations by scholars of black Pentecostalism argued that the notion of "otherworldliness," a key doctrine of this religious group, was apolitical. For example, Gary Marx has contended that Pentecostals were one of the least politically active religious groups in America. However, more recently, scholars of black Pentecostalism have explored its political dimensions. Hans Baer and Merrell Singer, as well as C. Eric Lincoln and Lawrence Mamiya, have noted that many black Pentecostal ministers were active in the mainstream political arena. Before and during the cold war, black Pentecostals in Brooklyn were an important political voice. The tenets of Pentecostalism were expressed fervently and publicly by parishioners and their leadership.[27]

Dozens of black Pentecostal churches were created in Brooklyn in the 1940s and 1950s and were supported by the efforts of the black working class. Members of these congregations offered a political critique of a society that set up barriers to exclude black people. They were neither right nor left on the political scale but created a political space that redefined the political dialogue. They offered a critical political analysis based on how they saw the world. They were not unaware of the issues of the cold war but argued that one could not find a social solution to the plight of people by turning to any "man-made" doctrines. U. L. Corbett, a member of the Church of God in Christ on the Hill, argued that Communism and the "American system" were both evils. One had to "walk and talk in the name of the Lord" in order to find peace. Samuel Gibson, who joined the Deliverance Evangelistic Center in the 1950s, noted that the "saints" rejected the "pleasures of the world." Maritcha Harvey, a member of a Pentecostal church in Bedford-Stuyvesant, argued that in the 1940s and 1950s the members of her church were faithful only to holiness and no other system.[28]

These arguments by followers of Pentecostalism did not exclude them from cold war politics but gave them a rhetoric by which they could enter the debate. They argued that a strict interpretation of the Bible was the only way to liberate people from eventual doom and destruction. For them "walking and talking in the name of the Lord" was the only sure political method to transform the world. Their remedy was to attempt to redefine politics by offering an alternative vision. Instead of focusing on the material they contended that one could only find peace, joy, and harmony by focusing on the spiritual. This view was a critique of a society that denied blacks access to material wealth. They simply attacked the criteria used to measure success and offered an alternative model that was attainable by poor people. It is not surprising that black Pentecostals mainly attracted members of the black working class.[29]

Conclusion

The literature on black religion has mushroomed over the last twenty-five years. Historians, sociologists, journalists, and others have produced numerous monographs, biographies, and textbooks exploring the lives of religious figures, a variety of black religious institutions, and sacred doctrine. These works have provided a greater insight into the relationship of race and class and the various black religious communities in America. As noted, an important focus of some scholars has been the political cultures of black churches. When discussing the black left before and during the cold war, historians and other scholars should also include the black religious community in its many dimensions. In spite of the harsh repression of left forces during this period, the black religious community was a center of hot ideological debate. To be sure, the black religious community was not unified, but its diversity puts this community at the center and not at the margins of cold war politics.

CHAPTER 3

The Pentecostal Preacher as Public Intellectual and Activist

The Extraordinary Leadership of Bishop Smallwood Williams

The oppressed are losing confidence in the legislative process. Political hypocrisy and procrastination and the rising tide of Wallacism [George Wallace] and do nothingism is not contributing to the tranquility of the Nation. In my judgement, there has been an ample and admirable display of patience on the part of the oppressed. . . . Frustration and cynicism are now gripping the hearts and minds of our people. The present civil rights leaders are losing control of the masses. New civil rights groups are being formed whose devotion to the nonviolent concept has faltered.[1]

A nationally known civil rights leader, politician, journalist, or well-known "black public intellectual" did not utter this forecast of the demise of the nonviolent civil rights movement and the emergence of black power. On Sunday April 19, 1964, a Pentecostal preacher by the name of Smallwood Williams expressed these views before his congregation. These were unusual words, even in 1964, for a Pentecostal leader, because most Pentecostals expressed little faith in a social protest movement whose aim was to alter the political culture of the nation. However, Bishop Williams was unique among black Pentecostal preachers. Central to his brand of Pentecostalism was a strong political message advocating racial and social justice and the reworking of the political consciousness of Americans. He was careful not to privilege modernist notions over premodernist ideas but blended both perceptions.

The objective of this chapter is to examine the ministry of Bishop Smallwood Williams, one of the leading black religious figures of the twentieth century, and how he reformulated and used black Pentecostal culture to create a political discourse for civil rights. To be sure, Bishop Williams's use of religion challenged popular perceptions of Pentecostalism. Conventional notions depicted Pentecostals as hyperreligious Christians who divorced themselves from worldly concerns. Williams, founder of the Bible Way Church of Our Lord Jesus Christ World Wide, Inc., contested this particular religious image by promoting a brand of Afro-Christian liberalism that blended left-of-center politics and Pentecostal religious notions. During the post–World War II period, Williams became one of the most vocal Pentecostal leaders of his generation. He urged his fellow clergy to fulfill their "Christian duty" by becoming advocates for the poor, the racially oppressed, and the downtrodden. At the same time, he was attempting to convince white America to broaden its notion of nationality by challenging an exclusive form of cultural citizenship.

Williams helped shape a brand of Pentecostalism that interpreted and placed national political events in a spiritual context without straying from important Pentecostal tenets. It was because of his ability to articulate a Pentecostalism connected to political ideology that made Williams an important black public intellectual. Long before the academy helped produce a number of black scholars who became spokespeople and leaders in the African-American struggle for equality, black ministers used their churches as arenas in which to communicate, organize, and lead black people. These ministers were usually associated with mainline churches, such as Baptist, African Methodist Episcopal, the African Methodist Episcopal Zion, and the predominantly white denominations. Williams was one of a handful of Pentecostal leaders who, before and right after the Second World War, used Pentecostal culture in a political manner.[2] He, in particular, contributed greatly to the political and intellectual debate of the post–World War II period by manipulating the language of the cold war era and using it in the fight against racism. He was able to interpret national issues by using an intellectual vernacular that could appeal to ordinary African Americans. He did this by relying on many forms of discourse, including the sermon and the written narrative. Although in his sermons he attempted to appeal to an audience that valued rationality, his discourse was also part of an oral folk tradition that reached its audience by arousing their emotions. He communicated with his audience by attempting to make them feel as well as think. Through his charismatic style by using what Herman Gray calls the "structures of feeling," Williams provided an avenue of knowledge.

Besides speaking out in the public arena on behalf of African-Americans and the poor, Williams became a political activist, challenging racial segregation and the conservative politics of the state during the cold war era. However, instead of advocating the building of a grassroots movement, and connecting race with gender, class, and sexuality, his brand of leadership was grounded in individualism. It emphasized a patriarchal model of the black family. While he opposed a racial essentialist approach that excluded blacks from political and cultural citizenship, he held on to a gender essentialist view. At the same time that he rejected a biological conception of race, he became a strong advocate for traditional conservative relationships between men and women. In fact, he used the essentialist conceptions of gender roles in his quest to combat racist views of blackness. Williams advocated a private as well as public patriarchy that reinforced notions of manhood. Not only did he think that men should dominate the public spheres of politics and religion, he also subscribed to men controlling the sexual and domestic realms of life.

In 1972 scholar William H. Becker argued that the "models of black manhood provided by the black church constituted one of its most important contributions, over the years, to the cause of liberation." Becker notes that these models are found in the "biographies, sermons, histories, and conference minutes of the black churches, and are manifested in the lives and work of significant black churchmen. . . ." However, Becker essentializes manhood and takes as a given that reaching manhood is the highest objective of black churchmen. Although he recognizes that there exist various models of manhood and that each model is dependent on a host of factors, such as "temperament of leaders," and the "ebb and flow of racism," he nevertheless, presents manhood characteristics as a "natural" phenomenon. Leadership, self-assertion, independence, black identity, vocation, are the measures for judging manhood.[3]

This chapter takes a different path than Becker. It is more than a biographical sketch or an examination of the economic and political exploits of an important religious leader who struggled to expand the meaning of citizenship. It looks at how a Pentecostal figure became an advocate for certain black representations in his quest to overcome racial obstacles set up to exclude African Americans, and other groups, from the body politic. When it comes to examining the civil rights struggle, the social and political story has been exhaustively investigated. There exist many works on the campaigns and activities of movement leaders and "ordinary people." To a lesser extent, the socially constructed categories of citizenship, gender, and sexuality have also been a focus of the historiography. This chapter builds on works that examine African-American history through the prism of gender. Through Williams's life story we can see how civil rights leaders constructed maleness and manliness in their battle for racial equality and inclusion in the state. He challenged whiteness not only by appropriating fixed categories of gender but also by divorcing white skin from citizenship. An examination of the life and activities of Williams provides an opportunity to examine how citizenship looks to a person who belongs to a socially and culturally marginalized group.[4]

The Construction of a Man "Born to Lead"

Autobiography was the means used by Smallwood Williams to present his life to the general public. Like other public figures who have presented their lives through biographical descriptions, Williams's work, *This Is My Story*, explains the forces that led him on the path to leadership. Hence, early on, Williams attempts to convey to his readers that he was selected by God to become a leader of his people. A central theme of the work is that Pentecostal culture helped shape his life and guided him.

Smallwood Williams was born in Virginia in 1907, and at the age of eleven he moved to Columbus, Ohio, with his mother and stepfather. (His natural father had died when Williams was an infant.) When he was a child, his mother joined Bishop Robert Lawson's Church of Our Lord Jesus Christ of the Apostolic Faith (COOLJC), a Pentecostal organization established in 1919. This Holiness-Pentecostal group, like others, has three tenets. The first tenet, being born again, occurs when a person professes his belief that Jesus died for his or her sins. The second, living a sanctified life, means that the reborn person must attempt to live a life like Christ's. This entails trying to avoid all transgressions. The third, baptism by the Holy Spirit, means that one has to experience the Holy Ghost as dwelling within one's body. The sign that the Holy Spirit has entered the person is manifested by speaking in tongues. However, the COOLJC distinguishes itself from other Pentecostal groups by rejecting the Holy Trinity and arguing that Jesus is the only one and true God. Unlike other Pentecostal groups, it also rejects divorce and ordination of women as ministers.[5]

Williams's autobiography describes a journey from an unsaved to a saved life devoted to God. According to Williams, in March 1919, at the age of twelve, he had the "greatest" experience of his life. He experienced a "new birth." He was born again. The old self that was sinful died, and a new self that was immersed in Christ was born. "I was so 'drunk' with the power of the Spirit that two deacons in the church had to help me home." Williams selected the word *drunk*, suggesting a state of intoxication in which one has no control over his senses, in order to create an image of a person who literally has surrendered control to the power of the spirit. The episode, according to the bishop, was a reenactment of Acts 2: 15–1: "For these are not drunk, as ye suppose, seeing it is but the third hour of the day. But this is that which was spoken through the prophet Joel: And it shall come to pass in the last days, saith God, I will pour out my Spirit upon all flesh; and your sons and your daughters shall prophesy, and your young men shall see visions, and your old men shall dream dreams...." This Bible verse is used by Pentecostals as evidence that God's followers experience his Spirit as manifested through visions, dreams, prophesy, tongues, and other "gifts." They have adopted an approach that throws into question modernist notions. Rationality is pushed aside, and the supernatural is given more value. As political scientist Pauline Marine Rosenau notes about postmodernist thinkers apply to Pentecostals. "All that modernity has set aside, including emotions, feelings, intuition, reflection, speculation, personal experience, custom, violence, metaphysics, tradition, cosmology, magic, myth, religious sentiment, and mystical experience takes on renewed importance."[6]

Consequently, Williams asserted that God had selected him to preach the gospel. An important notion among Pentecostals was the belief in the call, a prerequisite for the ministry. It is the belief that God directly contacts the believer, either in a dream, or through prayer, vision, or other personal forms of communication, and calls the person to the ministry. Williams claimed that he was summoned by God, and at the age of sixteen traveled to New York to preach at Lawson's Refuge Church of Christ at a revival. He became known as the "Boy-Wonder Preacher." By eighteen, he had been ordained in the COOLJC.[7]

Williams's autobiography also addresses contemporary social issues, particularly race, class, and gender, through the lens of Pentecostalism. As in the autobiographical works of W. E. B. Du Bois, Malcolm X, and other black figures, Williams details racial episodes that had an impact on his life. His autobiography and sermons describe his encounters with racial discrimination and how such experiences shaped his consciousness. These experiences were what historian Robin D. G. Kelley calls "rites of passage." The Pentecostal bishop wrote that his early education was less than idyllic. As a child in Lynchburg, Virginia, he attended an overcrowded segregated elementary school. He recalls that there were a hundred students in his class and he received only a half day of instruction at the same time that white children received a full day of instruction in well-equipped schools. After graduating from the elementary school, he was forced to attend a poorly equipped segregated junior high school that was called the "chicken coop." According to the bishop, he was quite aware that he was receiving a less than adequate education because there was a new modern brick school near his house that only white children could attend. This experience spelled out for Williams the meaning of white privilege. White skin meant that one had the right to adequate schooling, employment, housing, and other resources. Blackness, on the other hand, was universally devalued. Williams noted that even those blacks who were able to climb into a higher economic position were seen as less than human by the white society. For Williams the greatest social evil was racism, because it denied black people the opportunity for success by devaluing them.[8]

Williams's narrative does not dwell only on racial discrimination. Though he was raised in a racist society, his family served as a counterforce to the humiliations he suffered. Williams praised his mother for fostering his moral character and developing in him a sense of self-worth. According to the Pentecostal bishop, his mother was hardworking, kind, and generous and devoted to her children and husband. She was a person of "faith" and "an uncompromising optimist." He gave her credit for being a motivator. It was she who encourged him to pursue his ministry.

Williams also grew up in a world where African Americans constructed communities that helped foster self-esteem and worth. The church community, the most important institution in Williams's life, stressed the view that all its members were children of God and selected to be saved. He was worthy of sainthood and to preach the word. Nothing could be more important in a person's life than to be one of God's children. That vision of spiritual self-worth, ingrained in Williams, countered any notion of inferiority inculcated by a racist society. [9]

Williams contended that the Church of Our Lord Jesus Christ was nurturing and helped build his self-esteem by emphasizing that he, like all its members, was a saint regardless of his age, sex, or race. It did not matter what those on the outside of this religious community thought of them or what steps the larger society took to deny them dignity. They made the argument that they were in constant communion and fellowship with the Almighty and were assured of life everlasting. Moreover, for Williams and others of the early Pentecostal movement, there was little social distance between the home and the church. Williams and his family spent a great deal of time in the church, giving all of their available time to the COOLJC. The Pentecostal church became an important social world for him. He not only attended church on Sundays but also was active in COOLJC during the week, joining many of its auxiliaries. In fact, church leaders were viewed as patriarchal figures. Williams noted that, aside from his mother, bishops Lawson and Karl Smith, the pastor of the church in Ohio he attended, had the greatest influence on his character. They were the models whom he attempted to emulate. Their assertiveness, their ability to articulate and move a large audience, and the admiration they received from their congregations were inspiring to the young Williams.[10]

To be sure, COOLJC helped shape Williams's view on race. The Pentecostal movement in its early days was an interracial one. Whites joined the Church of God in Christ and worshiped with its black members. In fact, Charles Harrison Mason ordained white as well as black ministers. Pentecostal Assemblies of the World, created right after the Azusa Movement and led by Bishop Garfield T. Haywood, was an interracial group until the 1920s, when its white members left and formed Pentecostal Churches, Inc. Black Pentecostals have always stayed away from racializing their theology. This was also true among the leadership of COOJLC. Williams recalls that Lawson's church had an interracial congregation and he witnessed white children "rejoicing in the name of the Lord." In his autobiography he compared this sight to the day of Pentecost when people of various nations received the Holy Spirit and began to speak in tongues. As a teenager, Williams's notion of race was being shaped. Although he would experience racial animosity from whites, that was not his entire experience. The sight of white children worshiping in the same place with black children, along with portions of the Bible that transcended race, led him to a nonnationalist view. The fact that whites could be led by a black man was a challenge to white supremacy, because white racists claimed that blacks were inferior and incapable of leadership. The presence of white congregants in Lawson's church was evidence that they, like blacks, had to come to the Lord and humbled themselves. Their willingness to be led by a black man upheld the proposition, at least in the religious realm, that all were equal in God's sight. God poured out his grace to "all flesh." The fact that he compared this experience to the day of Pentecost demonstrated the power of Pentecostal culture and how it used the spiritual models as guidance for interpreting and understanding race relations. Pentecostal beliefs helped Williams to demystify whiteness and deracialize a society that racialized humanity.

Williams's views on race were reflected in his writings and sermons. As a leader of the Apostolic movement, he consistently warned blacks not to adopt an antiwhite sentiment because there were good whites who struggled for black freedom. His advocacy of an interracial society included criticism of Marcus Garvey and Malcolm X. In his autobiography he criticized Garvey and his movement because he believed Garveyism was simply "antiwhite" and ignored many whites who worked for racial equality. In a sermon entitled "The Future Belongs to Them That Belong to Him," the bishop contended that Malcolm X "was a talented, a gifted eloquent speaker. I disagree with Malcolm, in that I believe that it is unfair and inaccurate to castigate or blame a whole race for the evil that some practice."[11]

In addition to helping mold his conception of race, Pentecostal culture helped form his views on gender. The COOLJC's position that women were banned from the ministry reinforced the view that leadership was natural to men because God made it that way. When Williams broke away from COOLJC and formed the Bible Way Church of Our Lord Jesus Christ World Wide, Inc., in 1957, he continued the practice of banning women from the ministry. Whenever he referred to ministers in his writings or sermons, he always used the masculine pronoun. Moreover, Williams's acknowledgement of his mother's contribution in shaping his life excluded any mention of her helping him to develop leadership competence. The attributes needed for leading people, including assertiveness, public speaking ability, and administrative skills, among others, were not traits he identified with women. Further, his characterization of these traits as "gifts" given by God implied that leadership was not a process of socialization but a spiritual endowment conferred by God on those found deserving. In contrast, his mother's contributions were restricted to the more feminine virtues of devotion, kindness, and generosity. Although he notes that these traits were important, they were not the ones he turned to when declaring his manhood. The COOLJC did not differ from the larger patriarchal society on the role of women. Clearly, he adopted the larger society's view that a woman's role was confined to the private sphere.

After his graduation from high school in 1927, Williams moved to Washington, D.C., to organize a congregation. Like other ambitious black working men and women who established ministries, Williams first attempted to attract a following by preaching in the streets and establishing a tent service. His early ministry on the streets of the nation's capital first attracted a following of twenty. Soon after, he rented an old theater for $27 a month. He noted that rent for the theater was too expensive for a small congregation, so the church rented a storefront. However, as the congregation grew and accumulated funds, it was able to buy two lots on New Jersey Avenue to build a church. By 1936, the congregation was able to buy a plot of land and construct a new building. It was the collective effort of the Bible Way members that raised money that led to the purchase of a church building.[12]

Williams's world view was molded not only by a Pentecostal culture but also by institutions of higher learning. At the same time that he was establishing a church, he also was pursuing a degree at Howard University's

School of Religion. His efforts made it evident that a duality existed in Williams's world view. He essentially became immersed in two worlds, one of African-American folk religion, the other of academic learning and scholarship. Throughout his life, he managed to commute between these worlds while most of his fellow Pentecostal clergy remained far removed from—and often antagonistic toward—elite institutions of higher learning.

While at Howard, Williams was greatly influenced by Dr. Benjamin Mays, dean and later president of Morehouse College; Dr. Mordecai Johnson, president of Howard; and Professor Howard Thurman. For Williams, these men embodied a form of leadership that was noncompromising, truthful, and dedicated to saving the souls while bettering the worldly circumstances of African Americans. "Dr. Johnson, who held the post from 1926–1960, was a great inspiration to me in his strong position against racial discrimination. He was a bold and eloquently outspoken man, able to testify at congressional committees" and was able to raise the funds to develop and expand Howard University. Williams also recalls learning from Mays things "beyond the scope of church history and theology." Benjamin Mays was a race man who dedicated his life to improving the plight of black people. As Mays's reputation as a religious scholar and theologian grew in the United States and abroad, he criticized U.S. racial practices and treatment of its black citizens. Williams would also internationalize America's race relations by noting the global implications of America's racial practices. According to Williams, theologian Howard Thurman, an expert on mysticism, Eastern religion, and Gandhi's nonviolent philosophy, also influenced him. Thurman's universal view that all people were part of humanity and were worthy of the Gospel was a theme that Williams used in his ministry. Moreover, Williams noted that Thurman's book *Jesus and the Disinherited*, in which the author argues that Christianity was a "technique of survival for the oppressed," was a great inspiration to him. According to Thurman, "Jesus the idea" is an authentic fellowship embracing Christians and non-Christians who seek a religious experience. His Jesus embraces all, including the disinherited. Universalism became a major theme of Williams's ministry.[13] Thurman addressed the issue of segregation in a 1943 article entitled "The Will to Segregation." The theologian contended that the "most fundamentally important thing that must be done is to relax the 'will to segregation' that through the years has become the American technique for control of the Negro minority." Thurman's essay examined segregation in American institutions including business, church, and state, and its psychological impact on victims as well as perpetrators. When the church gives up segregation, Thurman maintained, it can truly be Christian.[14] This view on segregation would be at the heart of Williams's political arguments.

Other works by Thurman that greatly moved Williams were *The Negro Spiritual Speaks of Life and Death* and *Deep Is Hunger*. According to Williams, these books helped him developed a passion for reading and thinking about theology and philosophy. He gave these men credit for helping shape his intellect and leadership qualities. They represented the kind of black men he wanted to emulate.[15]

Williams did not earn a degree from Howard. In 1947 the Bishop graduated from the American Bible College in Chicago. Besides his theological education, Williams had some legal training. He took classes at the Robert Terrell Law school. Hence, Williams was shaped by the two very different worlds of Pentecostalism and higher education. From Pentecostalism he developed a world view that emphasized that God was a constant intervening force in one's life. For Williams, Christianity was a religion that helped those oppressed by racism and class exploitation.[16] But unlike more radical ministers, who emphasized mobilizing the oppressed to confront social injustice, he accepted the notion that God selects men to lead others out of the social quagmire. From higher education, he developed a sense of the social gospel and the incentive to fight for racial justice and a passion for worldly knowledge.[17]

His social concerns were evident in his early ministry. He focused on the material as well as the spiritual because of the different social and material conditions of blacks in Washington, D.C. "Pastoring in the inner city of Washington meant more than delivering a Sunday morning sermon, performing a marriage or eulogizing the dead. A pastor has to be the 'angel' to the temporal as well as the eternal needs of his people." The bishop noted that because racially restrictive clauses assured that blacks were relegated to slums where they faced horrendous conditions, he made his ministry twofold. He wanted to spread the gospel and address the racist deprivations endured in the nation's capital.[18]

Bishop Williams was motivated by public and religious service, but he was also an ambitious man who wanted to climb the ranks of social leadership. He clearly wanted to reach a position of visibility and power in his profession. For any person seeking leadership, part of reaching that goal lies in gaining a position of authority. Although he was loyal to Lawson and served as general secretary of the Pentecostal body for almost thirty years, and also became president of the Sunday School Association of the COOJLC, Williams was denied the position of authority he desired within the COOLJC. In 1957 he and five other officials of the Refuge group decided to break away from Lawson's organization because Lawson was unwilling to share power with Williams and the others. Williams wanted to be recognized as one of the leaders in COOLJC. Hence, Williams organized Bible Way Church World Wide Inc. as an independent body. Today that Pentecostal organization has established several churches in most urban centers and asserts that it has over 100,000 members.[19]

Williams's Articulation of Leadership, Class, Citizenship, and the Nation-State

I made a lot of Pentecostals uncomfortable. I never purposely set out to be unpleasant, but my emphasis on pragmatic preaching was leading me to get involved in areas where few in my church had ventured. Under my leadership in the late fifties and sixties ... members of Bibleway were getting involved in places that didn't make us particularly popular with some Pentecostals— Christian unity and cooperation ... I had the ability ... to see beyond denominational differences and religious prejudices to apply Pentecostal theology to practical areas of living. That gift of mine wasn't particularly appreciated. No doubt many Pentecostals, like many Christians in many other denominations, were threatened when they took a step outside their own door. This is true to this day, despite all the talk of the ecumenical movement.[20]

Although Pentecostals were known for focusing solely on the spiritual and not the material concerns of people, Bishop Williams's ministry greatly stressed humanity's need for material welfare. In his sermons and writings the Pentecostal bishop called on his fellow black clergy to become involved in the political arena in order to help fight for economic and social justice for African Americans. Because they were selected by God to be leaders, they had an obligation not only to their fellow parishioners, but to God. As men of God, black ministers had to be concerned with God's children. The legacy of slavery and racism, Williams contended, also made it imperative that the black clergy become involved in the struggle for civil rights because racial injustice was the greatest evil in America. As noted, Williams embraced the notion of spiritual gifts. It was the Supreme Being who gave them leadership qualities. Since God had endowed these men with such gifts, they had the obligation to care for the material as well as the spiritual needs of his people. This line of thought connected Pentecostal tenets with social action for material well-being. For Williams, there was no separation between spiritual and secular well-being. The Bible thus connected the premodern with the modern world and the spiritual with the material. It was a blueprint for spiritual salvation and social justice. The minister's obligation was to help people struggle against racial oppression.

Despite Williams's emphasis on the eradication of racial oppression, the issue of class did not escape his attention. His observation and experience during the Depression helped shape a moderate class analysis that was based more on the moral position of leaders than on economic determinism. He contended that the reason for poverty and unemployment had to do with Herbert Hoover and the Republican Party becoming "bedfellows with big business [and] making empty promises to poor people and provisions for the rich." The Pentecostal bishop claimed that the Bonus March had a greater impact on him than almost any other public event. Veterans of World War I who lost their jobs during the Depression demanded early payments of veterans bonuses that Congress had authorized. These men were not eligible to collect the bonuses until 1945, but their economic plight drove them to lobby for them. Although a bill passed Congress over the president's veto allowing veterans to collect 50 percent of their bonus, it did little to relieve the economic suffering of the men. In the spring of 1932, 17,000 veterans marched on the nation's capital to get Congress to authorize payment. They established a shantytown, or Bonus City, in Washington, in an area known as Anacostia Flats.[21]

When the bonus bill the veterans wanted was defeated in the Senate, thousands of them remained in the shantytown with their families. General Douglas MacArthur, the army chief of staff, ordered the army to disband Bonus City. Soldiers turned on veterans with tanks, guns, and tear gas. Two veterans were killed, and several were injured. According to Williams, the government's response to the marchers was evidence of the Hoover administration's indifference and disdain for the poor.[22]

The cruelty of Hoover's government to men who had made great sacrifices in service to their country led Williams to the conclusion that the state had fallen into the hands of apologists for corporate America. However, despite his position on the dominance of corporate power, he did not urge the working class to aggressively pursue its own interests. He did not point out the harsh reality of capitalism and its contradictions. Instead he based his argument on the moral obligation of leadership. Although he attacked the industrial elite, his critique was based on its failure to meet its moral responsibility. According to the spiritual sage, men in leadership were required to behave in a moral manner; a harmonious society, he contended, can only occur when people seek God. In that regard, Williams did not stray from his religious world view.[23]

The bishop's interpretation of the Bible and search for solutions to racial and class oppression led him to the position that the state, as well as its leaders, was obligated to pursue the people's social welfare. Besides being followers of Christ, all people were also citizens of the nation-state.

Williams maintained that no one should be barred from full participation and social security in a state declaring itself democratic. Countries were required to behave in a moral fashion. A nation should model itself after the Kingdom of God. It should not exclude anyone because of race or ethnicity or religion. It should follow in Jesus' footsteps. The Pentecostal leader asserted that the New Testament verses were proof that the mission of Jesus was taking care of the physical and spiritual well-being of his people and no one or no entity had the right to deny his objectives. In fact, he claimed that the measurement of the state's moral position was how well it provided for the least among its citizens. "There is a moral responsibility of government to help the poor and disadvantaged. The acceptance of this principle is a difference between the sterile, barren, starvation political philosophy of the late President Herbert Hoover's administration and that of the late President Franklin D. Roosevelt's liberal humanitarian administration of social conscience and concern for the poor and the disadvantaged."[24]

One can detect in Williams's writing Du Bois's notion of "a double consciousness." However, he used the concept not to describe a divided racialized self, but to stress the duality of human nature. Pentecostals were *in* the world and *of* the world. They existed in the spiritual and secular spheres.

The Pentecostal bishop contended that believers had to be aware that they were spiritual beings and citizens of the state; thus they had to serve two masters. They should follow Christian principles, but as citizens of the state, they had an obligation to participate in the political process. Williams found justification for his political activism in the Bible. To be political was to be Christ-like.

> In my pastoral ministry, I have been profoundly interested in the two-fold good. I tried to make good saints and good citizens of my people, the people of God, those inspired by my shepherd, I am as concerned about their social lives as much as their spiritual lives. "I have come that they might have life, and that they might have it more abundantly." These words of Christ clearly express His deep concern for the quality of His people's lives. As His representative, and as an agent for the Kingdom of God, His interests are my interests, His concern is my concern.[25]

His view that the state was the best vehicle for helping the poor and assuring racial equality was formed by New Deal liberalism. After voting for the first time in 1932, the bishop asserted, "I learned a critical lesson during the election: If the economic problems of the country could be solved through the political process, then the pressing social and racial conflicts could be solved through the same process. The liberalism sown in FDR's New Deal policies had laid the foundation for progressive change." Williams was not opposed to a civic-oriented culture and to moral uplift. In fact, he held the view that blacks had to be active in civil affairs and not wait for the state to act in their behalf. But he saw politics as "an indispensable instrument of a people's participation in the function of government through the electoral process. Its purpose is a good, not evil. To neglect to exercise your political duties as a voter because you're lazy, apathetic or indifferent is wrong." The Pentecostal bishop was of the view that people were obligated not only to be conscious of the spiritual but to try to be good citizens and at the same time loyal followers of Christ.[26]

Williams's fight was not limited to voting rights and the right to equal public accommodation; he intended to change a form of citizenship that seemed fixed in the conscious of white Americans. He realized that citizenship was not just a legal category but a cultural one. Hence, a great deal of his energy was spent attempting to reshape a cultural citizenship. Aihwa Ong contends that cultural citizenship is dialectical, determined by the state and its subjects. According to Ong, the state's hegemonic approach is opposed by subjects who attempt to negotiate this form of membership in a community. Hence, it is a dual process of making and being made. Cultural citizenship is practices and beliefs that grow out of "negotiating the often ambivalent and contested relations with the state and its hegemonic forms that establish the criteria of belonging within a national population or territory."[27]

Smallwood Williams challenged a cultural citizenship that used racial, class, and gender markers to define membership in the community. These markers dated back to the European settlement when citizenship was limited to white men of property and excluded people of color and women. The settlers brought with them their race and gender biases and reinforced these biases through law. Although by the end of World War II legal racial barriers to citizenship were attacked by the federal government as well as by civil rights groups, cultural determinants of citizenship were ingrained in the minds of many white Americans. They clung to the belief that blacks stood outside of the realm of citizenship and were not entitled to the privileges and responsibilities that went along with being citizens of the state. Williams became part of what scholar Renalto Rosaldo labeled the "dissident traditions of struggle for first class citizenship."[28]

Williams opposed white political demonization. He advocated a citizenship that would lead not only to a fairer distribution of resources but one that would lead to white Americans recognizing blacks as partners deserving all the rights and privileges that come along with being a citizen. His fight was to change cultural barriers to citizenship by universalizing the concept. In order for this to happen, he knew, white Americans would have to see blacks not as threats to their own personal security or to the nation, but as law-abiding, God-fearing, intelligent beings.

Despite Williams's elaborate explanation of the duties of the individual and the responsibilities of collective entities, he put limitations on the notion of human agency and depicted God as consistently active in human affairs. Emphasizing an important theme among Pentecostals, he contended that God had his hands in world events and people were limited to either following God or rejecting him. However, the rejection of God, he warned, would lead to harsh consequences. God would eventually punish those who rejected him. Punishment was interpreted as personal but also as a collective experience. Nations as well as individuals could be punished by the Almighty. Hence, the notion of social sin was embraced by the bishop. Poverty and racism were collective sins, and God would punish those societies where such evils existed. But God was not a vengeful being. He was benevolent and constantly tried to rescue not only individuals but also nations. Williams interpreted God's relationship with humanity as paternalistic; God was the Father, while people were simply children dependent on the Almighty. If his children stepped out of line, God would punish them. This view was similar to the male–female relationship. Men were naturally and spiritually dominant and rightfully placed in a position to lead , whereas the dependent women were relegated to the private sphere.

A good example of this political-Pentecostal theory was Williams's spiritual interpretation of the New Deal. By placing Franklin D. Roosevelt in a religious context, he remained true to the religious notion of limited human agency and God's selection of men for leadership. For Williams, Roosevelt was simply carrying out God's will. According to the leader of the Bible Way Church, although it was God who created the Depression because of America's rejection of him, He attempted to relieve suffering by giving America

Franklin Delano Roosevelt. "God was trying to speak to us at that time, but we failed to hear his voice. He sent Franklin Delano Roosevelt with a heart of love, sympathy and benevolence for all." Williams portrayed Roosevelt as an agent of God and a person who had great insight and benevolence and was willing to use government properly to eradicate hunger, poverty, and suffering. The bishop praised FDR for guiding the nation back to a moral path when he helped provide for the disinherited. According to Williams, God blessed America. However, when America turned its back on God, the Almighty punished the nation by calling FDR home.[29] New Deal liberalism and its stress on the expansion of government as a solution to social problems of concern to Williams was presented not as a step forward into the age of big government, but as a case of faith and deliverance. By juxtaposing the notion of otherworldliness, Williams relied on the Old Testament theme about the relationship between the Hebrews and God. Central to the Covenant, God delivered the children of Israel from oppression in Egypt because they maintained their faith in him as the one true God. If a person or collective entity believes in God, that person or group would be delivered from affliction in the here and now, not just in the hereafter. This theme, central to Afro-Christian faith and emphasized by Pentecostals, connected Williams to his religious roots. Indeed, his interpretation of American history closely resembles biblical narratives. Moreover, placing history in a religious context was a way of appealing to an audience that embraced a religious world view. Just as important, it rescued faith from being overpowered by a secular interpretation of history.

Because of Williams's historical interpretation and reliance on faith and deliverance, one should not be surprised that he attempted to connect the Jewish diaspora with the African-American diaspora. In a sermon in 1949 the bishop linked blacks and Jews by focusing on the common experience of suffering atrocities, inflicted on the Jews by the Nazis and on blacks by Jim Crow violence. A large part of humanity suffered because some felt that they were superior to others. Like his teacher Howard Thurman, Williams attempted to establish a spiritual commonality between Jewish and black suffering. The Jew and the black were brought together through the memory of their suffering. They had been victims of demonic practices of governments and dominant cultures. But as victims and as a people who had a close relationship with the Supreme Being, they were together in the camp of righteousness. Over forty years before cultural critic Paul Gilroy argued that suffering was an important tie between blacks and Jews because of its redemptive power for humanity, Bishop Williams used suffering as a paradigmatic act. The paradigm was the suffering of the Hebrews, who had a special relationship with God, and of the blacks, whose suffering was a reenactment of this biblical tale. Williams was suggesting that, despite their pain, the faith of African Americans in God would lead to their liberation. The children of God would not continue to suffer eternally. Eventually, their tormentors would be brought to justice.[30]

Williams's description of the spiritual journey of blacks and Jews was an attempt at constructing a history that united humanity. It also portrayed blacks in a more positive light then contemporary historical scholarship. A year after Williams delivered his sermon, historian Stanley Elkins published his work *Slavery: A Problem in American Institutional and Intellectual Life* comparing African Americans in bondage to Jewish concentration camp victims. According to Elkins, the horrors of the slave experience reduced African Americans to passive Sambos. While Elkins's work can be considered progressive, because it challenged an earlier literature that saw the peculiar institution as paternalistic and beneficial to blacks, it is problematic, because he focused on victimization. Williams's sermon, on the other hand, sees black suffering not as debilitating but as a marker of their righteousness and closeness to God.[31]

In spite of his emphasis on a spiritual interpretation of history, Williams was not antileft, and he certainly did not join the anti-Communism network of the 1940s and 1950s. Although he warned of the dangers of Communism, he was willing to work with the Communist activist Annie Stein in a campaign to desegregate the restaurants of Washington. He belonged to a group of ministers during the campaign that held rallies, raised money for the campaign, and recruited people to demonstrate at restaurants that practiced segregation.[32]

Williams's strongest criticism was aimed at the right. As the nation entered the cold war period, the Pentecostal pastor lashed out at what he claimed was a resurgence of American racism. Emphasizing his theme that God intervenes in human affairs, he declared that God used the Allies as "instruments of judgment" against this iniquitous beast and Hitler's totalitarian and disdainful philosophy of race hatred and dictatorship. He challenged racial authenticity by linking totalitarianism and evil, not with the Communist governments of the world but with those that adopted a racial doctrine. Referring to racist governments as "beasts" was no accident. In the Gospel of John, the Antichrist is described as the beast. This was language that was familiar to any Christian believer. Williams was driving home the point that racism was the greatest social sin of a nation and must be expunged.[33]

While racism was depicted as a great social evil, interracial harmony was painted by the bishop as God's will. Thus, any state that stresses equality among races is a righteous one. Unlike black Christian radicals like George Frazier Miller and Milton Galamison, who attacked militarism as a social sin, Williams used no such language. In fact, war could be a sacred event. He portrayed World War II as a spiritual occurrence because it dismantled the racist Nazi state. The boundaries on human agency and God's willingness to determine the course of worldly events made war an instrument used by the Almighty to seek the harmonious interracial state of affairs among his people. According to Williams, Hitler was defeated not simply by military might but because black and white boys fought together. Hence God was on the nation's side.[34]

But if America was at a great stage of moral authority during the war, it soon lost its moral edge. According to Williams, "Hitler still lives," despite his defeat, because his racist ideology lives in the nation's capital. The Nazi leader, Williams declared, is "stalking publicly and boldly in public places in our city." He called attention to the segregation and the privilege of whiteness. "It is unthinkable, yet it is true. The same German that fought against this country in a major war can come to Washington, D.C., stop at downtown hotels, eat at restaurants, and utilize public facilities." But blacks that fought for their country were denied basic rights of citizenship. They were denied service at the large department and drug stores and lunch counters. Williams's message was clear: The United States had fought against Germany's racist government, but it did not address racism at home. Instead, the nation went on denying to millions of people born in the country their constitutional rights.[35]

Williams made an argument based on social justice, fair play, and common sense. The Pentecostal bishop used the art of moral suasion. He publicly asked how the United States could declare itself to be the champion of freedom while denying millions of Americans their basic civil rights. He did not miss the moral tone in the United States message that it was a God-fearing country concerned with human rights. Williams brilliantly used the theme that Hitler is still alive to drive home the message that although the U.S. fought a war against a brutal racist regime, it had not dealt with racism in the country's own back yard. This appeal to a moral consciousness also encompassed an appeal to logic. How could the United States fight a war to end racism abroad and allow it to exist in its own backyard? Realizing that the country was in a vulnerable position in the geopolitical struggle, he manipulated cold war rhetoric in order to win human rights for African Americans. It was not just an attempt on the part of the Pentecostal bishop to force the nation to adhere to the bourgeois principles of the Enlightenment. The solution was for it to embrace a Christian ethic. For Williams, God was not dead, killed by an overemphasis on the secular. The Almighty reigned supreme, and he remained the life force people needed for spiritual and material existence.

The Cultural Significance of Williams's Sermons

For cultural scholars music has been a notable form of African-American performance art. But folk sermons, or what religious scholar Albert Raboteau calls "chanted sermons," should not take a back seat to music. The preacher's sermons are greatly judged on their style of delivery. It is only when they spark emotion that they are considered successful by the congregation. Any preacher using this form of sermon must possess verbal communication skills that can make people "happy." Folk sermons are part of a black Diaspora verbal culture that is divided between content and delivery. The content of such sermons often stressed the importance of the written word. Williams's written sermons contained the exegesis and tools used by theologians trained at seminaries and the academy. But the sermons and how they were delivered were an essential concern of Pentecostal ministers and others who were part of the religiously charismatic culture. Williams's sermons appropriated and reconstructed biblical narratives in performances that stressed drama and communication through experience. The preacher's job was not just to make churchgoers think; it was also to make them feel. Its purpose was to help the worshiper reach God through a religious experience where one communicates by feeling. Parishioners came to church because they contended that their spirits needed to be touched by the Almighty. Thus emotion and oral communication ruled supreme over reason and the written word.

Cultural scholars have noted that this form of communicative dialogue among African Americans had its origins in a racist society that denied black people access to the written word. One of the most significant aspects of black Pentecostalism is that it retained and nourished this form of communication through music, holy dancing, testimony, speaking in tongues, the sermon and other rituals that relied on an antiphonal structure, or call and response. Although the written word became dominant in African-American communities by the late nineteenth century as blacks gained more opportunity to learn how to read and write, the expressive or charismatic sermon did not wither away. To the contrary, it enjoyed a resurgence with the Holiness-Pentecostal movement of the early part of the twentieth century, especially among working class blacks who flocked to these churches. For many of them, it remained an important form of communication, because it allowed blacks to reconceptualize themselves as saintly people, worthy of God's salvation.[36]

The charismatic sermon falls into the category of what postcolonial theorists call oral performance, a part of an alternative discursive economy. The oral performance is a challenge to the dominance of the "written sign." However, Bill Ashcroft, Gareth Griffiths, and Helen Tiffin contend that it is an exchange requiring those involved in it to be physically present with one another. "In practice the oral only exists and acquires meaning in the possibility of an immediate and modifying response, existing therefore only interactively with it with its whole speech or movement of event." Ashcroft, Griffiths, and Tiffin argue that, in the economy of communication, the "oral" is placed in an inferior position when compared to the written sign in the modern world. "In 'modern' societies the oral and the performative continues to exist alongside the written but it is largely ignored or relegated to the condition or pretext in many accounts." The one important arena where this view is challenged is the Pentecostal church.[37]

Many outside of the Pentecostal churches have declared that Pentecostal charismatic sermons are for the unsophisticated, the ignorant, the less than civilized, and that they are used by men who want to manipulate the poor. Williams realized the sermon's intellectual, political, and cultural importance. The written word was not the only means of conveying information to people. Blacks continued to rely on an oral tradition that questioned the domination of the text as the most important form of expression.

Williams's sermons were messages that dealt with sophisticated themes such as redemption, "unmerited suffering" and compensation, the meaning of grace, and God's dispensations. He usually stated the theme of the sermon, then informed the congregation of the verses from the Bible that were relevant to the theme. After elaborating on the theme for a few minutes, he then read one or two verses selected for the sermon. He would explain the verse and then follow up the explanation by applying it to contemporary conditions. As he continued this pattern of reading and explicating the passage, he became louder and more charismatic. As he became louder, he emphasized how God loved his people and the great sacrifice He wants to save their souls. Williams used the shout, yelled hallelujah, and on occasion sang. His actions led the congregation to join in the sermon, usually with emotional outbursts among parishioners. Many of them would respond to the sermon by yelling "amen," "thank you, Jesus," "go ahead and preach." Many would jump up uncontrollably, shouting, dancing, speaking in tongues, and crying.[38]

By the time the congregation responded to the words and actions of the preacher, the sermon had been transformed into a participatory act. Both minister and congregation were actively contributing. By their emotional outbursts, the minister and congregation were communicating to one another that they had been touched by the spirit. They had reached God through experience. But Williams never diverged from his theme; he constantly returned to it throughout the sermon. The third part of the sermon was the conclusion. The bishop usually paused and ordinarily stopped the shouting. He would end the sermon by speaking in a calm voice, inviting those who were not members of the church and were not "saved" to come and accept Christ in their lives.[39]

The bishop combined conventional Pentecostal practices with a stress on a seminarian approach that emphasized reading an ethical message and reaching God through rationality. His sermons sought God through both experience and reason. He managed to bridge the worlds of Pentecostalism and the academy by moving back and forth between them. Political messages were also evident in the bishop's sermons. Racism and segregation and the fight for equality were themes that he raised on a number of occasions. The sermon became a means of appealing to people through both reasoned discourse and emotional exaltation.

Stand Up and Be a Man: Williams and the Politics of Black Male Essentialism

Williams's message was not restricted to an intellectual elite. Although he focused on institutional racism, he was able to present a case against racial oppression and its humiliating impact on victims in a personal manner; consequently, he drew on the sentiment of his audience by making them feel his pain and suffering. A case in point is the story he told of his son Wendell being denied the right to ride on a pony in Washington, D.C. Although

Williams offered to pay three times the price for a single ticket, the park attendant refused to accept the his offer. The racist attendant, who claimed that he would lose his job if he allowed the child to ride the horse, was enforcing Jim Crow and trying to dehumanize black people by letting the pastor know that no amount of money he offered would persuade him to violate the doctrine of white supremacy. The attendant was informing Williams that he and his sons were niggers not entitled to what amounted to a white privilege. The goal of the racist attendant was also to crush in the child any spirit and initiative to succeed in a racist society. Clearly, the worst part of the experience for the Pentecostal leader was facing his little boy. The act of offering to pay more was a humiliating challenge to his manhood. But he did it in order to protect his son from the harsh cruelties of racism and to salvage his role as protector and provider for his child. He wanted to save both his child and himself from the emotionally debilitating impact of racism. When his son wanted to know why he could not ride the pony, the eloquent preacher could not find the words to explain. "There was no sensible answer to why daddy?" Racism made him incapable of carrying out his proper role. Williams had been challenged not only as a black man but as a father. What is also quite noticeable in his heart-wrenching narrative is that it is couched in a gender-specific language. While Williams challenges assumptions about the authenticity of race as a biological category, there is no such challenge when it comes to gender. The assumptions of universal sex roles are apparent in the bishop's writings. The role of the father as protector of the family is a given.[40]

The amusement park episode with his son Wendell did not grant Williams the opportunity to take action. Years later, when his youngest child faced racial discrimination, he was granted that opportunity. His view of manhood as loving father and protector would galvanize him to take action against Washington's public schools. In his autobiography he wrote about the impact of segregation on black children. The outspoken Bishop argued that the school system in the District was a "so-called dual school system." Black children were forced to attend overcrowded and underfunded schools. The school board, in its attempt to uphold segregation in Washington, D.C., sent black children greater distances to black schools although underutilized schools attended by white children were closer.[41]

Williams was not content just to raise the issue of school segregation in his pulpit or carry out a publicity campaign. As a preacher-activist and agent of God, he confronted the school system's racism by waging a personal war to eradicate segregation in the schools. He came to the conclusion that segregation was an attempt to dehumanize black people, and the most effective way to dehumanize people was to go after children. Being forced to attend overcrowded, inferior, understaffed schools sent the message to black children and their parents that they were entitled to less than white children. But his approach was not to organize a mass movement or to seek the assistance of parents in a challenge to institutional racism. The religious activist transformed the struggle for desegregation by portraying that struggle as a personal one. The battle he decided to wage was for the right of his five-year son Wallace to attend an all-white and better-equipped school. In chapter eleven of his autobiography, "Civil Rights Begin at Home," the Bishop declared, "The hardest political battle I ever fought began at home." Although there was a "nice school" near his home, Wallace was forced by the Washington, D.C., superintendent of schools, Hobert Corning, to attend a segregated school. "I have to spend quite a sum of money to take my son over four miles to a so-called Colored school," Williams protested. Although he raised the economic hardships he faced, his greater appeal had to do with his inability as a father, protector, and man to change the situation. He asserted that this horrible situation reduced him to less than a man.[42] The bishop realized that he could no longer tolerate this social injustice. "I decided I would stand up and be a man!" he declared. "I challenged the system personally and single-handedly."[43]

When the superintendent did not respond to Williams's telegram protesting his son's transfer, the pastor concluded that the school leader did not take him seriously. "Did he ever get the surprise of his life." His effort was filled with bravado. In early March 1952 he went to the all-white school with Wallace in order to enroll him. When the principal refused to accept the child, the bishop and his son visited a classroom where the pastor saw there were twenty-two empty seats. He sat with his son in the kindergarten class. Although school officials claimed that Williams was just a "visitor," the Pentecostal leader declared his action a "sit-in." In fact, he returned the very next day and attempted to return to the class. But school officials and police blocked the classroom door. The superintendent blocking the classroom door hoped Williams would act disorderly by attempting to push his way through him. He could then have him arrested. However, Williams evaded that trap and walked away. But he did not stop his protest. He found two chairs, and he and Wallace sat in the hallway of the school. Williams portrayed his efforts as his own response to his son's reassignment to an inferior segregated school. It is not certain at the time of his action if he was aware of the potential for setting off a larger protest. However, the superintendent of Washington schools was aware of the bishop's protest. He asserted that although "he [Williams] was not acting for an organization, everyone in the central administration became alarmed that his actions might set off a rash of sit-ins throughout the schools."[44]

Williams contended that he was willing to end his protest on the condition that the superintendent reassign his son to a less-crowded school that he originally attended. However, he decided to end his sit-in after a couple of days, claiming that his son Wallace was upset that he could not go to school. Within a year, a group of parents in Washington, D.C., who called themselves the Consolidated Parents Group of Washington, took action to end the segregated school system. The group filed a brief with the U.S. Supreme Court asking it to take action against the Washington school system. Instead of joining the parents' struggle, Williams remained true to his individualist model and insisted on painting himself as a "modern Moses" leading the battle. He described in his autobiography how he sought advice from Dr. Mordecai Johnson, President of Howard University who "encouraged me and said my efforts reminded him of Mahatma Gandhi's effort of no-violence, of passive resistance." He noted that "the same technique was later adopted by Martin Luther King Jr., who at that time had not emerged on the national scene." Johnson advised him to continue the struggle but to shift it from the classroom to the courtroom. Despite his recognition that parents had taken action, he did not join them. Instead, he paid an attorney a thousand-dollar retainer "and put myself more deeply in the fray." The bishop was claiming he was more than willing to become an integral part of the legal battle to dismantle segregation.[45]

Had the *Brown v. Board of Education of Topeka* case failed, Williams recalled, "I had been advised to be ready with my case—I was." Not willing to remain inactive during the deliberations on the *Brown* case, Williams gave a sermon on four radio stations on February 1, 1953, entitled "The Spiritual Significance of the Supreme Court." The sermon, reprinted in the autobiography, called on people everywhere to pray for the justices to make the right decision and asserted, "The Supreme Court under God Almighty . . . is the hope of this nation at this critical hour."[46]

Williams depicted himself as a man who was in the forefront of the struggle for racial justice. Before Martin Luther King Jr., there was Smallwood Williams using nonviolent resistance. While the Supreme Court considered the *Brown* case, Williams was ready with his son's case and praying for God to move the justices in the right direction. The activist Bishop went as far as to see himself as a misunderstood Moses. According to Williams, not only did whites attack him for his effort to win racial equality but blacks called him "crazy" for being too radical. He claimed that there were many blacks who would have preferred that he not rock the boat and anger the larger white society. Despite the attacks, he remained true to his manly tone and the notion that individualist leadership was selected by God. "It is important, if one would fight for the right to be able to take criticism, abuse, and suffer misunderstanding of his objective. It is a thankless task to fight for an unpopular cause—even your own people will oppose your effort and fight against you in your very trying to help them. Moses discovered this in Egypt 3,000 years ago when he was threatened exposure by one of his own people after he killed an Egyptian to save one of his own."[47]

His notion of protest was couched in gender-loaded language. Struggle, intolerance of social injustice, and liberation became synonymous with the attributes of manliness. Because of his concern with the issue of gender and as a public figure, Williams worked hard to construct an image of black maleness. He challenged the popular image of black men, represented by popular television sit-coms such as *Amos 'n' Andy*. These images portrayed

African-American men as playful, irrational, silly, incompetent, and lacking the capacity for deep thought. They had no initiative and desired immediate gratification. The cognitive mind was alien to black male images. Black maleness continued to symbolize black inferiority.

Williams countered by presenting an image of black men as assertive, intelligent, and willing to protect their family. Real men do not take injustice to family members lying down. They act. The strategy of reshaping the black freedom struggle into an attempt to reclaim one's manhood was a familiar theme articulated by other black leaders. From slave narratives to modern autobiographies the reclaiming of manhood was described. But asserting manhood in these narratives meant using violence. For example, Frederick Douglass wrote in his slave narrative about a physical encounter that took place between him and a cruel overseer who attempted to break his will. Douglass fought back, and stopped the assailant from beating him. It was in the battle and victory that the black abolitionist declared that the politics of masculine force was the ingredient needed for black freedom.[48] In the case of Douglass it was the defense of manhood that galvanized men to action. The path to liberation was through masculine assertion.

Richard Wright also captured this argument in his semiautobiographical *Black Boy*. In it he describes episodes where he resorted to violence in order to liberate himself from his family, which is portrayed in the work as a tyrannical institution, oppressing the human spirit. In one such occurrence, a distant uncle did not like the way that Richard responded when he asked him the time. When the uncle threatened to beat him to teach him a lesson, Richard swore he would resist; he warned his authoritarian uncle that if he put his hands on him, he would cut him with razors. When the uncle backed off, Richard responded "I knew that I had conquered him, had rid myself of him mentally and emotionally."[49]

The message in Williams's story is similar to Douglass's, Wright's, and others: Standing up alone to harsh and oppressive conditions leads to self-liberation. It is not in the collective but in the single-handed struggle that one finds one's manhood. The instant a man refuses to tolerate social injustice is the moment he stands up to be a man.

Gender is a socially constructed (and at times ahistorical) ideological process through which individuals are positioned and position themselves as men or as women. For Williams this Victorian form of manliness became a weapon in his fight for equality. He used a brand of manly identity rooted in late nineteenth- and early twentieth-century western culture that emphasized a hypermasculinity linked to power and authority. The attributes were intellectualism, honor, sexual self-restraint, bravery, strength, independence in spirit, "high-mindedness," and a powerful will. This definition of manhood, as historian Gail Bederman notes, was exclusive to white men and was used to deny that black men were manly. Black men did not measure up because they simply lacked these Victorian virtues. They were instead portrayed as weak-minded and cowardly. Williams challenged this exclusively white men's club of manliness by simply appropriating these characteristics and forging an image of a black masculinity.[50]

Bishop Williams's attempt to transform the struggle for school integration into the battle for decent treatment of his own family no doubt had great appeal in a society that clearly defined masculine and feminine behavior. It was quite appealing to a patriarchal society where manhood was synonymous with assertive behavior, intolerance of injustice, and the will to strike out even in a violent fashion. As scholars have noted, the cold war was not just a battle over political and economic systems. Cold warriors linked gender roles and sexual behavior to the fight against Communism. Feminism was portrayed as weak, irrational, emotional, and, at times, dangerous to the nation. Historian Elaine May argues that men who were portrayed as feminine were seen as sexual deviants who could easily be won over by internal Communists and so undermine the security of the nation. The major weapon to avert such a threat was a concept of masculinity that defined men as rough, individualistic, and willing to fight to defend their freedom, honor, family, and country. Any alternative behavior fell into the realm of the feminine and was viewed as weakness. Marriage and family became major weapons against subversion because men could present the proper male role to guard against deviant behavior and also guard against mothers who helped produce effeminate "sexual deviant" sons by overprotecting them. As May notes, fatherhood during the cold war period "became a new badge of masculinity." This concept clearly had no space for intellectuals, homosexuals, or weaklings.[51]

Instead of challenging this sentiment, Bishop Williams actually manipulated this cold war view in his struggle for racial justice. It is no coincidence that several photographs of Williams with his family are printed in Williams's autobiography; their presence authenticated his role as husband and father. The photos, along with the language of authenticity of black maleness, were a politics of representation. The serious look, no smile, clean-cut, clean-shaven, trimmed mustache, and suit sought to portray black men in a much more serious light. These images, along with his sermons and writings, reinforced the representation of an asexual being, divorced from the body, who engaged the mind. It was in opposition to the dichotomy that cultural critic Paul Gilroy has eloquently noted in western thought about race: "blacks are the body and whites are the mind." Williams's suit and tie were a challenge to the image of black male deviance and criminality. Williams was aware that he, like every other black person, was scrutinized by a white racist society and seen as other than a law-abiding citizen. The suit was a strategy to do away with the old racist signifiers. It represented his claim to be a decent, responsible, law-abiding man—a high-status member of the American mainstream. The formal wear strongly suggested a person of good character and deserving respect. Thus, the wearing of the suit was a direct challenge to the larger society's image of blackness.

In her critical examination of W. E. B. Du Bois's *Souls of Black Folk*, Hazel Carby criticizes one of Du Bois's self-proclaimed mentors, philosopher Cornel West, for attempting to link the patrician dress code to a masculine intellectuality.

> West's claim is that moral and ethical values of intellectual practice are inscribed in the clothed body, and these clothes secured the status of the intellect within. The clothes can then be read, unproblematically, as clear signs of intellectual worth.
>
> A comparison of the photographs of Du Bois and Cornel West demonstrates how the male body can be sculpted to model an intellectual mentor. But to define this appearance as the only acceptable confirmation of intellectual vocation, critical intelligence, and moral action is also to secure these qualities as irrevocably and conservatively masculine. Just as Du Bois constantly replaces and represses images of sexual desire (in his chapter on Atlanta) with evocations of a New England work ethic, so West equates the body and mind as disciplined and contained within a dark, severely cut three-piece suit, buttoned shirt, and tightly drawn tie.[52]

Carby's critique of West serves as well to describe Williams's linking dress to a moral and masculine politics. The representation of family members also serves as proof of his manhood. Members of his family appeared happy, wore nice clothes, and were in a comfortable household. Williams is seated on a couch wearing a light suit and a pair of wire-frame glasses. Sitting to his right is his son, Smallwood Jr., who is dressed in a dark suit. Mrs. Williams is to the left of the bishop. She is dressed in a suit and is looking at her husband and Smallwood Jr. A daughter, Yvonne, is sitting in a chair to the far left of her brother Smallwood Jr. The youngest child, Wallace, is sitting on the floor next to a woman who is not identified. The caption under the photos reads: "The Bishop's greatest accomplishments, he often says, is the family he and Mrs. Williams reared in Washington. Each of the children, now grown, holds a responsible position."[53]

Despite her contributions to the building of Bible Way, Williams described his wife, Verna Williams, simply as a helpmate. As the church membership increased, Williams asserted, "She helped me by organizing various clubs, directed our Radio Chorus for more than thirty-five years," and was an "excellent manager and bookkeeper." These were important accomplishments, but Williams couches them in terms of serving a greater need by contending that "she took an avid interest in every facet of my work and life." So her managerial skills do not stand outside of his work but are instead seen as contributing to his ability to lead. He praised her for being a wonderful mother and a good homemaker who furnished "our home and church with great taste."[54]

Williams's ability to display to the public his success as a husband and father helped move his private world into the public realm. His family stood in contrast to the popular and social scientific literature that portrayed the black family as dysfunctional and disorganized and black males as irresponsible. He wanted to demonstrate to readers that the institution of fatherhood transcends race. The bishop contended that he, as a black man, was a good and loving parent. The caption's claim that Williams's greatest accomplishment was the family he and his wife had reared points out that he embraced the American virtues of the all-caring parent. Caring parent denoted one's humanity. The two, manliness and fatherhood, became synonymous. By declaring himself a successful father, he was demanding credibility and respect as a man. He was asserting the humanity of people of African origins. This image served both black and white audiences. For whites it was a direct challenge to racist stereotypes of blackness. For blacks it served as signifier of identity.

Central to Williams's attempt to construct images of black maleness was the issue of control, both physical and psychological. The scene of the bishop escorting his son to the all-white school and sitting with him in the classroom was an attempt to show the public that he was carrying out his role as a patriarch and as a man who was standing up to the system. The notion of independence was wrapped in the cloth of an assertive masculinity that ruled out any alternative model.

Williams's religious conceptualizations of the civil rights struggle as a challenge to manhood led him to adopt an individualist approach to struggle. As noted earlier, although he participated with other ministers and hundreds of demonstrators in Washington, D.C., in integrating restaurants in the late 1940s and early 1950s, the Pentecostal bishop did not bother mentioning this campaign in his writings. He did write about his involvement in the D.C. Coalition of Conscience formed in 1965 after a homeless mother of five was denied housing by the district welfare agency and eventually died of a blood clot in a psychiatric ward. However, he ends the episode of the story by noting that the case "inspired me to seek government aid in providing low and medium income housing for the people of our city."[55]

Moreover, although the bishop does not mention it, Verna Williams was also involved in the struggle, as a *Washington Evening Star* article notes. While the Pentecostal leader met with school officials, his wife accompanied their son to the all-white school. Hence, she was also critically involved in the struggle to break down the walls of segregation in the public schools of Washington, D.C. However, his focus was on his activities and his interpretation of the struggle to desegregate the nation's capital. This was not merely a case of Williams boasting of his accomplishments while ignoring the work of others. In his stress on leadership he emphasized the role of the sacred, particularly God's agency and his manipulation of moral men to bring about change. Social protest movements that stressed ordinary people's ability to bring about change contrasted with Williams's view of the limitation on human agency and God's intrusiveness in human affairs. This individualistic approach and view that God selected male leaders to make change led Williams to compare himself to such prophets as Moses fighting

Pharaoh and John the Baptist. Like Moses whom God used to warn the pharaohs, Williams asserted that he was being used to tell the modern pharaohs to honor God by upholding racial and economic justice. In chapter 10 of his autobiography, "The Prophet-Statesman," Williams asserts that the minister is a man of God and "must be like John the Baptist, crying in the wilderness of the asphalt jungles in the ghetto." Williams went as far as to claim that he was a prophet whose mission was to serve his people. "The prophet ofthe Eighth Century before Christ [Ezekiel] identified himself with the struggles and aspirations of his oppressed and enslaved people. And I, a twentieth-century prophet and a servant of God and the people, make no apology for use of the means of government, politics and all other legitimate means to free our people."[56] This strategy of linking the ancient text to current affairs was an appeal to those who held a Christian outlook or world view. As a modern Moses he was an agent of God, acting in His behalf. Thus, Williams's cause was not simply fair and reasonable; it was nothing less than sacred.

Bishop Williams's masculine imagery was not only used in his fight for racial justice, but also deployed against his critics. The Julius Hobson episode is a case in point. In July 1972 Hobson, the head of the Washington, D.C., branch of the Congress of Racial Equality (CORE), publicly criticized Williams by accusing him of building an expensive temple, living in a mansion that contained a huge portrait of the bishop, and taking a Cadillac with him to Europe. "Now I have worked in the churches in the town and I have tried on many occasions to appeal to them on the worldly hopes men set their hearts upon. I've been very interested in having discussions with ministers regarding the social problems in the community," the CORE leader asserted in an editorial that appeared in *The Washington Post*. But, according to Hobson, though he was invited to speak at Bible Way, he failed to have a serious conversation with the bishop. He accused Williams of exploiting his congregation. "He [Williams] took up a 'love' offering, he took up a minister's travel offering and then he took up a regular [offering]—he took up five or six offerings. So when he got to me to speak, I got up and said, 'Goddammit, if this is Christianity, I want no part of it and this son of a bitch is stealing from you, and the thing is, he's not just stealing your money, he's stealing your minds.' And I refuse to be a part of this. And I walked off."[57]

Williams attributed Hobson's attack to "his serious illness." While giving credit to the civil rights leader for his struggles, the bishop noted that "Mr. Hobson's illness is not only physical, but has also affected his once brilliant mind." Williams refuted Hobson's claims. Williams pointed out that Hobson was never invited to speak at Bible Way. "The only automobiles I have ever shipped abroad anywhere were a pick-up truck and a jeep, which were sent to Liberia, West Africa, as a gift to the Bible Way Mission School for our educational outreach for African children in the village of Tapeta, 250 miles from Monrovia." The bishop wrote that he had to make no apologies for living in a nice house. In fact, he worked hard to help provide decent housing for medium- and low-income African Americans in Washington's Northwest area. Blacks, regardless of their class position, should be entitled to a decent place to live he said. More important, Williams revealed to the nation that he possessed the Protestant work ethic because he was able to provide his family with a decent home. "While Mr. Hobson was making noise and appearing on television, I was and am working." The masculine tone of Washington's rebuttal is evident. His reference to Hobson's "making noise" was not just his way of displaying his disagreement with using a politics of protest, but also of implying that Hobson's methodology was irrational. Making noise is not constructive engagement. It is equated with hysteria, and is unproductive. By contrast, Williams was a good provider for both his family and the black people in Washington. His brand of serious politics resulted in benefits.

By classifying Hobson as a sick man, Williams placed him outside of the category of leadership because he was an irrational person. Hobson's cancer took away his independence because it affected not just his body but his mind. Because he was not a rational thinker, he could not be held responsible for his actions. Instead, Williams blamed the *Post*. It was the *Post* that manipulated Hobson's condition in order to sell newspapers. In fact, Hobson was portrayed as a victim of the *Post*.[58]

Conclusion

Williams's manly, individualist, and patriarchal approach is at best a paradox, containing negatives as well as positives in the struggle for black liberation. Despite its attractiveness, his individualist approach to struggle had its limitations. That Williams adopted this model (like so many others) has to be faulted because such an approach did not advocate a broader grassroots protracted movement. It viewed leaders as important and ignored a more democratic approach that embraced the involvement of others. The civil rights movement that emerged during the cold war period relied not only on important men, but on thousands of people across the nation.

Moreover, another problem with Williams's approach was that it did not see other forms of oppression interlocked with racism. The interlocking system of racism, sexism, class exploitation, and gay and lesbian bashing that lead to inequality is denied in a masculine and patriarchal model of protest. His use of manliness helped reinforce the sexist notion that women were irrational beings, incapable of leading and participating in struggle. While challenging the dominance of whiteness, he said nothing about sexual and gender oppression. An emphasis on fixed gender behavior stresses a Victorian masculine authenticity that would not consider alternatives to the popular view of men and women's roles in a society. Thus gay and lesbian groups that experienced discrimination were invisible to Williams.

Williams's attempt to create a universal black manly image ignored the reality that structural forces play a major role in defining and shaping manhood. Cultural critic Kobena Mercer notes:

Patriarchal culture constantly redefines and adjusts the balance of male power and privilege, and the prevailing system of gender roles, through a variety of material, economic, social and political structures such as class, the division of labor and the work and home nexus at the point of consumption. Race and ethnicity mediates this process at all levels, so it is not as if we could strip away the "negative images" of black male identity which is essentially good, pure and wholesome.[59]

It should be noted that Williams's sexual politics was juxtaposed to the reality that women played a significant role in church culture. They were leaders of choirs, Sunday schools, and auxiliaries. As leaders of various church organizations, they organized events, raised money, and reported to the congregation on their activities. Because of their activities, they managed to carve out public space and remained in the public eye of the church community. Moreover, black women outnumbered black men in the congregation and were able to have a voice in the church through music, testimony, and other participatory rituals. Just as important, although Pentecostal churches were known for adopting a strong fundamentalist view, gays and lesbians functioned in the churches with impunity. This is because, in part, music is central to the church service. Consequently, the church relied on musically talented people to sing, lead choirs, and play musical instruments. Black Pentecostal churches became more tolerant of gays and lesbians, especially those who possessed musical talents. In the midst of acclamation of the masculine gender model, church parishioners challenged and destabilized this model with alternative ones.

But the construction of a black manhood had its merits. It was both a sociological and psychological strategy. It was an attempt to transform the thinking of people in a race conscious society. To be sure, in a society that portrayed black men as social deviants, criminals, lazy, instinctual, clowns controlled by their emotions and libidos instead of their minds, Williams's social construction of the black patriarch served a useful purpose. It was an attempt to counteract racist notions by publicly portraying black men in control of both public and private spheres. Because he was able to draw the spotlight and grab some public attention, Williams represented the black male as caring father, devoted husband, and a race man. He carved out some room for black men in the intellectual and political life of the larger society.

Williams's black manhood model should be seen in opposition to other models that emerged during the post–World War II period, in particular, the cool jazz image that was personified by trumpeter Miles Davis. Davis's autobiography highlights his artistic work, but it also tells the reader how he created and maintained a black hypermasculinity. While Williams's manhood model was steeped in a Victorian and religious construct, Davis's was grounded in secular images that were enormously misogynist, violent, and sexually exploitive. Davis notes that he learned at an early age from his father to be "cold." He describes admiringly how men, including his father, were brutal to women and included an episode in which his father punched his wife (Miles's mother), knocking "a couple of teeth right out of her mouth," after she locked him out of the house. Davis leaves the reader with the impression that his mother had provoked her husband into striking her.[60] He also notes how the jazz singer Billy Eckstine's brutalizing of a woman reassured Miles of the singer's masculinity despite his "soft" look.

> B [Billy Eckstine] was so clean and fine back in them days that women were all over his ass. He was so handsome that I used to think he looked like a girl sometimes. A lot of people thought that because B was so handsome that he was soft. But B was one of the toughest motherfuckers I ever met. One time we were in Cleveland or Pittsburgh and everybody was waiting on B outside his hotel in the bus, ready to go. We were about an hour late in leaving. Now here comes B out of the hotel with this fine woman. He said to me, "Hey, Dick, this is my woman." She said something like, "I got a name, Billy, tell him my name." B turned around and said, "Bitch, shut up!" He slapped the shit out of her right there. She says to B, "Listen, you motherfucker, if you wasn't so pretty I'd break your motherfucking neck, you jive bastard." B was just standing there laughing and shit, say, "Aw, shut up, bitch. Wait til I get some rest. I'm gonna knock your fucking ass out!"[61]

For Miles, violence was an affirmation of manhood and a tool used to enforce male dominance over any woman who challenged it. So Eckstine's actions were to be admired because he proved that although he looked "soft," he behaved like a man and because he was more than willing to put a woman in her place.

Boxing became Davis's favorite sport and Sugar Ray Robinson became his role model because he was cold and had the ability to knock anyone out. When constructing the cool jazz image, Davis emulated Robinson because he was confident, fearless, had the ability to inflict pain and he was someone who was a sharp dresser. In fact, Davis's explanation of why he spent a great deal of time discussing Ray Robinson in his autobiography is that he became "the most important thing in my life besides music. I found myself even acting like him, you know, everything. Even taking on his arrogant attitude. Ray was cold and he was the best and he was everything I wanted to be in 1954."[62]

The cool persona, for Davis, consisted of being "rebellious, and black, a nonconformist, being cool and hip and angry and sophisticated and ultra clean, whatever else you want to call it—I was all those things and more. It also meant being able to have women."[63]

Davis admired men like his father, grandfather, and Sugar Ray Robinson because they didn't "take shit." According to Robinson, "My grandfather was something else, didn't take no shit off no one." On the other hand, women were viewed as a burden causing trouble or as trophies to measure one's manhood. While he painted his father in almost saintly terms, he portrayed his mother as intolerant and controlling. "But my mother would whip the shit out of me at the drop of a hat." His father encouraged his creativity while his mother was an obstacle.[64]

Davis had no hesitation about brutalizing and inflicting pain on women he wanted to control or who were nuisances to him. In his autobiography he revealed the lengths to which he was willing to go in order to maintain his control. As a patriarch, women were suppose to pay him the highest respect or face his wrath. Recalling the time he struck his first wife, Frances Taylor, Davis couched his physical assault in the category of jealousy. "I loved Frances so much that for the first time in my life I found myself jealous. I remember I hit her once when she came home and told me some shit about Quincy Jones being handsome. Before I realized what had happened I had knocked her down. . . ." He confessed that that was not the last time he hit her or other women he would marry, particularly when they demonstrated independence. He battered Cicely Tyson because she annoyed him. He had told her that he did not want a particular friend of hers calling the house, but she protested and he struck her. In fear of being hit again, she fled to the basement of the house and called the police. According to Davis, "What really bothered me about Cicely was how she wanted to control everything in my life." But it is Davis who attempted to assert control by using violence. Even though he admitted that Frances Taylor was a superstar and a very talented dancer, "probably the premier black female dancer," it made no difference to the jazz trumpeter. "But I made her get out of that because I wanted her at home with me. Later when Jerome Robbins personally asked her to do the movie version of *West Side Story,* I wouldn't let her do that or *Golden Boy* with Sammy Davis Jr., who asked her himself when we were playing in Philadelphia."[65]

Apparently, he did not mind that women were sex workers. When he was pimping in 1951, he claimed he "had a whole stable of bitches out on the street for me." But unlike Frances, who was independent and developing her own career, Miles's "bitches" were working to service him. "But it wasn't like people thought it was; the women wanted someone to be with and they liked me. I took them to dinner and shit like that. We'd get down on the sex thing, too, but that wasn't much, because heroin takes away your sex drive. I just treated prostitutes like they were anybody else. I respected them and they would give me money to get off in return. The women thought I was handsome and for the first time in my life I began to think I was, too. We were more like a family than anything." His claim that they were like a family indicates an extreme form of patriarchy that emphasized complete dominance over the women's bodies.[66]

The contrast between Williams's and Davis's configuration and expression of black manhood is quite stark. Although both were patriarchal and used to define their manliness, Davis's was ruthless, exploitive, and individualistic and showed no concern for the women. Williams, while highly paternalistic, centered on the goal of advancing the race.

Williams's greatest contribution to religion and politics was his ability to combine Pentecostalism to a political discourse that allowed for many to participate in the political arena without sacrificing political beliefs. His stress on individualist politics should not be seen as egotistical but as a means of remaining true to one's faith while carving out a map for political involvement for Pentecostals and others.

Scholar James Cone argues that the advocacy of freedom and hope has been an important component of African-American religion. The message of hope and the advocacy of freedom were central messages of Bishop Smallwood Williams. Without a doubt, his activism for social justice was not only a product of his theological training but was also rooted in the black Pentecostal church. Black Pentecostalism needs to be studied not simply as an aspect of African-American religion but also as a formative element in African-American social thought, literary expression, and political activism. Black religion and black Pentecostalism have been a part of the cultural and political landscape of the country and have had a dramatic impact on American society. One of the most important contributions of African-American religion has been the shaping and the nurturing of black leadership. Black Pentecostalism is no exception to the rule.[67]

CHAPTER 4

The Reverend John Culmer and the Politics of Black Representation in Miami, Florida

The Reverend John Culmer was the best-known and most respected black leader in Miami during the 1930s and 1940s. Still, despite his notoriety and prominence, he goes almost unnoticed by scholars. The Episcopalian priest receives little attention in books and articles on Miami's historical past. Paul S. George and Thomas Petersen note only that Culmer was a member of a black advisory group that helped secure public housing for blacks in Miami. Author Marvin Dunn's *Black Miami in the Twentieth Century* takes an uncritical but more extensive look at the Episcopalian priest. However, there is little assessment of Culmer's leadership.[1]

Throughout his career as an Episcopalian rector, Culmer dedicated himself to improving the social conditions of black people. To a large degree, the political climate helped mold his political activist approaches. Culmer adopted an accommodationist style. Operating in a harsh racial climate, he attempted to improve race relations between the dominant white majority and black minority and win concessions for blacks without committing major impairment to the city's apartheid system. The Episcopalian priest was heavily engaged in a politics of "possibility" and retained a hope and faith in the benevolence of white elites. He was working in a period when there was little militant activity in the black community that challenged the Jim Crow structure in Florida. Moreover, he was a leader when few white allies were willing to participate in a militant battle against Jim Crow. Consequently, Culmer keenly manipulated a certain segment of the larger white society by promoting a congenial relationship model between blacks and whites in the hope of winning concessions for African Americans from white elites.

Culmer relied on a class-based politics that portrayed the black elite as the guardians of a black bourgeois culture. The rector of Saint Agnes Episcopal Church portrayed himself and others of his class as law-abiding, congenial, hardworking people who embraced middle-class values, opposed crime, and deserved respect. A politics of respectability was evident in his style of leadership. Moreover, Culmer used an indirect challenge that maneuvered around the contours of white supremacy without demanding its immediate destruction. He became the rational negotiator who was able to work with the power structure for goods and services to the black masses. Harmonious relations were not merely an objective but a means to secure benefits for those of African origins. The core message of his leadership was that whites as well as blacks, even in a Jim Crow society, were good-natured and could get along. Connected with the Episcopalian priest's methodology of shaping black and white representation was his vision of the state. Culmer's state was not one in which rulers imposed or regulated the relationship between the races. The best government was one that allowed the good nature of human beings to determine their affinity and well-being.

Scholar Peta Stephenson notes: "Racial or ethnic identities are not always externally imposed, and may be invoked as political resources by subordinate group members themselves. The stigma of inferiority usually attached to oppressed groups may be inverted to incite political mobilization against oppression."[2] Culmer took part in cultural politics by attempting to reshape the black image. He used the signifiers of class, race, and nation in the unending black liberation struggle.

Miami's Black Community

Throughout its history Miami's black community was socially stratified. Many of its black residents were made up of people from the black diaspora. Historian Raymond Mohl notes that by 1920, 5,000 people from the Caribbean, the majority from the Bahamas, made up 50 percent of the black population of Miami. Besides native-born African Americans, Jamaicans and Haitians flocked there seeking economic opportunities. Blacks worked as laborers in clearing land for construction projects, draymen, stevedores, and hotel porters. Some labored as mechanics, leather tanners, tailors, blacksmiths, and gardeners. Black working-class women worked as domestic workers, laundresses, nursemaids, and cooks.

Despite their efforts at finding economic success, many blacks were relegated to live in an area known as Colored Town, later called Overtown. The formation of Overtown confirms the view that residents of ghettos do not create them. On the contrary, those with power, including politicians, realtors, bankers, and white homeowners who fear black encroachment, form and maintain these segregated and dilapidated areas. Their major objective has been to contain black bodies in designated areas. For decades Colored Town was the only area of Miami in which blacks could live. Many of the houses were rundown shacks owned by white absentee landlords. By 1930, 25,116 blacks lived in this black community, and most lived on city blocks that contained three to fifteen shacks. The conditions for most working-class blacks in Colored Town were overcrowded and unsanitary. Colored Town, like other black areas, did not receive adequate city services. Despite the fact that the area's population grew, few city services were provided Miami's black community. There were no playgrounds or parks; inadequate educational facilities led to a high illiteracy rate; and poor sanitation services resulted in a high incidence of disease.[3]

Socially, Colored Town and, later, Liberty City, Coconut Grove, and other areas of black concentration in Miami were not one-dimensional but rather heterogeneous communities. Despite the despair in Colored Town, it contained a black middle class. Many who made up the black bourgeoisie had migrated from other parts of the South. These were doctors, lawyers, teachers, dentists, pharmacists, small business owners, and clergy, and according to black attorney L. E. Thomas, they desired autonomy. By 1904, two black doctors practiced in Miami as well as two pharmacists. "The completeness of two drug stores operated by two black pharmacists," Thomas asserted, "makes it entirely unnecessary for us to leave our own section to purchase anything sold in drug stores. People's Drugs, the older store, has filled more than 40,000 prescriptions since 1925." Thomas contended that black professionals were not separate but worked to service the black community. "The stores have the unified support of the doctors, and together, it is safe to say, fill more prescriptions in proportion to the population than any Negro druggists in the South."

But doctors and pharmacists were not the only black professionals that were dedicated to the community. Thomas declared that black lawyers in the city were serious professionals. He asserted that he and his fellow black colleagues were not "glorified notaries" with law licenses. "We mean the independent practice before the bar in our own rights, matching wits with adversaries and diligently pursuing the rights of clients as counsel and advocate." Thomas went so far as to declare that he engaged in a higher type of practice than was his privilege in his two years at the Detroit bar. According to the attorney, judges in Miami treated him with consideration.

It might appear that Thomas was attempting to deny the existence of Jim Crow in Miami. However, one should not dismiss his comments. On the contrary, his comparison of Detroit and Miami strongly indicates that the North was no bed of roses when it came to race relations and that the attorney might have experienced racial hostility in the North. It also suggests that not all blacks experienced Jim Crow in Miami in the same manner. Members of the black bourgeoisie, especially professionals, gained some benefits from racially segregated society. Segregated communities that were denied services by the larger white community were dependent on the black middle class. Likewise, many black business owners and professionals who were not allowed to operate in the white areas of Miami were dependent on a black clientele. Besides having a place to practice their particular professions and operate businesses, they were recognized as leaders and spokespeople of the community. "The importance of the business we handle is measured chiefly by our ability, diligence, character and the confidence Negroes have in their own." Moreover, at least some members of the white power structure recognized members of the black middle class as professionals.

Many black businesses operated in Colored Town. Historian Paul S. George notes that Colored Town's business district was predominantly black owned. "By 1905, it contained grocery and general merchandise stores, an ice cream parlor, a pharmacy, a funeral parlor, clubhouses, rooming houses, and an office of the *Industrial Reporter,* a black newspaper. A soft drink plant, professional offices, real estate brokers, insurance agencies, and numerous food and entertainment establishments later joined these enterprises." By the 1920s a number of nightclubs and dance halls operated in Colored Town and featured big-name entertainers such as Marion Anderson, Bessie Smith, and Nat King Cole.[4]

Members of Miami's black middle class attempted to address the social conditions of Colored Town. The Negro Uplift Association waged a battle against police brutality. But while some members of the black elite addressed institutional racism, others used the strategy of social and moral uplift. Though they advocated black self-sufficiency, they also became staunch advocates of molding black working behavior. By shaping black behavior into more acceptable middle-class behavior, they argued blacks would be accepted into the larger white society. Thus, they pushed the view that one must take responsibility for one's own life. Like the larger white society, they argued that virtuous demeanor would win favor with whites; therefore, racism was not the major culprit of the lack of black progress; the cause was indecent black action.

The black middle class complained about some of the activities of working-class people, including gambling, drinking, and "rowdiness." Saloons and bars operated in the northwest part of Colored Town, thus clashing with the Victorian virtues of the black middle class. Moreover, because of protest from middle-class citizens of North Miami, sexual workers operating there were forced by law enforcement officials to relocate into the northwest part of Colored Town, thus helping to create a red light district. The Civic League of Miami, a white civic organization, and later its black counterpart, the Civic League of Colored Town, launched an effort to clean up the area of "vice." Instead of targeting the racist policies of law enforcement and the denial of adequate services to residents, the Civic League of Colored Town called for a 8:00 P.M. curfew for children, the removal of sex workers from the streets, and the escorting of "good women" after 9:00 P.M.[5]

In addition to the Civic League of Colored Town, other strong advocates of uplift were the Negro Uplift Association of Dade County, the Dade County Women Civil Improvement Association, and the Adelphian Club.[6] The Adelphian Club, organized in the early 1920s, consisted of such notables as John Culmer, Luther O. Carey, a prominent real estate agent, and S. G. Dames, manager of the Miami branch of the Afro-Insurance Company. In addition to these groups, the Black division of the Junior Chamber of Commerce helped sponsor a Clean-Up Drive of Miami's black communities. Women were major figures in organizing clubs. Black women established a host of sororities, including the Beta Zeta Sigma chapter of the Delta Sigma Theta Sorority and the Gamma Zeta Omega chapter of the A.K.A Sorority. Non-Pareil Study Club, organized by women in 1927, encouraged education among African Americans. According to its 1941 calendar the Cwest Club was organized in 1920 by women because a "lot of time was being wasted" by black women. Their objective was to channel black women's time into constructive behavior. They hosted a number of "teas" and did charity work. The club's song reflected the group's philosophy.

Sewing and weaving,
Uplifting the coming youth;
And in our Leaving,
We hold our hands to you;
Self-improvement and others,
Are our tasks day by day [7]

The civic activities among Miami's black middle class demonstrates their faith in shaping black behavior. It accepted the notion that blacks, even in a Jim Crow society, were not victims, but agents who could shape their lives.

Culmer's Politics of Accommodation

John Culmer became part of a black elite culture that had heavily invested in good harmonious race relations in the context of Jim Crow. Culmer, who became the chief agent of uplift and accommodation in Miami, was born in the Bahamas in 1891 and grew up on a farm owned by his father. He left the Bahamas in 1911 to find a seminary in New York or Philadelphia where he could train for a career in the ministry. However, he was denied admission to a seminary in those cities because of racial discrimination. After a brief visit back to the Bahamas, he eventually came to Miami where he worked in low-paying jobs. Eventually he joined Christ Episcopal Church in Coconut Grove and served as its organist and Sunday school teacher.

Since Miami was a segregated society that offered blacks practically no opportunity for higher education, Culmer left the city and attended Oskaloosa College in Iowa, receiving a bachelor's degree in music. He then attended Bishop Payne Divinity School in Petersburg, Virginia, earning a bachelor of divinity in 1919. After his graduation he served as priest in charge of Saint James Episcopal Church in Tampa, Florida. [8]

After a successful career at Saint James, Culmer relocated to Miami and became rector of Saint Agnes Church, which had started out as an Episcopalian mission. Built in 1898, the church was one of the oldest in Miami. It had experienced some rough times. It first attracted people from the Bahamas because a large number of people from the island were Episcopalian. However, many of these early members were migratory workers who came to the city during crop season. Many of the new arrivals stayed, but by 1900 stronger immigration laws curtailed immigration. In spite of the law, the church began to attract people who were native born.

A schism took place in the 1920s when some members wanted the church to become part of the African Orthodox Church. As noted in chapter 2, Alexander McGuire, a follower of Marcus Garvey, established the AOC and modeled itself on the Episcopalian. However, McGuire argued that white symbols and white church officials should be replaced with blacks symbols and figures. The stress on racial pride and racial emancipation attracted some 400 people from Saint Agnes. They left the church to join an AOC body. Moreover, the church was experiencing some financial difficulty.[9] Culmer had had a very successful leadership at Saint James in Tampa by eliminating the church's mortgages of $25,000 and helping the institution grow. When he arrived at Saint Agnes, he inherited a divided church membership and a debt of $3,000. Under Culmer's leadership, Saint Agnes overcame its financial problems by raising money from the members and receiving a loan. It even managed to buy a new church building.[10]

Culmer's leadership strategy of developing trust among white officials in order to win concessions grew out of the harsh reality of black life in Miami. It clearly differed from Afro-Christian liberalism, because in Miami, blacks could not rely on the state to codify and institutionalize mechanisms to protect their rights. By 1936, thanks to the activities of progressives like Claude Pepper, Bowden Thomas, and the Citizens' Protective League, Florida abolished the poll tax. But even as it abolished the poll tax the state legislature passed a bill barring Miami blacks from participating in municipal primaries. Even southern progressives like Claude Pepper could not be counted on to support an all-out battle for black political empowerment. His opposition to the poll tax was not grounded in race but in his disapproval of how white workers suffered. Despite his liberalism, he clearly did not want to appear to southern whites as though he was opposing segregation. He openly claimed that he was not in favor of black enfranchisement. In a letter to a friend, Pepper argued that he was an ardent segregationist. " I certainly did not say anything, directly or indirectly, indicating that I believed in social equality because, of course, I do not." He further claimed that his fight against the poll tax was not because he supported black voting rights. "I thoroughly agree with your statement that you have not seen any great influx of Negro voting in Florida on account of the repeal of the poll tax. On the other hand, it definitely resulted in giving the right to vote to many people who were disfranchised by the poll tax." Pepper, like many southern progressives, made no room for racial equality when it came to their vision of liberalism.[11]

The government sanctioned Jim Crow; the Ku Klux Klan attempted to intimidate black voters. Author John Egerton contends that the racial terrorizing of blacks was common in the South. The author writes that "it was the eleven states of the old confederacy that built compulsory segregation and blatant white supremacy into laws and customs across the board, and that's what made them seem so different from the rest of the country in the 1930s."[12]

In Miami, a staunch Jim Crow city, African Americans faced discrimination and racial consternation. Throughout the 1920s, the Ku Klux Klan subjected blacks to attacks. On several occasions, the Klan paraded through the streets of Miami, attracting thousands. In 1925 the local chapter of the Klan estimated its membership at 1,500.[13] But its influence cannot be assessed by its membership alone. It became an acceptable fraternity among white Floridians. The acceptance of the Klan by white Miamians was indicated in 1925 when members of the Klan marched in the Fiesta of the American Tropics Parade in Miami on December 31, 1927. The racist-terrorist organization's presence in the city's celebration was so acceptable that in 1927 the American Legion gave an award to the Klan for the best float in the annual Independence Day parade. Lynchings, bombings, kidnappings, and beatings of ministers and others accused of promoting black equality were a reality in Miami. Anyone speaking out against racial injustice could easily become a target of the Klan. H. H. Higgs, a Coconut Grove black minister and president of the local branch of Marcus Garvey's Universal Negro Improvement Association, was kidnapped by the Klan in July 1921. The racist group accused the black preacher of advocating equality and interracial marriage. It only released him after he agreed to go back to the Bahamas. During the 1930s and 1940s, the Klan continued its campaign of intimidation against blacks and labor leaders who sought interracial cooperation. The Klan attempted to intimidate Charlie Smolikoff, the director of the Florida branch of the Congress of Industrial Organizations, by visiting his home.[14]

As late as the 1940s, racial terror was still a reality for blacks in Miami. The famed actor Sidney Poiter, who was born in the Bahamas and came to Miami in 1943 at the age of fifteen, quickly became aware of the reality of racism in the city. Soon after his arrival in Miami, Poitier got a job delivering packages for Burdine's Department Store. According to Poitier, "I joined a cadre of little black kids who made up deliveries on bicycles."[15]

Poitier recalls delivering a package to a wealthy area in Miami Beach. When he rang the doorbell, a white woman demanded to know what he wanted. After he told her he was there to deliver a package, she told him to go around to the back of the house. Unaware of the protocol, the teenager asked why he had to go around to the back of the house. When the woman became angry and slammed the door in his face, Poitier, unaware of the import of his actions, broke a Jim Crow rule: he left the package at the front door and walked away. This small act was seen as an act of defiance. He had not only failed to respect white womanhood, but also challenged the South's racist etiquette. He had refused to act in the manner required of blacks in the South. By simply leaving the package at the front door, he put his life in mortal danger.

Two evenings later, returning from the movies with one of my cousins, I noticed that my brother's house was completely dark—at a very early hour—which seemed a bit peculiar. As we approached the porch, voices from within the house whispered, "Get on in the house. Come on in the house." We stepped inside and found the whole family moving about in an atmosphere of heavy tension as if they were under siege. In hushed tones, my sister-in-law asked accusingly, "Where have you been?" We said we had gone to the movies. "Did you see those white men?" she inquired. I said "No," and she said, "They had on robes and hoods. They said they were looking for you. We've got your clothes packed. We've got to get you out of here." It still didn't scare me. I'd heard about the Klan and the nightriders, and white folks who were always trying to intimidate black folks but I wasn't frightened by them. Possibly because I didn't know any better at that time, which was due in part to my spending the first fifteen years of my life free of the crushing nega-tive self-image hammered into black children by this system, in this Miami, in this America. Under cloak of darkness I was hurried out of my brother's house and ten miles across town, to Uncle Joe's place on Third Street, where my brother had made arrangements for me to retreat. I settled in there and imme-diately started looking for another job, having been told by my brother never to go back to Burdine's.[16]

Poitier's experience demonstrated the means which Jim Crow Miami would take to uphold the racial order. There were no deviations, not even for a boy of fifteen who was unfamiliar with the American South's racial customs.

And if the Klan attacks were not bad enough, blacks were targets of a racist police force. Numerous beatings and killings of blacks were carried out by police officers with impunity. Blacks were usually accused of moral crimes—gambling, prostitution, disturbing the peace. Police chief Leslie Quigg was well known for his harsh treatment of blacks. In 1925 he was tried for killing a black man. A 1928 grand jury found that Quigg recruited racist whites to his police force and assigned them to Colored Town without offer-ing them any training. The report also accused the police chief of using the electric chair as a form of torture to get confessions. Charlie Smolikoff was arrested on a bogus traffic violation. The reason the police targeted the labor leader was due to his organizing effort of black shipbuilding workers in 1943. Moreover, police raided the home of other CIO organizers in 1948 in an attempt to stop interracial union organizing. It was under these repressive conditions that militant collective activism was curtailed.[17]

Instead of risking immediate reprisals by traveling the more militant path and alarming the vast majority of whites in the city, Culmer attempted to win support from whites in power by arguing that blacks were not a threat to the social, political, and economic order of the South. Absent from his message was any emphasis on black political and economic empowerment. Instead, he became an advocate of the notion of white benevolence and good faith. Throughout his career in Miami, Culmer contended that the true objective of blacks was harmonious race relations within a racist society. He constantly reassured whites that Miami's black population only wanted to take steps to maintain a good relationship between the races. In his effort not to be seen as a challenger to the Jim Crow system in his campaign, the politically moderate priest stressed the obligation of blacks to improve black life. Culmer adopted what historian Neil McMillen calls a "feasible limits" approach as a means of confronting white supremacy. According to McMillen, feasible limits is a form of low drama resistance, not involving direct-action campaigns. "Black spokesmen frequently demonstrated for better jobs, better schools, and full citizenship rights. But neither massive street demonstrations against economic and educational discrimination nor voter registration campaigns designed to arouse the disfranchised black underclass were within the realm of possibilities."[18]

Culmer was a part of the generation that arose after the first Reconstruction period. Its leadership in business and law and in the black churches selected a strategy of accommodation to whites in exchange for economic benefits. To his credit, Culmer pushed the boundaries of Jim Crow in his search for political gains and improvements in health care and living standards for Miami's black population. In the Episcopal priest's conciliatory approach there was an emphasis on racial solidarity as well as harmonious race relations. Clearly, he was aware that physical contact with white society required that blacks obey a set of Jim Crow etiquette rules that only humiliated them. These rules were a means of dehumanizing African Americans and upholding white supremacy. An attempt to improve conditions in the black community and to encourage blacks to become more self-reliant helped create an organic black community that offered an alternative to the larger white society's constant racial attacks. Hence, his rejection of political agitation and his reliance on white benevolent action and black Miami's ability to transform itself into a "nobler" race was a means of uplifting their spirits as well as improving their material condition.

An example of Culmer's white benevolence and black obligation message is in the *Miami Herald*'s exposé on slum life. As a result of these articles, describing the horrendous conditions of the slums that blacks occupied in Miami's Colored Town, the mayor appointed him to a committee that investigated slum conditions. Thanks to his efforts, ten blocks of a slum area were condemned and a federal housing project was built in Liberty Square. He also took credit for the development of playgrounds and the planting of trees in black areas.[19]

Culmer's approach extended beyond seeking decent housing for blacks; he even used a nonthreatening approach to raise the issue of voting rights. The rector's argument for black enfranchisement rested on the view that blacks must pull their fair share. He asserted that blacks must not be given special treatment but they must be obligated to fulfill their duties of citizenship. Those duties included voting. For Culmer, there was no denying that blacks were citizens. But instead of arguing that the lack of the franchise for blacks had to do with white supremacy, he placed the burden on blacks. They simply had to live up to their responsibilities as citizens. When it came to granting blacks the franchise, Culmer argued that the way to freedom was an individual and group responsibility. Democracy, according to the rector of Saint Agnes, meant no special treatment or favors to minorities but everyone pulling their own weight. The vicar of Saint Agnes did not carve out an expansive role for the state when it came to race relations. He placed emphasis on the civic responsibility of whites and blacks.

In order to help reach his objectives the priest, along with other black ministers of the interdenominational Ministers' Alliance, created "Good Citizenship Sunday." According to Culmer, the ministers and other speakers designated one Sunday in June to speak on the "duties, responsibilities, privileges and benefits of Good Citizenship." Educational mass meetings were held at Saint Agnes and other churches, and ministers gave instructions before primaries and general elections.

Good Citizenship Sunday was more than an attempt at mobilizing black political power in Miami. Such a move within a Jim Crow society could have been seen as threatening. Culmer was aware that attempts by blacks to vote in the South often led to assaults and murder. In order not to arouse or send out a direct challenge to white political dominance, Culmer declared that the organizers were going to stress social uplift. The vicar did not hesitate to try to extract benefits from the most ardent racists. As director of publicity for the Interdenominational Ministers' Alliance, Culmer contacted H. Leslie Quigg, chief of police of the city of Miami, to inform him that the black ministers were going to sponsor a "Better Citizenship" campaign in June. Culmer informed Quigg that the group planned to print placards and distribute them to blacks in public places. In addition, he told the chief that the Alliance wanted to establish a speaker's bureau made up of men and women who would give short talks wherever black people congregated. The placards would inform people that obscenity is objectionable and "crap shooting" is "unnecessary." They would also stress to blacks that crowding on sidewalks and spitting on them were obnoxious acts. Culmer's letter won Quigg's support, in part because of the transformation of public space. Instead of asserting that public space occupied by black citizens was going to be used to sabotage white supremacy by mobilizing them for political empowerment, Culmer convincingly argued that it was going to be used as an arena to mold black working-class behavior.[20]

Culmer's letter also reflected his attitude toward the black working class. Like many of the black elite, the rector peddled the notion of cultural essentialism and was quite critical of black working people. Although he rejected racial authenticity, Culmer, with his stress on Victorian virtues, had little tolerance for behavior outside of what he considered proper. Hence, working-class forms of recreation, which included gambling (playing the numbers and shooting dice), congregating in the streets, listening and dancing to jazz, blues, and other forms of secular music, and frequenting bars and saloons, were looked upon unfavorably by the Saint Agnes vicar. Instead, the black middle class attempted to reshape the black working class by pushing a social uplift agenda. He attempted to convince the working class to adopt more middle class, socially acceptable forms of behavior.

The juxtaposition of strategies on the 1939 election between Culmer and the more militant Sam Solomon, exposes the rector's allegiance to accommodation. Solomon, a journalist and political activist, rallied blacks to the polls by urging them to stand up to the Klan. His position ruled out compromise and appeals to white terrorists or the white power structure to allow blacks to vote. Instead, Solomon adopted the position advocated by W. E. B. Du Bois that defied racists by demanding that blacks be granted the franchise. For Solomon, the agent for black political empowerment was not the white power structure but simply blacks going to the polls. In contrast, Culmer sought the black franchise by relying on the assistance of the white ruling class. The rector noted that he and other ministers wrote a letter to the city's clerk in 1939. The letter requested that he "take such precautionary measures, as, in your judgment, you deem necessary to insure the protection of new voters from racial violence at the polls, as well as to avert any occasion for disturbance of the peace and harmony of the races."

Culmer contended that this letter to the clerk brought assurances from him that the rights of blacks seeking to vote would be protected. The assurance from "the powers to be," according to the priest, "gave the Negroes courage and inspiration to march to the polls undaunted and unafraid." Culmer asserted that the police, "upon whose shoulders the responsibility for any racial uprising had been squarely placed, performed their duty admirably."[21]

Culmer's praise for whites helping secure the franchise for blacks went beyond law enforcement. The priest contended that the appeal to vote was not challenged by the white press. In fact, he asserted, it supported black enfranchisement. Moreover, Culmer argued that his appeal to the city clerk was beneficial despite demonstrations by the Ku Klux Klan because he felt that the white supremacist organization would not dare challenge law enforcement or public opinion. He implied that institutional racism was no hindrance to black progress. In fact, those institutions were supportive of black rights. Thus, there were no demands for the destruction of Jim Crow practices or a call for a democratic approach that would involve unifying the black community across class lines in the struggle against racism. Instead, he adopted an elitist approach that involved black leaders negotiating and appealing for protection and tolerance from the larger white society.[22]

Culmer's disdain for Sam Solomon was quite evident in his writing. Although he did not accuse the militant leader of lying about the record of the black ministers of Miami and only wanted to set the record straight, the tone of the letter is apparent. He claimed sarcastically that Solomon had been "sky-rocketed" to fame and had become the "Moses of the Negroes of Miami" and their "proud Savior." The praise heaped on Solomon by the press, was ridiculed by Culmer.

Congratulations, commendations and invitations flood Mr. Solomon's desk. Among them is an invitation to be guest speaker at the opening session of the thirtieth annual conference of the NAACP. The Conference was held in Richmond, Va.... Notables were there from every section of the nation. There to hear Mr Solomon tell of his triumph in Miami. Over the Klan. Over disease and filth. Over opposition at the polls. Such a recognition must have made our "hero" proud of himself.[23]

The rector's ridicule of the more militant leader was not just a personal attack but was politically motivated. The praise of Solomon indicated that his approach won favor with blacks; thus accommodation was in danger of being replaced with a more militant approach. In defense of his approach, Culmer listed the accomplishments of the Interdenominational Ministers' Alliances, which included the creation of the Negro Citizens League, Citizenship Day, and the letter to the clerk requesting police protection on election day.

Culmer's stress on harmonious race relations, winning concessions for people of African origin, and his nonconfrontational strategy, were evident in his struggle against police brutality. In 1938 the Rector of Saint Agnes, on behalf of the Alliance, published a letter calling on the chief of police to end the reign of terror created by Officer R. B. (Schoolboy) Simpson. Simpson had killed three black people within a seven-month period. However, his complaint was not based on the fact that Simpson killed black people without punishment. He did not talk about the black community being victim to a homicidal, out-of-control cop. Nor was there any mention of human rights violations, or any protest against institutional racism. Instead, the priest appealed to white officials by claiming that Simpson was disturbing the "peace and harmony of the races." The letter called on the white interdenominational ministerial alliance, white women's clubs, and other civic groups to cooperate with his ministerial organization in having the officer transferred. In his letter Culmer challenged the notion that blacks were outside of the law. Despite its conciliatory tone, he attempted to challenge white society's portrait of blacks as criminals by declaring that they were peace-loving and law-abiding citizens.[24] Culmer's attempt at forging black representation as law abiding was a challenge to the then popular view that they were criminals not deserving to be treated as citizens of the states.

Key to Culmer's nonconfrontational strategy was his depiction of race relations in the South. He did not view race relations as horrible. Instead, he portrayed the South as a model of cordial race relations. Because of their long history of close social and geographical location in the South, blacks and whites had the greatest amount of respect for one another. He depicted the history of race relations in the South as an evolutionary process in which both groups worked hard at coming to terms with their existence in the region. Experience was the great teacher. The perpetrators of racist ideology were northern whites. He was publicly critical of Northerners and their policies. For example, he lashed out at the New Deal liberalism. In a letter to Earl Brown, managing editor of *The Amsterdam News*, the priest asserted that since the poll tax had been abolished in 1936, hundreds of blacks had voted in the May primary. He contended that New Deal policies had bene-fited those who had been the "recipients of its charities" and bad for "those who prefer to work for an honest living." Blacks had not received their share of benefits from the New Deal. He noted that blacks had not received their fair share of FHA loans. The rector viewed the expansion of federal power as a means of denying blacks an equal share of resources. For Culmer, only a society that was based on merit could benefit blacks.

Race relations in the South, according to Culmer, had improved. In fact, the priest contended that blacks could receive "more consideration" if petty jealousy did not exist among black leaders and if blacks as a whole had una-nimity. Culmer went so far as to argue that when northern whites come to the South, they were more antagonistic toward blacks than "well-to-do dyed in the wool crackers." Their behavior was based on their desire to impress southern whites.[25]

In a letter to one of the managers of the boxing committee of the munici-pal stadium, Stephen Munulty, Culmer demonstrated to what lengths he would go to win white support in his attempt to convince the officials to allow blacks to attend the events. The rector asserted that he was "not one of those so-called 'smart Northern Negroes' who have recently come to your city with new-fangled revolutionary ideas." His appeal was to assure the larger white society that he was not demanding equality or challenging white dominance. There was no discussion in his letter that people should be seated on an integrated basis. "This legitimate request," according to Culmer, "should not be interpreted as a desire on the part for social dealings. In fact, it is not even contrary to Southern practices.... It is just downright fair to your colored taxpayers."[26] John Culmer attempted to place blacks in the Republic, not as alien beings who were not eligible for entitlements from the state, but as loyal citizens who deserved fair treatment. The assertion that they were taxpayers was used as an argument that they should be able to attend a publicly operated facility. His use of persuasion and his silence on the issue of nondiscriminatory seating was an indication of what he saw as feasible objectives in a racist society.

Culmer's portrayal of blacks as loyal citizens of the state put him on the side of the anti-Communist crusade. His declaration that the Klan, after it paraded through Colored Town, stood for the "highest ideals of Ameri-cans and their banner is the cross of Christ" seems bizarre. He went as far to claim that blacks who "believe in the cross have noth[ing] to fear: But, sin-ners, be warned!" The Klan march, the rector of St. Agnes wrote, was only a warning to those blacks who "are inclined to accept communistic doctrines." The rector's words not only demonstrated his awareness of white Southern anxiety over black equality but their fear of Communism. He asserted that the "evil of communism has not yet crept in among blacks even though there are other evils." Appealing to the white terrorist organization, he assured them that their march was not necessary because "no race is more loyal to

American ideals than is the Negro. For those ideals, he has fought and bled and died. And he will do it again. He has never sold out to the enemy."

One might argue that Culmer had acquiesced to white power and that his effort to ease white fears was harmful to blacks. This view cannot be denied. To rely on the good will of those who benefit from white dominance revealed a certain naïveté on the part of the rector. But such a reading of his words without consideration of alternative meanings overlooks his effort to present the black image. An integral factor in his approach was convincing white Southerners that blackness was not synonymous with an antagonist force and perfidious to American principles. He did portray the black body and mind as flawed entities. But they were not innately defective. They were clearly in need of guidance. However, with guidance and uplift, they could easily be resurrected morally and socially and made into productive beings like their white counterparts. Despite their faults, they had redeeming qualities, including loyalty to the state and its white constituents. They were not outside of the boundaries of citizenship but should be recognized as constituents deserving respect and the protection of the law. If for no other reason than their loyalty, they were entitled to live in peace and not be victims of racial terror.

The nonconfrontational approach used by Culmer in order to win concessions from the white elite was meant to convince them that blacks had the same interest as white citizens. The pastor pushed the theme of common ground on several occasions. On January 12, 1941, Culmer delivered an address over radio station WKAT in Miami assuring whites that black people were not seeking "social dealings" but material improvement. Attempting to build bridges and deracialize black and white relations, the priest contended blacks only "ask for adequate protection against our common foes—crime and disease. Both are colorblind. The criminal who kills a black man may some day go colorblind and kill a white man. Criminals must be punished. Germs too are colorblind and the places that breed them should be eradicated." Although he did assert that discrimination led to black poverty, the common approach meant not challenging white supremacy but adopting white society's image of the black working class as criminal and diseased beings. Instead of attacking white racism, Culmer went so far as to assert that blacks from slavery to today remained loyal to whites. Thus, there existed a linkage between both racial groups.[27]

Even when Culmer represented blacks, arguing on their behalf about working conditions, he never gave up his search for common ground through a nonconfrontational rapprochement. A case in point was his letter to John D. Wing. He complained that the segregated area of the downtown bus terminal that serviced the black community was located in a dangerous area. Hundreds of blacks lined up in a small area near passing trains without barriers to protect them. He asserted that blacks had complained to him about the conditions and he was speaking in their behalf. However, whatever militancy was in his letter was sacrificed when he reminded Wing he had support among the white business community because he was willing to try to alter the behavior of black working people. "When employers complain to me that my people are not giving them a fair day's work, I do not hesitate to tell them to be loyal and faithful servants; to respect those in authority over them; to live peaceably with their neighbors; to save their earnings; to buy homes to invest in war bonds; to realize that they are a minority group and as such cannot enforce their demands even though they may be right." Culmer's conservative approach resembled Booker T. Washington's accommodationist strategy. It was an attempt to create a dialogue between black and white Americans by focusing on a politics of possibility and respectability. Culmer, like Washington, ruled out a broader strategy that would lead to a fairer distribution of resources. He also came to the conclusion that the remedy for blacks was not the creation and maintenance of the welfare state that helped provide assistance for the poor. Instead, it was the creation of a better spirit and atmosphere where blacks and whites would have respect for one another and could live in harmony. However, whites would only have respect for blacks when blacks were worthy of it. Central to this view was that white racism was not endemic or pervasive to American society. Whites in power determined the state of race relations before the 1950s in Miami. It was only by their recognition that blacks could be appointed to bodies that addressed issues that were pertinent to them.

Culmer's representation of blacks as loyal, nonmilitant, and deserving of all rights of citizenship challenged the popular view that blacks were genetically inferior. He was attempting to reclaim blackness from white racist notions of black people. On the other hand, while attempting to portray blacks in a positive light, his view portrayed the black working class as being caught up in a culture of despair.

By the 1950s Culmer's approach of accommodation would give way to a more militant point of view and methods in the fight for racial equality. Nevertheless, Culmer's legacy is quite significant, because it provides a richer picture of accommodation as a tactic. Instead of viewing it as a means of acquiescing to white racism, it should be seen as a strategy employed by blacks to help bring about changes in a racial system that offered few other options.

CHAPTER 5

The Reverend Theodore Gibson
and the Significance of Cold War
Liberalism in the Fight for Citizenship

By the 1950s Theodore Gibson had become the most prominent black figure
in Miami, Florida. The Episcopalian rector led the Miami branch of the
NAACP and waged a fierce battle to desegregate the Jim Crow city. It was
under his leadership that the Miami branch of the noted civil rights organization faced its greatest challenge. In an attempt to discontinue the branch's
activism and eventually eradicate it, the state of Florida accused the civil
rights organization of harboring Communists and launched a campaign to
gain the organization's membership list. The Miami branch of the NAACP
refused to cave in to the state's demand and waged a diligent battle for its
existence. The battle between Gibson and the state would eventually be
settled in the U S Supreme Court, which ruled in favor of the NAACP leader.
Despite his activities and this major victory in the Supreme Court, Gibson
is barely mentioned by scholars, though he receives a mention in Eric
Tschechlok's "'So Goes the Negro': Race and Labor in Miami, 1940–1963."
Tscheschlok portrays Gibson as a militant voice that helped transform the
NAACP from a nonactivist to a more proactivist organization, challenging
racial discrimination. However, the author is silent on Gibson's anti-
Communist efforts and his fight to protect his and the NAACP's constitu-
tional rights. Author Marvin Dunn's *Black Miami in the Twentieth Century*
takes an uncritical but more extensive look at Gibson. However, he offers
little assessment of Gibson's leadership. One of the most insightful portray-
als of the fight between Gibson and the Florida Legislative Investigation
Committee is Robert W. Saunders's *Bridging the Gap: Continuing the Florida
NAACP Legacy of Harry T. Moore*. Saunders, who served as head of the
Florida NAACP, recalls how he and members of the NAACP stood up
against the legislative body. But Saunders's personal account relied, for the
most part on his memory.[1]

Throughout his career, Gibson, like Culmer, dedicated his life to improving the social conditions of black people. However, the leadership approach
of the two differed because, in part, almost two decades separated their periods of activism and they therefore operated in different social and political
contexts. To a large degree, the political climate helped mold their political activist approaches. While Culmer adopted a politics of accommodation,

Gibson became the symbol of the militant integration movement. He emerged during a moment of crisis in the 1950s and 1960s, when fierce civil rights campaigns were blossoming and successfully dismantling harsh racial barriers to public accommodation, education, housing, and employment. The Supreme Court's *Brown* decision, the Montgomery bus boycott, the attempt to integrate Central High School in Little Rock, the sit-ins and the formation of SNCC, and other national and local activities helped create an expectation that segregation and racial discrimination were inevitably doomed. Countless people throughout the nation in the 1950s and 1960s were galvanized in the fight against Jim Crow. Struggles for liberation in Africa, Asia, and Latin America against imperialist western powers threw into question the image of the passive colonial subject who was satisfied with his plight. Without a doubt, the atmosphere during this period made it easier for black leadership to demand and gain more than improved race relations. The major similarity of Culmer and Gibson was that both attempted to raise political consciousness among blacks and whites by making them aware of the black presence. However, it is in this context that Gibson, more than Culmer, problematized the ideology of racial hierarchy by challenging white privilege. Although the objectives of both were to present blacks as loyal, patriotic Americans who deserved the benefits of citizenship, Gibson's portrait of blacks rejected Culmer's image of black citizens as patient and loyal bystanders, waiting and relying on the good will of the larger white society. Gibson demanded an egalitarian relationship in which blacks would be treated as equal citizens of the state.

Gibson, by arguing that African Americans should be assured the rights and privileges of American citizenship because they were loyal anti-Communists, no different in their goals and desires than white Americans, demonstrated his embrace of the cold war liberal state. The attempt at forging images of militant integrationists who were loyal to country ruled out radical activities that might paint African Americans as lawbreakers or subversives. Thus, tactics outside of the law or association with left forces was not an option for Gibson and the NAACP. Gibson was not just in opposition to the state's black subversive image. He was critically engaged in a politics of patriotism, attempting to persuade the larger society that African Americans were loyal to the nation and therefore deserved to be treated as full citizens.

The Early Story of Gibson's Life

The story of Theodore Gibson is a Horatio Alger tale. Writer Carita Swanson Vonk has written the most extensive work on Gibson. A great deal of her book *Theodore R. Gibson: Priest, Prophet, and Politician* is based on Gibson's own recollection of his life. Although a single mother raised him, Gibson managed to become successful. His story, like that of so many other black leaders, is portrayed as a narrative of accent. Gibson was born in 1915 in Miami. His parents were Bahamians who separated when Theodore was a child. His father had little to do with him. Young Theodore was sent to the Bahamas to live with his maternal grandparents. According to Theodore, his grandfather, Ezekiel Smith, "was the only father I had. He was one of the first men I ever knew." Smith was portrayed as a strong and robust man who was a devout Christian. He spent a great deal of time with his grandson and helped mold his Christian beliefs. Absent from Vonk's tale of the shaping and molding of Gibson's character are women. There is no mention of Theodore's mother or grandmother when she focuses on character development. It is the grandfather who is presented as the molder of character. Hence, men mold character while women are portrayed as nurturers. Serving as a role model for his grandson, Smith became a leader in the Anglican Church in Georgetown, serving as a catechist. Gibson remembers that his grandfather sang and led the Georgetown congregation in song and prayer.[2]

Gibson's formative years were spent in Georgetown, a black enclave, and there he was protected from the more virulent forms of white racism. He was spared the attacks and insults suffered by blacks in Jim Crow America. Instead, his grandparents, his church, and the community helped built his self-esteem.

After living a few years in the Bahamas, Gibson came back to Miami in 1924 to live with his mother, who had remarried. According to the Gibson narrative, he attended and graduated from Booker T. Washington High School, and like many other people of African origins in Miami, he sought higher education outside of the city. He attended St. Augustine College in Raleigh, North Carolina. The college, a historical black institution founded in 1867, granted its first accredited bachelor's degree in 1931. Gibson graduated in 1938 and went on to Howard University Law School. While at Howard, he reevaluated his career plans and decided that he wanted to become an ordained minister. Gibson selected the ministry because he viewed it as the best means of addressing the plight of black people in America. After one semester at Howard University Law School he left and enrolled in the Payne Divinity School (later Virginia Theological Seminary). He graduated in 1943 and was ordained in 1944 at St. Augustine Episcopal Church in North Carolina. He was called to Christ Episcopal Church in Coconut Grove in 1945.[3]

Changing Winds

The most important civil rights organization in Florida during the 1940s and the 1950s was the NAACP. Harry T. Moore, a teacher from Brevard County who organized the Brevard NAACP in 1934, became the first executive secretary of the Florida NAACP in the late 1940s. Under his leadership the Florida state chapter of the NAACP fought fiercely against lynching and police brutality. It also struggled to integrate all public spaces. In the summer of 1949 Moore declared that the state chapter was raising money to help finance the cases brought by six students against the state university admissions policy. The state only granted scholarships to blacks who attended schools outside of Florida, whereas white students received scholarships to attend the University of Florida. By 1950 Moore attempted to have the United States Supreme Court decision in *Sweatt v. Painter* enforced in Florida. In *Sweatt* the High Court had ruled that Texas had not provided equal facilities when it established Prairie View Law School for Sweatt, the sole black student. It declared that the state had either to provide equal facilities for Sweatt or integrate existing facilities that had been provided for whites. In order to make a case for the enforcement of the Supreme Court's decision in Florida, Moore urged that the Florida chapters of the NAACP take surveys of local schools and compare them to white facilities. Once they found that black facilities were inferior, the chapters were told to petition the local school boards to take steps immediately to make black schools equal. They would then go to court if the boards refused to equalize the schools. Moore set the tone for the NAACP when he asserted, in September 1950, "We cannot afford to sit down and wait until our local officials get good and ready to provide equal facilities for Negroes. Neither can we listen to those of our own race who advise more patience and who argue that the state does not have enough money to do all of these things right now. Negroes already have been extremely patient. We have waited and begged for over fifty years, while local officials brazenly ignored the law and denied us equal opportunities."[4]

Another area in which the state NAACP vigorously fought was voting rights. In 1944 Moore led the fight in Florida to abolish the all-white primary and for universal suffrage by organizing the Progressive Voters League (PVL). The PVL became what biographer Ben Green called the "de facto political arm" of the Florida NAACP. By 1945 it was launching voter registration drives and increasing the number of black voters throughout the state. In January 1950, the state board of the civil rights group called for an all-out drive for the registration of blacks. Each branch was requested to set up a registration committee and cooperate with black churches.[5]

Moore's efforts made him dangerous to the guardians of white supremacy in the state. Not only had he sought to increase the number of black voters, he had also challenged Jim Crow terror in the South by calling for investigations into the slaying of innocent African Americans by law enforcement officers and vigilantes. On the night of December 25, 1951, Harry T. Moore and his wife, Harriette, were the victims of a bomb that was planted under their bedroom by members of the Ku Klux Klan. No one has ever been convicted of the murder. Harry T. Moore's hard work helped tens of thousands of blacks to register to vote in Florida. Just as important, his assertive leadership approach and willingness to directly confront the American apartheid system in Florida, helped forge a militant strategy for Florida's NAACP. In his memoir, Florida's NAACP leader, Robert W. Saunders, observes that despite the hope of white supremacists that Moore's assassination would silence civil rights advocates, the murder "made many Black citizens more determined than ever to fight for their rights.... For decades after the deaths, Black Floridians remembered the ultimate sacrifices of Harry and Harriett[e] Moore as they demanded the death of Jim Crow."[6]

The Miami branch of the NAACP clearly reflected the militant attitude in the fight for civil rights. It battled for adequate housing and education facilities and equal accommodations in public facilities in the city. The Miami branch went on record in March 1950 as supporting low-cost federal housing for the poor. In that same month it also fought against police brutality by calling for an investigation of the killing of a citizen in Liberty City by a black police officer. The killing was linked to racial disparities of services. The murder, according to the agency, indicated that the training provided to black officers as compared to white police officers was inadequate. In April black golfers began using the Miami municipal golf course. But when whites complained about the black presence, managers of the facility decided to enforce a policy limiting black access to the course to Mondays. With the support of the NAACP, the black golfers sued, demonstrating the civil rights group's goal was to eradicate segregation and discrimination on several fronts, including recreation.[7]

The Miami chapter of the NAACP pushed for better race relations. But its view of racial cooperation differed from Culmer's. He had sought the suspension of hostility and the gaining of white concessions in the form of additional services for the black masses but never made a direct assault on the racial caste system. The Miami branch of the NAACP now intended that blacks and whites had to be treated on an equal basis and not in a Jim Crow context. The organization announced in April 1951 that mayors Harold Turk of Miami Beach and William Wolfarth of the city of Miami would be keynote speakers at the first "Goodwill Inter-racial Meeting" sponsored by the Miami NAACP. The Miami group noted that the two speakers were qualified to address the meeting because they were "leaders in the field of human relations." Now it was not the larger white community that would stand in judgment on black leadership; the Miami branch of the NAACP was creating new criteria for determining which whites were friends or enemies of the race. Accordingly, those in the white community who worked to improve race relations between blacks and whites based on respect and equality were considered friends, and by implication those who were not willing to accept such criteria were not considered allies in the battle for equality.[8]

An indication that the Miami NAACP rejected accommodationism as a scheme to improve race relations came when W. A. Morris, president of the branch, sent a letter to William Wolfarth, mayor of Miami, complaining about a racist statement made by O. D. Henderson, director of public safety. Morris accused Henderson of attempting to associate blacks with innate criminality. The branch president accused Henderson of declaring, "You're not going to eliminate *bolita* [illegal gambling operations]. You're just kidding yourself if you think you can. A complete closedown would mean jailing everyone over there in the central Negro District." Morris noted that this was an attack on the good and responsible citizens of African origins who had contributed greatly to the city. He called for a retraction of the statement. Black ministers also joined with the NAACP in condemning Henderson's racist statement. J. N. Byrd and J. A. Roberts, representing a group of black ministers, insisted that this was a racist attack on the black community "to which the ministers of this area take severe exception." Both the Morris and the ministerial letters not only displayed an antiaccommodationist sentiment on the part of the NAACP and the black ministerial leadership, but also reflected class politics. They made no attempt to defend the activities of the black working class. Instead, Miami's black middle-class leaders criticized what it labeled as inappropriate working-class behavior. Gambling, numbers, congregating on public sidewalks, and loud talking in public were behaviors that were seen as detrimental to the race. The black middle class that was involved in militant action for civil rights struggle constructed an image of black people as law-abiding, possessing individual initiative, and essentially Victorian.[9]

The stress on middle-class mores, along with a race-specific agenda, did not lead the middle-class protest group to ally itself with labor. More important, many labor unions excluded blacks from their ranks, and that worked against an alliance with Miami civil rights organizations. The reality was that in Jim Crow America many labor institutions maintained white privilege. To a large degree, the black middle-class emphasis on race-specific solutions and the absence of a race and class agenda was adopted by many members of the black working class because there was no alternative. Consequently, the black middle class and working class in Miami teamed up to eradicate white privilege in the labor market and in the union hall. In March 1950 the Greater Miami Right to Work Committee was established to fight for jobs for black painters. The *Miami Times* reported that even though many jobs for painters were located in the black neighborhoods of the city, blacks were denied those jobs because they were not members of the union, a prerequisite for employment. The committee declared, "They will not stand idly by while one segment . . . faces starvation due to the shortsightedness and irresponsibility of the leaders of the building trades union." The committee called on the American Federation of Labor to end its policy of discrimination. The Reverend Edward T. Graham headed the Labor Relations Committee of the Negro Service Council. In March the group met with Building Trades Council representatives who pledged charters for locals of black craftsmen and to help them find employment. Although locals based on race would preserve segregation, the Labor Relations Committee of Negro Service Council's goal was to break white worker's monopoly on craft employment. Apparently, a gentlemen's agreement had been reached, and some jobs would go to "qualified black craftsmen" in the black community. However, despite the agreement, the Relations Committee accused the Building Trades Council of violating the pact.[10]

It seems the stress on race instead of class hindered the working class. But it was evident that there was little choice for black workers in a Jim

Crow society. White workers assumed that their white skin entitled them to employment and the exclusion of black workers. Thus, middle-class black organizations fighting white supremacy became the avenue for the black working class.

As late as 1963 the NAACP was attacking white privilege in the trade unions. After it had gathered a number of affidavits alleging racial discrimination in Local 7, Plasterers, Masons and Bricklayers International Union, the NAACP made plans to protest these alleged acts. The civil rights organization noted that it had forced the union in 1954 to open its ranks to blacks. Since then, however, only a few black workers had been assigned jobs by the union. Robert W. Saunders, the NAACP field secretary, noted that blacks were forced out of the union, which then reverted to the status of an all-white labor institution. The NAACP's fight against unions centered on white workers who attempted to uphold white privilege.[11]

One of the strongest alliances in the civil rights community in Miami was made between the NAACP and black ministers. Several ministers in Miami were active leaders in the NAACP, including Theodore Gibson, Edward T. Graham, L. C. Mickens, Thedford Johnson of St. John Baptist Church and president of the Baptist Ministers' Council, and S. A. Cousins, of Greater Bethel AME Church, one of the oldest and largest churches in Miami. Churches were used for NAACP meetings. For example, a meeting on June 13, 1949, of the NAACP branches on the lower East Coast of Florida was held at Mount Herman AME Church in Fort Lauderdale. Moreover, the NAACP turned to the black churches for support during its membership drives. Letters urging churches to participate in a membership drive were sent to churches in the Miami area. When the state NAACP launched an all-out drive to register 25,000 black voters, it announced that black churches would become recruiting grounds. The cooperation between the NAACP and the black churches over the issue of black voter registration was illustrated when the civil rights organization issued a plea for churches to recognize the fourth Sunday of each month as "NAACP Sunday." Churches were asked to take a few moments on that day to remind parishioners of the important work of the NAACP in southern states, including opening up Democratic primaries to black voters, improving school facilities for blacks, helping to abolish Jim Crow trains and buses, and saving the lives of blacks through the courts. Black churches became the major arenas for membership drives in Miami, and on several occasions the Ministerial Alliance joined with the NAACP in battle against racism. The NAACP and the Interdenominational Ministers' Alliance sponsored a mass rally at Saint John's Baptist Church in May 1950 after a successful membership drive. NAACP officials announced that its program included integrating municipal enterprises "maintained by common tax funds." A membership drive meeting was held at Mount Olivette Baptist Church in the spring of 1950. The pastor, Rev. L. C. Mickens, declared, "As long as we are afraid of losing a job or going to jail or even of dying while seeking our God-given rights, we cannot expect any better treatment because nobody ever made any progress through fear." These words addressed a major concern and problem that the NAACP faced in the South. For many southerners, membership in the NAACP could lead to economic terrorism and to physical threat carried out by state and local officials as well as white vigilantes. Miami, like other parts of the South, attempted to eradicate the civil rights group. In order to combat the fear of white retaliation, the NAACP and members of the black clergy attempted to persuade church people to join and dedicate financial resources as well as their time to the group.[12]

It should also be noted that in its pursuit of racial justice, the Miami branch of the NAACP helped forge alliances and developed a civil rights community. One such alliance was formed between Jewish and black Americans. The American Jewish Committee, temples and synagogues, and individuals contributed to the NAACP and to the fight for freedom. The American Jewish Committee endorsed and financially contributed to the civil rights organization, as did individual rabbis. The NAACP, in part, must be given credit for creating a venue for cooperation. Its fund-raising and social events featured American Jews. The Southland Singers, a Jewish folk chorus, along with the Booker T. Washington choral group provided music for the first Goodwill Interracial Meeting at Bethel AME church in 1951. Leaders and activists in the American Jewish community were eager to become involved in the fight for racial justice in Miami. Gloster Current informed Gibson in January 1957 that Rabbi Benno M. Wallach of Temple Sinai in North Miami and formerly from a reform congregation in Merrick, Long Island, had asked to serve in some capacity in the Miami branch.

When Gibson became head of the Miami branch of the NAACP in the mid-1950s, the political atmosphere had changed. Civil rights militancy in that city had replaced Culmer's accommodationist approach.[13]

Cold War and Civil Rights

As noted, Gibson emerged during a period when there was a great deal of ferment for integration. Besides the emergence of social protest movements throughout the nation, the judicial branch of the United States government had sided with those struggling for integration. In fact, the 1954 Supreme Court decision in *Brown v. Board of Education* had a tremendous impact on the civil rights community, particularly, the NAACP. The court's unanimous decision helped frame the argument used by proponents of integration used when challenging segregation. A major argument used by civil rights community was based on social and political democracy. The advocates of this idea indirectly challenged race by arguing that in a democracy there should be no racial barriers to citizenship; therefore, black and white Americans were entitled to the same rights. This concept was evident in Milton Galamison's statement to the members of his grassroots organization, the Parents Workshop for Equality in New York City Schools, which fought for school integration in New York City. "In an integrated school," Galamison declared, "your child will receive the benefits of a democratic education that will enable him to live, play and work with children of all backgrounds. Your child will develop a better appreciation of himself as a human being—born free and equal in dignity and rights with other children." Gloria Ray, one of the Little Rock Nine, a group of African-American high school students selected by the Little Rock, Arkansas, school board to integrate Central High School, also advocated for social and political democracy when she said at a press conference, "I am thankful for having a chance to fulfill my educational desire and for being a citizen in a country where the federal government respects and protects the rights of all its people." Gibson, like others, turned to the *Brown* decision when arguing for the sameness notion. In a letter inviting Dade County schools to a meeting to discuss integration, he quoted from the Supreme Court's decision. "We conclude that in the field of public education in the doctrine of 'separate but equal' has no place. Separate educational facilities are inherently unequal." The pastor's militancy was linked to the optimism of the 1950s.

But the modern civil rights movement materialized during the cold war. This period witnessed the ascendancy of the anti-Communist network and its successful campaign to stamp out forces on the left. The network included the executive and legislative branches of federal and state governments, industry, the Catholic Church, trade unions, civil rights organizations, and state and local government anti-Communist investigation committees. This massive labyrinth helped create a climate that turned left or progressive dissent into a criminal act and an act of disloyalty, even treason. The NAACP became part of the anti-Communist network and adopted a cold war liberal position that embraced social reforms, but at the same time it attempted to purge Communists and other left forces from mainstream institutions, unions, political civil organizations, and even their own ranks. At its forty-first annual convention in 1950 the NAACP adopted an anti-Communist resolution calling on branches to exclude anyone who was not in accord to the NAACP's position to "strengthen American democracy." The leading civil rights organization reinforced its 1950 resolution at its forty-third annual convention. "We reaffirm the anti-Communist resolution adopted at the 1950 Boston Convention supported by an amendment to our Constitution by the National Board restricting membership to those who support the principles and program of NAACP, which were strengthened and clarified by the Convention in Atlanta, Georgia, in 1951." The national leadership of the NAACP waged a campaign against Communist infiltration. Thurgood Marshall, who was the NAACP's lead attorney in the *Brown* case, feared the growing mass movement for civil rights because it would make Communism, Communists, and their activities popular among blacks. Because of his fear that Communists would infiltrate the civil rights organizations, he cooperated with J. Edgar Hoover and the FBI. In fact, Marshall became Hoover's leading source of information on the activities of the leading civil rights leaders.[14]

Reflecting the national and local sentiment, the Miami branch of the NAACP lived up to the challenge posed by the anti-Communist network. Lucille Black, membership secretary of the branch, contacted Gibson and informed him that it was reported that Mrs. J. E. Dixon, a member, said she had been sent to Cuba by the NAACP to observe the activities of Communists among the people in the rural areas of the country. Black requested that Gibson look into this situation, essentially to see whether the Miami branch had been infiltrated by subversives. Not willing to just hunt for Communists in its ranks, the Miami NAACP openly expressed its patriotism, painting its members as loyal Americans. When the organization hosted an event featuring Thurgood Marshall, not only was the national anthem sung but "America the Beautiful" was recited by the audience.[15]

The NAACP's expression of patriotism and anti-Communist sentiment was not just hyperbole or theatrics on the part of Gibson and the organization; on the contrary, it was an attempt to define the black presence in America and the relationship between blackness and citizenship. The proclamation of citizenship was a message to the nation that as black Americans they were also loyal to the state. Gibson and other NAACP members were challenging racial nationalism by engaging in what historian Gary Gerstle calls "civic nationalism." From the country's early history, racial nationalism defined citizenship in America. According to Gerstle, "People held together by common blood and skin and by an inherited fitness for self-government." Both the constitution that supported slavery and the 1790 law limiting citizenship to white men upheld this racial nationalism. Throughout the nineteenth century and for most of the twentieth century racial nationalism remained in place.

However, as Gerstle contends, racial nationalism was challenged by a civic nationalism. This concept embraced people across racial and ethnic lines and defined citizenship by behavior rather than natural features. A key factor leading to a growing popularity of civic nationalism was the cold war. The cold war helped usher in new concerns and new fears that would occupy American thought for decades. The battle against Communism and the measures used in that fight, including propaganda, convinced many Americans that the enemy was not racial or ethnic but was determined by one's ideology. On the other hand, this view gave to racial and ethnic groups that had been excluded from both legal and cultural citizenship an opportunity to win recognition as members of the nation with full legal status. As Gerstle notes:

> The black radicals Paul Robeson and W. E. B. Du Bois were persecuted for their Communist sympathies, but other black activists, ranging from World War II veterans to southern preachers such as Martin Luther King Jr., found in the 1950s a more favorable climate for civil rights agitation. The Supreme Court delivered its momentous *Brown v. Board of Education* decision outlawing school segregation in 1954, a moment of acute Cold War tension. These

developments revealed an incipient shift in criteria determining how the nation would draw its boundaries and define who could or could not belong to the American nation. Large majorities of Jews, Catholics, blacks, and other minorities would benefit from this shift, for as long as they agreed to stay away from communism and ideas associated with it, they found their opportunities for inclusion in American society enhanced.[16]

Several African-American leaders and organizations were fearful that the smear of Communism could derail their push for civil rights. Just as important, many were also aware of the opportunities for inclusion in American society that the cold war period had provided. Clearly, it was becoming more difficult for the United States to ignore racial discrimination at home during the postwar era when it declared itself the preeminent democratic power and labeled the Soviet Union a slave state. Racial discrimination in the United States became fuel for the Soviet Union's propaganda machine. Legal scholar Mary Dudziak contends that, in a bipolar world, "it was frightening to see the Soviet Union capitalize on America's 'Achilles' heel.' Soviet propaganda exploited U.S. racial problems, arguing that American professions of liberty and equality under democracy were a sham." But the Soviet Union and its satellite states were not the only countries to notice the differences between the United States' ideals and its practices. Nations in the developing world and in Europe criticized America for denying African Americans equality, adding pressure on U.S. officials to address the color line at home. As Dudziak notes, racial nationalism was contested by the federal government in part to improve the United States' position in its fight against Communism.[17]

The contest between Communist forces and the United States for allies also helped to diminish the importance of racial nationalism. The Soviets and the American Communist Party tried to win allies among African Americans and others by depicting the racial practices of the United States and linking them to the inherent flaws of capitalism. This tactic put the United States on the defensive. No longer in a position to ignore racial discrimination, the federal government filed amicus briefs in support of the National Association for the Advancement of Colored People's efforts to end school segregation, including the *Brown* case.[18]

Many in the African-American civil rights community were more than willing to prove their loyalty to the nation by becoming actively involved in the campaign to wage a war domestically as well as in the international arena in order to stamp out Communism. Spokespeople in the civil rights community when battling for equality stressed a civic nationalism condemning Communist attempts to influence them and at the same time emphasizing their rights as American citizens to full equality under the law. Terrence Roberts, one of the Little Rock Nine, made this clear when he told the press of the devious behavior of Communists. "I know that Communists enjoy taking advantage of situations such as these to twist the minds of people of the world. But I'm thankful that in America their actions are being foiled through the actions of many democratic minded citizens."[19]

At the same time that Gibson was portraying the Miami branch of the NAACP as patriotic and loyal to the United States, he attempted to equate militancy for the cause of integration as democratic and segregationists as anti-American. This method was evident in Gibson's letter to the editor of *Look* magazine in May 1958. He responded to Governor LeRoy Collins's call for moderation on the issue of race. Gibson claimed that the NAACP believed in the "broader values and more fundamental principles of our founding fathers and our U.S. Constitution, rather than upon the laws and statutes of a state determined to maintain segregation." He asserted that patience did not mean submission to undemocratic practices, moderation did not mean refusal to try to obtain equality of civil rights, and gradualism did not mean "never" or stagnation in the status quo of tradition and Jim Crow. Attempting not to appear like a wild-eyed radical, Gibson wrote that the civil rights organization only sought legal redress when all other avenues had been exhausted. It could not be seen as acting in "irresponsible haste." Gibson rejected Governor Collins's suggestion that an interracial commission be set up at the federal and state level with its members selected by southern governors because then it would consist of people selected by men who supported segregation.

Gibson argued that democracy could not exist in a society that denied citizens basic rights and that the democratic rights of black citizens should be recognized immediately. Governor Collins's calls for moderation rang hollow because, as Gibson declared, one could not be moderate when freedom was denied blacks because of their race. "Negroes, like other American citizens, feel within their hearts the desire for recognition as human beings, and striving toward the ideals of democracy." According to the NAACP leader, "It must be planned and executed by those who would like to achieve a just solution of this challenge in democratic living." When fighting the cold war, one had to fight racial inequality. Gibson painted the struggle for racial justice as an all-American venture.[20]

The decision to engage in a discourse of anti-Communism was intended, in part, to convince the larger American society that African Americans were loyal Americans and deserved to have full citizenship. Blacks were not challenging America or refusing to accept that America was a great country. For Gibson, black representation should not have been associated with those on the fringes, those disdainful of American values. He meant to counter the notion that people with dark skin were unpatriotic and were not entitled to the benefits and opportunities of the American nation-state. On the contrary, blacks were loyal and patient and it was time America acted by granting them full citizenship. This view was evident in Gibson's response to a *Miami Herald* writer who accused the NAACP of disrupting the harmonious race relations between blacks and whites. "The position of the NAACP is this. We are not denying any progress made, but we are disturbed about the length of time it has taken Negroes to be permitted to participate wholly in the American society. We are also cognizant of the great difficulties encountered in the struggle up to now. Negroes are not seeking something extraordinary or impossible. They are only asking for rights already theirs and guaranteed to them many years ago along with the rest of the citizens of the United States." Rights were not determined by race or class status. There was no mention of social uplift as a prerequisite for rights or as a means of winning social favor with whites. What is clear is the notion that blacks, as citizens, were due these rights. While Culmer was more closely allied to the Booker T. Washington approach, Gibson's militancy was in the camp of the militant integrationists. "The NAACP is not satisfied with changes already made because they have been too long in coming, have come about too far apart, and have been too bitterly won when they have finally arrived," the Episcopalian priest declared. "We ask for acceptance of Negroes as participating American citizens with privileges of using their guaranteed rights."

Gibson versus the Florida Legislative Investigation Committee

The "loyal American" approach of Gibson was highlighted in the battle between the NAACP and the state of Florida beginning in 1956, when the Miami branch of the venerable civil rights organization became a prime target of the anti-Communist campaign led by the Florida Legislative Investigative Committee (FLIC).

Despite the fact that there was a weakening of racial nationalism in the 1950s, the South had not abandoned this concept. In fact, it dug in its heels in an effort to protect racially distinctive citizenship. Southern NAACP chapters became a major target for white southerners because, as civil rights scholar Aldon Morris notes, "Whenever the NAACP won a legal contest, it served to delegitimize the white racist system in the eyes of blacks." By the early 1950s, as the NAACP filed a number of lawsuits to end segregation in public schools, a coordinated southern attack was launched against the venerable civil rights organization in order to defeat its campaign of desegregation. Several groups intending to uphold white supremacy, including the Ku Klux Klan, White Citizens Council, and southern states' rights associations, sought to crush the civil rights movement through economic reprisals, intimidation, and violence. However, it was not only vigilante groups that tried to end civil rights activities in the South but also state and local governments. Several southern state governments attempted to force state and local NAACP chapters to submit their official records, including membership lists, as a means of intimidating them. Virginia, Texas, Arkansas, Alabama, Louisiana, Florida, and other southern states created special investigative committees, which led to indictments, fines, and imprisonment of NAACP officials. These tactics to stop the NAACP's drive to win full citizenship rights for blacks revealed a coordinated effort on the part of the South to relegate African Americans to second-class citizenship.[21]

However, in an age where there was mounting national opposition to
racial discrimination, racial markers alone could no longer be employed to
define black citizenship, especially when the battle took place in the federal courts. Hence the opponents of racial justice sought to connect racial
nationalism in the South to anti-Communist efforts. Historian Thomas
Borstelmann argues that white political elites in the South opposed the
national Democratic Party's position on civil rights by "elevating the rhetoric
of anti-Communism as a more widely acceptable cover for segregationism."
Borstelman argues, "White southerners increased their use of anti-Communist
rhetoric after the *Brown* decision as part of a strategy to equate integration
with Communism." Desegregation efforts were depicted by white southerners as attempts by Communists to destroy the social order and bring about a
Bolshevik revolution. In an effort to derail the forces struggling for equality
and economic democracy, southern states placed the red tag on civil rights
and labor organizations as well as individuals involved in the antiracist campaign. The upholders of racial nationalism were more than willing to participate in the language of civic nationalism to relegate blacks to the status of
second-class citizens. They were trying to confine blacks to the position of
citizens without political power. In her book, *Divided Minds: Intellectuals and
the Civil Rights Movement*, professor of journalism Carol Polgrove contends
that the "Cold War gave racist politicians an opening to badger anyone likely
to speak up for racial change. The equation of racial change with communism continued to be drawn with relentless regularity. The same Cold War
that provided liberals with an argument for racial change provided opponents with an argument against racial change. Since the Russians used the
American racial situation to smear the United States, were not Americans
who advocated racial change behaving suspiciously like Russians? In the
minds of many southern whites, the very idea of whole-scale social reform
imposed by a central government was a communist idea."[22]

To be sure, Theodore Gibson and members of the Miami NAACP were
conscious of the FLIC's efforts to portray them as an immoral force
attempting to break southern customs and law. Gibson was aware that this
battle could not just be fought only in the courts; it also entered into the
political and cultural arena. Historian Gary Gerstle contends that African
Americans, fearful of being accused of Communism, "were quick to disasso-
ciate themselves from black organizations that harbored Communists...."
Gibson's fear of Communism went deep. Indeed, he became aggressively
anti-Communist, signifying a awareness that he could gain large political
dividends by it. By broadcasting his disdain for Communism not only was he
trying to save the NAACP's civil rights organization from being tainted as
subversive and protect its members from harassment but he also was using
anti-Communist rhetoric as a means of forging an identity of the loyal
American who deserved full citizenship rights.[23]

The confrontation between the NAACP and the state of Florida thus
turned on the meaning of citizenship for African Americans. The winner of

the contest over who should define citizenship would determine the legal and social status of African Americans. The state wanted to limit blacks to a second-class citizenship and relegate them to the lowest socioeconomic position in southern society. The FLIC wanted to continue denying blacks an adequate education and decent housing and the right to vote. By denying full citizenship rights, the state assured the survival of white supremacy and domination. Indeed, the demand by the Florida Legislative Investigation Committee that the NAACP turn over its membership list would have given the anti-integrationist force the capability of intimidating the membership of the Miami branch in its quest for full citizenship rights. The mere knowledge that the state had such a list would most likely have caused panic among the membership; some members might decide to leave the organization, and potential members would be dissuaded from joining. Such results would have stopped the NAACP from pursuing its aim of tearing down legal barriers to social equality.

In 1956, under the direction of State Senator Charley Johns, an arch segregationist, the Florida state legislature established the Florida Legislative Investigation Committee (FLIC). Johns, from Bradford County and president of the state senate, had served as acting governor of Florida from 1953 to 1955. Notorious for his racist views, Johns once opposed a law to unmask members of the Ku Klux Klan. The committee hired Mark R. Hawes as its chief counsel. Hawes, from Tampa, also served as chief counsel to the Florida Association for Constitutional Government, an organization described by state field secretary of the NAACP Robert Saunders as a "racist" outfit. The FLIC's objective was to investigate organizations suspected of subversive activities. It had the power to subpoena witnesses and hire investigators in the quest to root out subversion. Although the committee claimed that its goal was to root out subversion, its first target was the NAACP. Johns and other committee members were disturbed by the NAACP's efforts to eradicate segregation in the South. In a January 1957 report, the committee claimed the NAACP's effort to dismantle segregation in the South was progressing at an "alarming" rate. The committee asserted it wanted to slow the pace of integration.[24]

In its attempt to restrict black rights the FLIC laid out its case against the NAACP. It painted the civil rights organization as subversive, controlled by Communists who were not only antithetical to American principles, but also out to destroy southern society. In an attempt to reveal the subversive nature of the NAACP and its effort to destabilize southern society, the FLIC raised the specter of racial commingling and miscegenation. The mini-HUAC accused the NAACP of formulating a "plan calling for the full, complete and absolute integration of the races in this country in every phase of American life by 1963. This includes the removal of all legal prohibitions against intermarriage of the races." The "investigative" state body further attempted to instill fear by noting that not only was the NAACP trying to prevail by desegregating the South and dismantle the southern way of life, but it was winning the battle. "The NAACP is directly responsible for securing the decisions of the United States Supreme Court holding separate but equal facilities in education, both elementary and at the higher levels, to be in violation of the United States Constitution. Having secured these decisions, the NAACP has set itself up as a sort of executive arm of the federal courts to execute the integration decrees of federal courts which, standing alone, are not self-executing under the law."[25]

Portraying the NAACP as a devious and sinister entity, the FLIC claimed that the civil rights organization was not representing the "poverty-stricken" but those of means and even soliciting "plaintiffs without their knowledge." This accusation strongly suggested that the NAACP was unethical and that its take-no-prisoners approach forbade locals from compromising with local authorities. More important, the FLIC depicted the civil rights group as one that operated outside of the law. "Although the NAACP has done business in Florida for many years, the charter of the national association was never placed on record with the Secretary of State, as required by law, until after the enactment of the authority under which this committee was created." The accusation was clear; the law only covered those who were morally correct and did not apply to those who were deemed to be out of step with the southern moral code. "The great bulk of the NAACP's activities, above described, are in the opinion of counsel contrary to the spirit and letter of the canons of ethics and general laws governing the conduct and practice of the law; and amount to an abuse of the judicial processes of the courts in which these cares are carried on."[26]

The FLIC was not content to just declare the NAACP out of step with the South's moral and ethical code; it labeled the civil rights organization a criminal outfit. It accused "certain attorneys for the NAACP" of engaging in "unethical conduct in violation of the canons of ethics governing the practice of law in Florida." It further accused witnesses called by the NAACP to support its case for integration of possibly committing perjury. The FLIC even requested that if such allegations were found to be true, the authorities should institute "proper proceedings against any such offender."[27]

In its crusade to crush the NAACP, the FLIC held hearings in February 1958 both in Tallahassee and in Miami. Claiming that it was searching for reds within the venerable civil rights organization, it subpoenaed several NAACP officials throughout the state, as well as other activists for civil rights. Although the NAACP attempted to stop the committee from subpoenaing its members by asking a circuit court to rule on the constitutionality of the FLIC, the civil rights organization failed to convince the judge. It also failed to convince an appeals court that the committee did not have the constitutional right to question it. Undaunted by the courts' rulings, NAACP officials decided that they would not cooperate with investigative committee by refusing to answer any questions that violated their constitutional rights.[28]

On February 26, 1958, the FLIC conducted a hearing in Miami. The committee claimed that it was concerned with "activities with various organizations which have been or presently operating in the field of, first, race relations, second, the coercive reform of social and educational practices and mores by litigation and pressured administrative action. . . ." The committee also declared that it was concerned with "Communist action and Communist infiltration and control over the NAACP." The committee accused the civil rights organization of being "uncooperative" because its members refused to answer questions and submit its membership list allowing the FLIC to discover the "exact nature of Communist penetration and influence in the NAACP in Florida." The investigation committee called the NAACP "obstructionist" and went as far as to accuse it of using tactics similar to the Communists.

At its Miami hearing the committee questioned Ruth Perry, the secretary of the Miami branch of the NAACP. After it failed to force Perry to submit the membership list, one member of the committee, Representative Cliff Herrell of Dade County scolded her by asserting, "Any person who fails to cooperate with the committee is not fit to be a citizen of the state of Florida." Another FLIC member accused the NAACP of harboring Communists. The FLIC members' attack on Perry was a form of racial and cold war politics. Despite her white skin, the claims that Perry was not fit for citizenship and was protecting Communists was essentially labeling her not only a subversive but also a race traitor who was forfeiting her citizenship rights by allying with the civil rights group. The FLIC cited her for contempt.[29]

When testifying before the Florida Legislative Investigation Committee, Gibson read a statement noting the anti-Communist strategy of the Miami branch, countering the claim that the civil rights organization was subversive. He informed the committee of the intolerance the civil rights group had for communists.

> I think it is, we should say, for the benefit of this Committee, that since 1950, when our National Congress met in Boston, we took—we passed resolutions excluding from our ranks any and all persons who may have subversive tendencies. I think I am correct—as a matter of fact, I know I am correct, that each year thereafter we have passed a similar resolution reaffirming our position, and let me say that if this Committee knows of anybody who is said to be and has been proven to be a member of any subversive group and you would give me, as the President of the Miami Branch, that person's or those person's names, we through implementation by the Congress, we are authorized to exclude, put out of the organization immediately, forthwith, any such person.[30]

The anti-Communist position, publicly confessed by Gibson, was to indicate the organization's intense effort to eliminate the left from its presence. Gibson further developed his anti-Communist–loyal American position in his statement before the FLIC. He arranged his statement to focus on three major points. The first point centered on the anti-Communist argument. While noting that he had not brought the membership list with him, he reminded the committee that he had in the past told it of the steps the national organization had taken since 1950 to eliminate Communists from its ranks and the measures his organization had taken to assure that there were no Communists in the leadership. He noted that he had also brought to the attention of the committee J. Egar Hoover's statement congratulating the NAACP on its "success in keeping the organization free of Communist infiltration. " By noting Hoover's congratulatory statement in his book *Masters of Deceit*, Gibson was claiming authenticity for the civil rights organization's struggle against America's enemies. A ringing endorsement from the nation's leading foe of Communists was the best testament to of the NAACP's loyalty to America and of its fervent commitment to the anti-Communist crusade.

Although he could not assure the committee that there were no Communists among the rank and file of his branch, he nevertheless declared the national leadership and he were taking vigilant steps to purge any Communists who might be discovered operating in the NAACP. According to the rector, "If it is brought to the attention of anyone in the NAACP that a member is engaged in subversive activities, steps will be taken to sever his relationship with the organization. The organization's policy has been strictly enforced in the Miami branch during the past five years of my administration."[31]

Gibson's second point was that the submission of the list would jeopardize the safety of the NAACP. He emphasized his willingness to check the names that the committee submitted to him and tell them whether or not they were subversive. However, not to appear as though he were violating the law, Gibson reminded the committee members of his reason for not handing over the membership list. He claimed that the fear of reprisals by the state on the civil rights organization would be widespread. "All that the general public will understand, and particularly members and prospective members of the NAACP, is that the NAACP membership is subject to the scrutiny of Florida officials." Simply put, Gibson's argument was that the submission of the list would directly hurt the NAACP's hold on to its members.[32]

Gibson's final point was the need to protect his rights as a citizen. He accused the committee of violating his First Amendment rights. "In our judgment this is as gross an interference with freedom of association and freedom of speech and will have as great a detrimental effect to such freedoms as if we were required to turn over the names of our members to the Committee." In his defense, Gibson returned to the NAACP tactic of ridiculing the southern opposition to equality by describing it as unpatriotic: "While the activities of the Association in fighting for freedom from racial discrimination and for equality for Negroes may seem revolutionary to the present power structure in Florida and in respect to the mores of the South, it is true to and in accord with the most fundamental tenets of the American social order." Gibson concluded his statement by offering to cooperate with the Committee: "However, that cooperation will not extend to the point of allowing the Committee to violate my constitutional rights, the constitutional rights of the NAACP or the constitutional rights of the NAACP members and contributors."[33]

Even though he was declaring his rights as an American citizen and at the same time his opposition to the committee's attempt to trample on those rights, he said nothing about the rights of individuals who might have been members of political groups considered subversive. Gibson offered no defense of those whose views were unpopular during this period of anti-Communist hysteria, nor did he extend full First Amendment rights to them. Like the committee, Gibson was according constitutional rights only to those who were deemed loyal to the country. The talk of the NAACP policing its own ranks to purge "subversives," and its willingness to cooperate with the FLIC to hunt for Communists among it ranks, helped to define Gibson's and the NAACP's meaning of citizenship. It was a citizenship based on a way of behaving deemed appropriate by American cold warriors. Left-leaning activists and thinkers were simply not included in Gibson's definition of citizen.

Despite Gibson's argument, the FLIC held him in contempt. A state trial court claimed that there was no social reason why Gibson should not submit the membership list to the FLIC. The court ordered the Miami NAACP president to appear at a July 27, 1960, FLIC hearing with the list. But when the activist priest refused to produce the list at the July meeting, a state circuit court on August 30, 1960, held Gibson in contempt, sentencing him to six months in prison and fining him $1,200. Gibson appealed his sentence before the Florida Supreme Court. He was granted a stay of execution by the state court while he appealed.[34]

In its brief before the Supreme Court of Florida, the FLIC continued its strategy of portraying Gibson and other members of the NAACP who refused to cooperate with the committee as criminals, not deserving to be protected under the law because they were involved in a devious subversive plot. Mark R. Hawes, the chief counsel of the FLIC who prepared the brief, described the appellants' brief as "nothing more than leftwing literary intellectual garbage never recognized, to the writer's knowledge, by Courts generally, and certainly not by this Honorable Court as authority for anything." This accusation was made to counter Gibson's attempt to paint himself and the NAACP as loyal Americans. Hawes attempted to internationalize the civil rights struggle by portraying Gibson and the organization as part of a fifth column undermining the nation's values. The counsel even labeled the NAACP's magazine, the *Crisis*, as the organization's "own official propaganda organ."[35]

Hawes hammered away at what he described as the major arguments of the appellants. He ridiculed the claim of Gibson and the members of the NAACP that the trial judge erred in overruling their objections that forcing them to submit the list was a violation of their constitutional rights. Hawes also criticized Gibson's accusation that the trial judge committed error by overruling Gibson's objection to appearing in front of the FLIC because even before his appearance it had manifested bias and prejudice against him and the other appellants.

Hawes contended that the Supreme Court's ruling in *NAACP v. Alabama* (1958) recognized the sovereign state's ability to require an organization to produce the membership lists of the NAACP, providing "a controlling justification and state interests could be demonstrated." In support of the state, Hawes argued that there was justification and it was in the state's interest to gain the membership list. "In the hearing presently under stay by this Court's order, the Appellee is attempting to determine in essence, the degree of penetration, infiltration and influence the Communist Party apparatus has made on several organizations in the State of Florida, which organizations are active in certain vital phases of life in this State, such as race relations, litigation, labor and education." The state was simply trying to determine whether the Communist Party had taken over the NAACP. Although Florida's subversive statutes were no longer valid and the legislature did not have the legality to enact other subversive laws (because the federal Smith Act had preempted them), the state legislature had the "authority and power to enlighten itself through investigation on the subject of communism, as a part of its legislative process under Article 5 of the United States Constitution." He claimed that Florida had a right to "make application" to the U.S. Congress to call a convention to consider amending the Constitution. However, in order for Florida or any other state to take such action, it first had to launch an investigation to determine whether such an act was warranted. Wrapping his case in the Constitution, Hawes claimed that Article 5 granted to the states the "right to initiate proceedings to amend the Federal Constitution in any manner that various State legislatures desire." There was no discussion by Hawes of Florida denying blacks their constitutional rights; he argued only on what the committee perceived as the political leanings of the NAACP and the State's "constitutional right" to investigate it.[36]

The state's justification, according to Hawes, was also based on his assertion that the appellants did not deny the accusations of the state; they simply argued that the state lacked the legal grounds to investigate the civil rights organization. The counsel for the FLIC also claimed to have "expert" witnesses who were able to identify Communists in the Miami branch of the NAACP. One such expert, J. B. Matthews, who had served as director of research and counsel for HUAC from 1938 to 1954, had assembled files on Communism for that committee and "spent a lifetime in the study of communism and subversion." Hawes magnified Matthews's credentials by pointing out that he possessed files that filled twelve rooms and that every security agency of the U.S. government had relied on him. According to his testimony, the United States Communist Party tried to infiltrate personal and ideology into organizations and to influence the "actions of organizations after infiltration." Matthews, who testified before FLIC on February 10, 1958, claimed that he could provide documents proving the affiliation of NAACP officials with the Communist Party.[37]

Matthews claimed that the "Communists are at work, with their customary fanatical dedication, in stirring up trouble in the field of public school integration in the South." The expert witness also accused the CPUSA of working for over thirty years in "the field of agitation among Negroes." They had, according to Matthews, set up fronts to persuade blacks to join the Communist cause. "The Communists favor racial amalgamation and assert that a Communist revolution would speed up the process." Although the NAACP is not mentioned in the pamphlet, the reference is clear. "The Communists have established friendly contacts with the Negro leaders of most of the recent integration incidents in the South."[38]

Hawes also claimed that he had the names of 150 "past and present card-carrying members of the Communist Party who do now, or have in the last few years, lived in the State of Florida" and that based on "sworn testimony" some party members were members of the NAACP. Moreover, the anti-Communist resolutions of the civil rights organization were evidence that Communists had infiltrated the organization and the state needed to know to what degree the party was dominating it.[39]

The state painted the NAACP as a notorious organization bent on creating havoc in America's racial order. It threatened the very existence of southern society by attempting to break its most precious taboo on interracial sex. The state paid no attention to the claims of equal treatment under the law and the rights of full citizenship to black Americans. Instead, it equated integration with the lust of black men for white female bodies.

Attorneys representing Gibson argued that the NAACP had a protracted history of opposing communism and that the Miami chapter was just as anti-Communist as its national organization. The argument, however, did little to convince the court. The Supreme Court of Florida ruled that the FLIC was entitled to subpoena records of the Miami-based civil rights organization. The court declared that Gibson was not legally obligated to submit the membership list to the committee; however, he did have to have it on hand when he was questioned by the FLIC and refer to the list when answering questions at the hearing.[40]

The defeat left Gibson with one final legal option, an appeal to the United States Supreme Court. The high court agreed to hear the case soon after the state's court decision. However, almost two years passed before the Supreme Court ruled in the case.

The Supreme Court's decision, handed down on March 25, 1963, was a confirmation of Gibson's argument. That was evident in the Court's embracing of a citizenship devoid of racial definitions. However, the High Court did not reject the state's argument because of the illegality of silencing people because of their political beliefs. It held that the state did not have ample evidence proving that the NAACP was subversive. According to the court, the committee did not call alleged Communists before it. "It is not discovery of their membership in that Party which is the object of the challenged inquiries." Instead, it was the NAACP and Gibson who were the subjects of the investigation. "There is no suggestion that the Miami branch of the NAACP or the national organization with which it is affiliated was, or is, itself a subversive organization. Nor is there any indication that the activities or policies of the NAACP were Communist dominated or influenced by the CP. In fact, this very record indicates that the association was against Communism and has voluntarily taken steps to keep Communists from being members." The Supreme Court's claim that the state's case was flawed because it failed to prove that the NAACP was subversive, helped legitimize Gibson's social construction of the loyal American–anti-Communist model.[41]

To be sure, the Supreme Court found the FLIC case unconstitutional and in violation of the Fourteenth Amendment of the U.S. Constitution. But its opinion noted that the state failed to prove its case because it did not have enough evidence to connect the NAACP to Communism. Throughout the opinion, the Court emphasized the anti-Communism and the "nonsubversive" nature of the NAACP. "The entire thrust of the demands on the petitioner [Gibson] was that he disclose whether other persons were members of the NAACP, itself a concededly legitimate and nonsubversive organization.... The prior holdings that governmental interest in controlling subversion and the particular character of the Communist Party and its objectives outweigh the right of individual Communists to conceal party membership or affiliations by no means require the wholly different conclusion that other groups—concededly legitimate—automatically forfeit their rights to privacy of association simply because the general subject matter of the legislative inquiry is Communist subversion or infiltration." The Court's decision was based on the "fact that the record in this case is insufficient to show a substantial connection between the Miami branch of the NAACP and the Communist activities which the respondent committee itself concedes is an essential prerequisite to demonstrating the immediate, substantial, and subordinating state interest necessary to sustain its right of inquiry into the membership lists of the association."[42]

The Supreme Court's decision reflected the growing racial liberalism of the federal government in post–World War II America, traceable in large part to the geopolitical concerns of the cold war. To be sure, it is historically incorrect to claim that the Court in *Gibson v. FLIC* and in other cases acted out of concern solely for cold war politics and apprehension over the United States image abroad. The postwar racial liberalism in America has many roots, including the work of social scientists on race relations; the changing demographics of northern urban centers and their impact on the political process; the growth of the New Deal political coalition, which included labor, progressive southern Democrats, members of the national Democratic Party, and African Americans; the emergence of a radical labor movement, particularly the CIO unions that fought for racial equality; and the persistent civil rights struggles across the nation. These were just some of the players who helped bring about a more liberal attitude on race in America. These forces attacked America's color line, weakening its grip over the nation.

But one should not dismiss or downplay the cold war's contribution to emerging enlightened racial policies during this period. Just as important was the growing awareness among civil rights leaders and others of the United States anxiety over its position in the world and how groups on the margins used the tension to their advantage. Scholars have noted the detrimental impact of the anti-Communist hysteria on civil liberties and how it curtailed left voices in labor and other segments of society. They have explored how those seeking social change used this period to help in the fight for democracy. The pivotal role that images and identity played in the fight for equality has been less explored. The NAACP's and Theodore Gibson's loyal American–anti-Communist image was a key component in this vital struggle for citizenship.

Scholar Godfrey Hodgson has argued that the cold war of the 1950s and 1960s helped produce an "ideology of liberal consensus," that is, according to Hodgson, "the ideology that held that American capitalism was a revolutionary force for social change, that economic growth was supremely good because it obviated the need for redistribution and social conflict, that class had no place in American politics." Throughout American society and its institutions, Hodgson contends, there was little dissent from the "broad axiom of consensus," and those who did so were ignored. So even liberal forces, such as Democrats who were involved in Americans for Democratic Action, pushed a politics of responsibility, taking aim more at Communists and the left than at offering a strong critique of America.[43]

Hodgson also notes that during this period there was an acceptance of labor and minority groups; only those on the extreme right and left were not drawn into the "big tent" of the consensus. While Hodgson is correct about the growing acceptance of labor and minority groups and critical dissenters were pushed to the sidelines, he ignores the wide variety of forms and critiques that many within the "big tent" used. Even within the accepted code of behavior, people found ways of dissenting. Historian Eric Foner contends, "Black organizations now embraced the discourse of the Cold War, while using it to advance their own aims, thus complicating the idea of freedom while helping to cement Cold War ideology as the foundation of the political culture." Gibson and the NAACP, while accepting the "liberal consensus," managed to formulate a critique that juxtaposed American ideals to American practices and it was the racial practices that came under harsh criticism. By declaring their embrace of freedom, democracy, and constitutional rights for every citizen, Gibson carved out a less than perfect critique. Its major focus was on a political agenda that lacked any critical analysis of class, gender disparity, or other forms of structural inequality. In fact, after the FLIC lost its battle with the NAACP, it turned its attention to investigating and harassing homosexuals. Nevertheless, his critique greatly assisted in eradicating legal barriers to racial discrimination. The elimination of the Jim Crow system would greatly assist people of African origins in Miami and elsewhere in gaining access to political power, and, just as important, it would help African Americans to be seen as belonging to the nation.[44]

A. Philip Randolph, ca. 1930s. (Courtesy of Chicago Historical Society)

Public Mass Meeting

— HELD BY —

Chicago Division
Brotherhood of Sleeping Car Porters

Sunday Afternoon, April 22,

3 P. M.
AT

Metropolitan Community
... Church ...

4100 SOUTH PARKWAY

A. PHILIP RANDOLPH
General Organizer,

will discuss every phase of the Strike Situation, and also the "So called offer to Settle with the Pullman Porters," so prominently played up by the Pittsburg Courrier.

The success of the Brotherhood is of vital interest to all Negro workers. Learn more about it at this meeting.

Everybody Welcome   **Admission Free**

CHICAGO DIV. HEADQUARTERS
224 EAST PERSHING ROAD
M. P. WEBSTER, Organizer   GEO. W. CLARK, Sec.-Treas.

◆ 101

Flyer announcing a public mass meeting of the Brotherhood of Sleeping Car Porters at the Metropolitan Community Church on April 22, 1928. (Courtesy of Chicago Historical Society)

Milton A. Galamison (fifth from left) with wife, Gladys, next to him, holding their son n.d. (Property of author)

Bishop Smallwood Williams and his son Wallace sitting in the classroom of an all-white school in Washington, D.C. (Courtesy of Yvonne Williams)

Bishop Williams' Family Portrait. "The Bishop's greatest accomplishment, he often says, is the family he and Mrs. Williams reared in Washington." (Courtesy of Yvonne Williams)

Portrait of Rev. John Culmer. (Courtesy of the Museum of South Florida)

Rev. Theodore Gibson (left). (Courtesy of the Museum of South Florida)

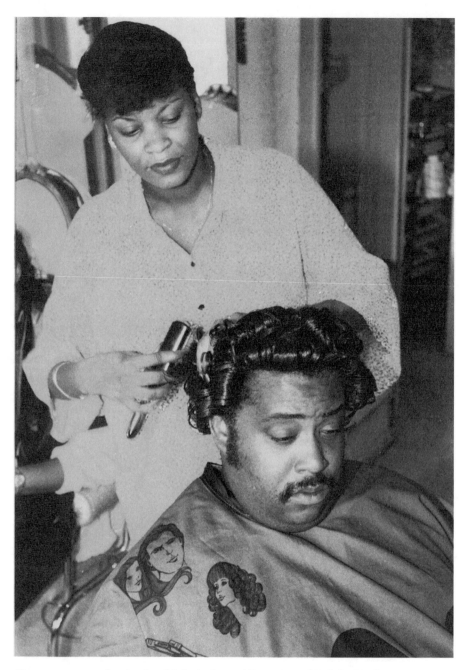

Sharpton at a parlor having his hair done. (Courtesy of Ralph Ginzburg)

Sharpton at a radio station with a new look. (Courtesy of Ralph Ginzburg)

Sharpton in police wagon during the Diallo protest. (Courtesy of Azim Thomas)

CHAPTER 6

"A Natural-Born Leader"

The Politics of
the Reverend Al Sharpton

The Reverend Al Sharpton's most vocal critics have painted him not only as an opportunist, ambulance chaser, and a media hound, but as a political radical who is to blame, in part, for the deterioration of race relations and for the raw exploitation of New York City's African-American communities. Newspaper columnist and social critic Jim Sleeper contends that Sharpton and other black militants ignore the economic hardships faced by African-Americans and excuse crimes committed by black criminals. Instead, he plays the "race card" and thrives on a politics of racial division. According to Sleeper, the dishonesty of local black leaders such as Sharpton, who lie about white attitudes and are supported by guilt-ridden white liberals who defend the lies, is the major cause of racial tension in New York.

Sleeper, who portrays himself as a liberal insider and a supporter of liberal causes, argues that white ethnic groups support only certain aspects of liberalism. Although they live in racially homogeneous neighborhoods and may not like blacks, white ethnic groups support initiatives to give blacks a fair shake because they believe that anyone should have an opportunity.[1] What they oppose is anyone being given benefits and breaks without working for them. Thus, Sleeper joins a long list of people railing against "preferential treatment" for blacks in order to explain that not all white resentment against the black presence is based just on race. He does not deny that ethnic groups have excluded blacks and Latinos from their neighborhoods, but this blemish does not diminish the good done by these white ethnic communities. They actually symbolize what is grand about the concept of community. They represent the Victorian virtues of hard work and honesty. Hence, Sleeper reconstructs the image of white neighborhoods as romantic utopian communities that suppress differences for the good of the whole.

In his attempt to portray a romantic New York past, Sleeper quotes a friend and a former colleague who grew up in a racially mixed neighborhood in the city. According to Sleeper, his friend declared that New Yorkers are not liberal but tolerant. Sleeper cites his friend's comments because he wants to drive home the point that white New Yorkers hold the principle that everyone should be given a chance to succeed, no matter their race, color, or creed. The author argues that New York's white working class adopted a civic culture that consisted of the basic belief in human self-worth, respect, hard work, and decency.[2] Ethnic neighborhoods played an important role in the city because they were places that instilled civic culture.

It is apparent that, while Sleeper does not blame white ethnic groups for the city's racial divide, blacks are prime targets for the author. According to Sleeper, it is a group of militant blacks or "race hustlers" who are to blame for New York City's racial climate. "What exists today is a group of 'professional blacks' (not to be confused with black professionals) who developed a predictable stake in expanding the boundaries of racism in pursuit of moral and practical exemptions from social obligation, done much to restore faith." In fact, the journalist contends that the neoconservative labeling of all blacks as criminals is an overreaction, but not entirely their fault. It is a response to a group of local black race hustlers and their white apologists who argue that a white genocidal conspiracy is responsible for black crime.[3] Sharpton is part of the Brooklyn-based insurgents who have no legitimate answers to the plight of poor people. Sharpton ignores the economic factors that helped create the underclass, as well as personal responsibility.

Sleeper displays a profound ignorance of the work of social and cultural historians who have, during the last three decades, published numerous works providing evidence that, throughout American history, African Americans have forged cultural strategies to address the economic, political, and social realities of their situation. Instead, the former *New York Daily News* columnist relies on the words of the late historian and cultural critic Christopher Lasch. Sleeper writes that Lasch "reminds us of the black sociologist E. Franklin Frazier's observation that the black man's 'primary struggle' in America 'has been to acquire a culture—customs, values and forms of expression which, transmitted from generation to generation, provide a people with a sense of its own integrity and collective identity.' Only within such a culture can individual dignity be nourished and cohere." Preparing the groundwork for the right-wing ideologue Dinesh D'Souza, who claims in *The End of Racism* that blacks suffer from a civilization gap (culture gap), Sleeper contends that race hustlers like Sharpton attempt to prey on the culturally challenged black community and fill the black cultural void by substituting racial ideology. "Can an embattled minority acquire a culture through politics, especially a politics that defines itself primarily as a struggle against the white racist devil? Those who think so defend not a culture in the classic sense but an ideology and, to my mind, a delusional system, a separate reality." Sleeper would have his readers believe that the politics of professional blacks, including Sharpton, is a politics of resentment "irresistible" to "angry" blacks thus reducing civil-rights activism to the politics of "victimization." Blacks are portrayed as constant victims of a white racist genocidal policy. Sleeper accuses Sharpton of engaging in racial posturing.[4]

In high praise of Jim Sleeper's *Closest of Strangers* Christopher Lasch claims that the work "carries so much conviction." Like Sleeper, Lasch contended that Sharpton was part of the "black elite" who used the race card for their own self-interest. Lasch painted black nationalism as a defense of the particular, while integration embraced commonality. The demise of the civil rights movement created an avenue for a new black leadership to emerge and manipulate a divisive racial rhetoric. Joining such prominent voices as Arthur Schlesinger Jr. and others who are involved in the "culture wars," Lasch attacked the champions of cultural diversity, labeling them extreme nationalists, rejecting universal vision. "[I]t is no longer a matter of asserting (in the manner, say, of Marcus Garvey or Malcolm X) that blacks have nothing to gain from integration into a corrupt society, a society that refuses to practice what it preaches. Now it is Western Culture as a whole, Western rationalism as such, the very notion of a common tradition or a common civic language or a set of common standards, that is said to be necessarily and unavoidably racist." While noting the shortcomings of integrationists (their goal should have been giving blacks an avenue to join the common society, not to achieve upward mobility), he goes after the "professional black militants" for racial polarization.[5] These militants have demanded "a new politics of collective grievance and entitlement." They attempt to succeed by claiming blacks are the perpetual victims of white racism and therefore should be held to a lesser standard than whites when it comes to deciding the criteria for jobs and entrance into the university. Lasch asserts that Al Sharpton, notably in the Tawana Brawley case, where he defended a fifteen-year-old girl who falsely accused police officers of raping her and leaving her to die in a lot in Wappingers Falls, New York, is typical of black professional militants who reject the common standard. The author is not content to argue that class is more significant than race. He goes on to argue that racism is irrelevant as an explanation of black poverty in New York.[6]

Like Sleeper and Lasch, neoconservative author David Horowitz contends that Sharpton has squandered the moral legacy of Martin Luther King Jr. In fact, Horowitz accuses Sharpton and other black leaders of making a living from blaming whites for the problems of blacks. The minister, according to Horowitz, is nothing more than a "convicted liar," an "anti-Semitic racist" who has "ruined people's lives." In the eyes of this neoconservative thinker, Sharpton is an analogue of the former Ku Klux Klan leader David Duke.[7]

It should be noted that Sharpton's critics cross racial lines. For example, Harvard University's sociology professor Orlando Paterson refers to Sharpton as a racial arsonist and has expressed dismay that the minister from Brooklyn has managed to climb to the top of New York City leadership. *Miami Herald* columnist Derrick Z. Jackson was disturbed by Sharpton's gaining the national spotlight during the debate at the Apollo Theater in Harlem between Al Gore and Bill Bradley in 2000. "I was sick when I saw him ask the first question, because it is difficult to believe, thirty-five years after so much terrible struggle, that the leadoff batter at the Apollo was a man who has built his credibility on politics so toxic they would shame DuPont." He called Sharpton the "black folks' Richard Nixon" and "Pat Buchanan."[8]

Despite the criticism and demonization heaped on Sharpton by Sleeper, Lasch, and a host of others, few writers have been able to shed light on Al Sharpton's intellect and politics. These assertions do little more than construct a simplistic image of the minister from Brooklyn. They completely ignore his use of cultural symbolism, his reinterpretation of race and politics, and his efforts to transform himself. In their construction of Sharpton, these critics create a person who serves their conservative argumentation for the causes of the racial divide in New York and the nation, but tell us nothing about this complex figure. Since the early 1990s Sharpton has become a significant political presence in New York City and the nation. He came in a respectable third in a four-person race in the Democratic senatorial primary in 1992, receiving over 72 percent of the black vote. The best example of his growing success is his showing in the 1997 Democratic primary for mayor. The flamboyant minister captured 32 percent of the vote, almost forcing a runoff election between himself and Ruth Messinger, who received 39.9 percent. Although his notoriety cannot be denied, political figures who would not have been seen with Sharpton a few years ago now embrace him publicly. The head officer of the NAACP, Kweisi Mfume, attended a party in Sharpton's honor in the summer of 1997 and called the minister "a man for our time." The Reverend Jesse Jackson declared that Sharpton had been there when he needed him, adding, "I am here now because he needs me." Former Mayor Dinkins, who has harshly criticized Sharpton in the past and backed Ruth Messinger for mayor in 1991 instead of Sharpton, praised the activist minister. Sharpton attended Emancipation Day celebrations in Barbados during the summer of 1997 where one speaker called him an "international figure" who is "respected throughout the world as a freedom fighter." His political prominence in New York State was made evident when in the summer of 1998, the three leading Democratic candidates vying for the Senate sought the endorsement of Sharpton's organization, the National Action Network. *Time* magazine writer Jack White contends in his article "Big Al's Finest Hour" that the activist minister deserves praise for urging calm after four police officers were found innocent for shooting to death an African immigrant by the name of Amadou Diallo. White joined those who argued that there is a new Al Sharpton by writing that the minister has the making of a "moral leader."[9] Sharpton has been the central figure in a protest movement against the policing policies of former New York mayor Rudolph Giuliani. The protests attracted thousands of people across racial lines and involved prominent figures as well as ordinary people.

The political success of the minister from Brooklyn cannot be explained simply by asserting that he is a hustler and that his supporters are dupes of a con artist. Sleeper and other critics have put Sharpton in a vacuum, as though he is a static character and his politics have not evolved over time. They see him as a manipulator of the poor, ignorant masses, ignoring the cultural and political context that fosters Sharpton's success. Moreover, both critics and supporters present him as a one-dimensional character, ignoring the periodization of his politics. Sharpton has been continuously involved in the construction of racial images of New York politics, and he has been continuously defining his relationship to the political construction. To gain a better understanding of Al Sharpton, this chapter examines both his early and later politics and how he places himself on the political map. Throughout the 1980s, Sharpton's actions and language painted a New York City that was similar to the South in its racial politics. While constructing such an image, he used cultural symbols as forms of opposition. In the absence of any strong social protest movement, Sharpton won support by relying on a charismatic leadership. Since 1991, as the political landscape has changed, Sharpton has attempted to reconstruct his image from an impulsive militant to a more responsible activist and politician. He has paid greater attention to electoral politics and tried to forge a progressive coalition across racial lines.

The Rise of Al Sharpton

Sharpton emerged during a period when New York City was undergoing rapid transformation. Manufacturing was losing its dominance in the city's economy and was replaced by finance, insurance, real estate, and advertising. Fewer workers were needed, and the best-paid positions went to a trained middle- and upper-managerial class. The lost manufacturing jobs were replaced by many insecure and low-paying jobs in the service sector. This trend toward marginalizing the working class was exacerbated by an attempt to reduce welfare. Author Bill Tabb asserts that Mayor Ed Koch, who served from 1978 to 1990, selected as his administrators people who would carry out a war on the poor, especially the minority poor. His director of human services told researchers that the number of people receiving welfare would be "what she wanted it to be"; by mid-1978, the rejection rate was almost twice that of 1976. In fiscal year 1977–1978, by limiting intake, rejecting applicants, and uncovering "ineligibles," the department had reduced the rolls by 40,000. In addition, many were forced into part-time work with no medical insurance. The increase in the involuntary part-time workforce was the result of declining opportunities for full-time employment. Most of these workers were not in their teens but were twenty years old and older, yet they were making the minimum wage.[10]

The increase in underemployment prompted a rise in the number of home-less families. Until the 1980s the homeless in the city had consisted of men and women without families. Throughout the 1970s, the number of homeless families remained constant at about 940. Most of these cases were due to temporary problems, such as fires and illness. However, throughout the 1980s the number of families without permanent housing increased, reaching 5,200 in 1988. Women who were unable to find jobs that would pay them a living wage headed most of the families. The Koch administration allowed lofts and tenements to be converted to luxury apartments through abatements, forfeiting millions of dollars in lost taxes, while limiting housing for the poor. Authors Jack Newfield and Wayne Barrett contend that realtors like Donald Trump, who contributed to Koch's electoral campaigns, received large abatements and zoning changes. Trump in fact received the largest tax write-off in the city's history; he got a $160 million abatement, over forty-two years, for renovating the Commodore Hotel into the "elegant Grand Hyatt." At the same time, single room occupancy hotels that once gave shelter to the poor were converted to upscale apartments for the emerging middle class produced by the newly dominant industries of the city. To make matters worse, the tax breaks combined with a shrinking middle class to increase the tax burden on middle- and working-class New Yorkers.[11]

Throughout the 1970s and 1980s black and Latino communities were being devastated by high unemployment, crime, crack, and teenage pregnancy. Harvard University sociologist William Julius Wilson has convincingly argued that the disappearance of jobs paying a living wage has led to the growth of an urban underclass trapped in poverty and crime. But Wilson's liberal suggestion that full employment be used to address the problems of the underclass was not the dominant view among policy-makers. Conservatives were winning the public debate on the causes of poverty. Instead of fostering a recommitment to fight racial discrimination or focusing on class as an aspect of black and Latino unemployment, conservatives emphasized the "culture of poverty" argument. They emphasized the dysfunctional behavior of the poor. Conservatives argued that welfare programs helped destroy the initiative and entrepreneurial spirit of welfare recipients and made them dependent on the state. The way to destroy this culture of dependency, according to the right, was to dismantle the welfare state. Such an action would force the poor to become self-reliant. The Democratic Leadership Conference, a neoliberal organization that emphasizes global free trade, a balanced budget, smaller government, and workfare over welfare, embraced the culture-of-dependency argument. In 1992 the Democratic Leadership Conference helped put into the White House one of its own members, Bill Clinton, who then pursued DLC policies, including "ending welfare as we know it."

Coinciding with the deteriorating economic situation for some New Yorkers, police assaults on citizens became a major issue. Under Mayor Ed Koch there were a number of highly publicized police brutality cases, including the Arthur Miller, Michael Stewart, and Eleanor Bumpurs cases. In 1978 police choked Arthur Miller, a respected businessman in Bedford-Stuyvesant, Brooklyn, to death. The police claimed that Miller had resisted arrest and that they had applied a chokehold as a "restraining device." Michael Stewart, a young African American, died in a hospital after being arrested and beaten into a coma by police in 1983. And Eleanor Bumpurs, a sixty-seven-year-old mentally disturbed woman, was shot to death by police who were attempting to evict her from her apartment. They claimed she had attacked them with a knife. Though there were several police officers in the apartment at the time, one with a protective shield, she was shot twice. The first shot hit her in the arm that had the knife; the second shot struck her in the chest.[12]

In every case of police brutality during the Koch administration, the mayor defended the action of the police. Blacks and Latinos felt themselves under siege. Instead of addressing the racial wounds that divided New Yorkers, Koch intensified the situation with his use of racial coding. He proclaimed that most blacks are anti-Semitic, later clarifying his statement by arguing that most black leaders are anti-Semitic. When demonstrators were protesting Koch's decision to close Sydenham Hospital in Harlem, a poor area in which infant mortality matched that of developing nations, the mayor ordered the police to break up the demonstration. During the Sydenham crisis, Koch met the cast of the Broadway musical *Ain't Misbehavin'* and insulted the black community when he put on an Afro wig and replied in a vernacular when someone remarked that it was hard to tell whether he was a Democrat or a Republican. He used inflammatory language when he called those on welfare "poverty pimps." Black leaders, such as Congressman Charles Rangel, of Harlem, and the Reverend Herbert Daughtry, of Brooklyn, challenged Koch and his policies. In particular, Daughtry organized numerous demonstrations against police brutality, demanded youth program and summer jobs for teens, as well as greater communication with black leaders, and protested the antiblack and antipoor policies of the administration. However, the city's black leadership was divided. Some supported the mayor, while others could not agree on candidates to challenge Koch in mayoral elections. Moreover, leftist groups and civil rights organizations that had been actively organizing people twenty-five years earlier had faded from the scene, replaced by the black power and, later, by more divisive voices of the new right and neoconservatism.[13]

Sharpton emerged during this time of rapid economic and social transformation, appealing to many because he addressed issues such as police brutality in a dramatic fashion; he seemed to be a strong black advocate against white racism. Like all charismatic leaders, Sharpton's public performance employed a politics of manhood, presenting himself as the embodiment of the bold black man who was not willing to tolerate any kind of injustice. For many, he became a symbol of defiance against police and racial assaults.

Sharpton's early public performance adopted civil rights and black power traditions. He appropriated the language of those past progressive movements and blended them into a unique oppositional style. He did what cultural critic Kobena Mercer calls "democratic equivalences," appropriating the goals and language of movements for democracy and applying them to his movement. By doing so he recreated civil rights and black nationalist paradigms. The minister from Brooklyn attempted to paint New York as the most racist city in the country, equating it with southern cities during the civil rights decades. Sharpton explains: "I think when people turned on the television, when we marched in Howard Beach and Bensonhurst, and saw people holding watermelons and calling people niggers—they never imagined that could happen in Brooklyn. If you had taken some people, brought them in a room, and showed them tapes of those marches, they would have thought it was in Birmingham in '63 or Selma. No one would have believed it was New York. I think that's one of the problems the media has with me—that I was able to tear the veil off racism in New York." In this text, Sharpton has two purposes. The first is to associate New York City with the image of southern racial terror and brutality of the Birmingham campaign of 1963, the Selma march of 1965, and other campaigns in the South that are retold in documentaries, public commemorations of the civil rights struggle, and in countless texts, monographs, and picture books about the movement. He has equated the racial violence and situations in New York during the 1980s and 1990s with the violence of the South that has become part of the official civil rights narrative. According to Sharpton, blacks were living in dangerous terrain, under siege by white racist mobs, and harassed by a brutal police state bent on denying blacks their civil rights. The second purpose is to position himself against New York's Jim Crow by presenting himself as a black revolutionary who is willing to put his life on the line for his people.[14]

Sharpton's assertion that the civil rights movement only arrived in the New York area when he brought it, completely ignores the protests and demonstrations led by the Congress of Racial Equality and by the black ministers and ordinary people of Brooklyn who challenged the racial practices of the construction trades in the early 1960s. He also ignored the struggle to integrate New York City schools led by Rev. Milton A. Galamison. Instead, Sharpton asserted that the militant civil disobedience movement in New York, grounded in the tradition of the southern civil rights movement, was his brainchild. Black New York had been waiting to make a statement for years because urban blacks in the North were used to limiting themselves to rallies and electoral politics. Sharpton wrote: "While I was thinking of Breadbasket, SCLC, Dr. King, and civil disobedience. I listened to Jesse Jackson and Jim Bevel and those men sit and tell stories about the Freedom Rides and lunch counters and I'd always thought 'Why can't we bring that to New York?'" He presented himself as a product of the southern civil rights struggle, gaining firsthand knowledge about protest strategies from leaders such as Jackson and Bevel. For Sharpton, it was the oral tradition passed down by the icons of the southern wing of the civil rights movement that was most appealing. It was the southern wing of the civil rights struggle and not its New York and northern campaigns that were being articulated by Sharpton because those southern events had become part of the "official" story and the collective memory of the nation whereas the northern ones are long forgotten and, for the most part, no longer a part of the larger civil rights narrative.[15]

Sharpton's actions were and continue to be reenactments of events of the previous generation, an attempt to recreate the southern civil rights struggle in the north. For example, after his arrest for the Day of Outrage demonstration in 1987, the Brooklyn minister borrowed a page from the history of the Mississippi Democratic Freedom Party, which had refused to accept two at-large seats at the 1964 Democratic National Convention, offered as a compromise of their demand that they be recognized as the legitimate Democratic Party of the state. "They had all the leaders in one cell, and about one o'clock in the morning Al Vann [the assemblyperson from Bedford-Stuyvesant] came into the jail and said he had talked to the Brooklyn D.A., Liz Holtzman, and that she had agreed to let the leaders go. But I said, 'No. We all have to go or nobody goes.' I remembered Fannie Lou Hamer and them, you don't leave anyone in jail."[16]

At the same time that he wrapped himself in the heritage of the civil rights movement, he also borrowed from the black power movement. Nowhere is this clearer than in the struggle against police brutality, where he used a colonization argument. Although he did not swallow the rhetoric of revolutionary black nationalist groups that claimed the black community was a colony and the police an occupied army, Sharpton has nevertheless asserted that the agents of law enforcement and the media inflict tremendous harm on people of color.[17] His struggle is against a police system that degrades blacks and steals their humanity. Like Malcolm X, Huey P. Newton, H. Rap Brown, and other black revolutionaries who were the personification of black manhood, calling for self-defense of black people and pointing out the significance of armed struggle, Sharpton has defiantly confronted the system by using words as his major weapon. His claim during the Tawana Brawley case that he was protecting black womanhood thrilled his audience because he pitted himself against "white racists." He was able to do what black men in bondage were not able to do, defend black womanhood. The rhetoric of manly defiance played on the emotions of African Americans. His slogan at rallies, "No Justice, No Peace," helped present him as a person militantly challenging the white power structure. The chant sent the message that white America cannot be assured tranquility if it is not willing to grant justice to blacks.

Sharpton's attempt to construct a manhood that was identified with a defiance to authority is clearly illustrated in the Tawana Brawley episode. His attacks on "white cops" for allegedly raping a fifteen-year-old were couched in a language of manly obligation to stand up against the violation and sexual exploitation of black women. By manipulating an African-diasporic collective conscious of a historical fact, of slave masters raping black women, Sharpton painted himself as one who was not going to idly stand by. Instead, he, along with Brawley's two attorneys, was bold enough to defy a governor, an attorney general, and a grand jury in their "pursuit" of justice.

Sharpton's faults and questionable activities are not important to his followers. Commenting on Sharpton's popularity, *New York Daily News* columnist E. R. Ship claims that the minister's "supporters either never stopped believing the Brawley take or have forgiven Sharpton his trespasses. It's political power they crave, and Sharpton seems their best hope for now." His followers dismiss accusations that he was once an FBI informant, a strategist in the Brawley fiasco, and is closely associated with boxing promoter and unsavory character Don King. They claim that any criticism of Sharpton is an attempt to smear his character. In fact, he continues his close association with King. In early 1998 at the "Hall of Justice," Sharpton's organization, the National Action Network, invited Kweisi Mfume and prominent local politicians to support Don King. What Ship misses in her analysis of Sharpton is his rhetoric of manly defiance. What impresses his followers is his ability and willingness to defy the power structure that is seen as the cause of their suffering. He uses an accessible language in a dramatic black religious style that is attractive. His followers see him as a man who is willing to tell it like it is, to "be real" and "stay black." As Donna Wilson, radio host of a morning talk show on black-owned radio station WWRL and staunch Sharpton supporter, said, "Al Sharpton was born to lead."[18]

One thing that has helped Sharpton attract a following is his speaking ability. He has perfected the patriarchal black preacher's style. In Afro-folk religion it is a style noted more for manner than substance. The loud, raspy voice, with its crescendos reaching a higher pitch as he moves through the narrative, makes his audience feel and experience his pain, anger, and excitement. What he says is not as important as how he says it. This style of oratory relies heavily on an antiphonal structure. Its success or failure is measured by applause, shouts, and yells of approval. In a setting that blurs the boundaries between religion and politics, Sharpton is successful because he is able to make his audience, like those at a good old-time revival, unite, galvanized by a spirit of righteous indignation or jubilant over a victory in a court battle or concessions made by the "enemy." Sharpton, like so many African-American ministers involved in politics, has managed to present the world to his followers as a simple battle between good and evil. His preaching style has been an important factor in his political ascendancy.

For years, style has been an essential theme of Sharpton's class politics. The minister's early image was a challenge to middle-class mores. His early disregard for dress suits and ties and his fondness for jogging suits and sneakers demonstrated an affinity with the young and the working class. While a suit represented establishment politics and those who had ties to the system, the jumpsuit symbolized a connection with those on the street, especially young people. They were more likely to have a rebellious spirit and see little difference between the black middle class and white politicians. Sharpton realized the usefulness of clothing style when forging an identity. In a *Village Voice* interview, the minister from Brooklyn claims he became conscious of the link between clothes and political struggle.

> Clothes are always important to any public figure, but it really became something that I watched when I was about 14 or 15, traveling with James Brown.... Then in the Movement, when I became Jesse Jackson's youth director in New York, I saw that he, too, would use clothes in a certain way. I never

saw Reverend Jackson wear a suit and tie until '72, '73. He wore turtlenecks, medallions, like I later wore. Between Jesse and James Brown, I learned that what you wore projected some of your message. So later in life, whether it was a jogging suit or a three-piece suit, I understood that people see you before they hear you, and a lot of what they hear they judge by what they see.[19]

Sharpton also realized that many young African Americans were not looking to political figures who associated with those with power. His jogging suits became like a populist's overalls, a clear message that he did not care about the proper and conventional wear when addressing top political figures. The message he was sending conveyed his solidarity with the black community. He claims that at "different stages in my life, when I was doing just street activism, I would wear just jogging suits, going on marches that mostly resulted in a night in jail. Why would you wear a suit if you're going to spend the night on Rikers Island?" Although Sharpton did not mention that he used jogging suits as a way of identifying with black working-class youths, nevertheless, he identifies the wearing of the outfits with his street activism.[20]

Sharpton's most notable feature has been his hair. The straightening of his hair is a challenge to an "authentic" black look that has been embraced by fashion designers appealing to a middle-class black clientele. The black power movement of the late 1960s and early 1970s challenged the Eurocentric look, attempting to replace it with African styles. Kente cloth, dashikis, and the Afro were symbols of an "authentic" African look. True blackness, according to supporters of black aesthetics, could only be associated with their interpretation of the African look. Straightening the hair was more Eurocentric and thus inauthentic. During this period, the conk had been critically wounded by the accusation that it was a symbol of cultural genocide and a denial of blackness. The late Kwame Ture, formerly known as Stokely Carmichael, captured this sentiment when he asserted in 1966: "A broad nose, a thick lip and nappy hair is us and we are going to call that beautiful whether they like it or not. We are not going to fry our hair for anyone."[21]

Although the politics of black power have faded, the aesthetics have lived on, promoted to and used by a growing black consumer market. The "natural" look has been captured by commercial capitalism, commodified, turned into a lucrative business. Millions consume Johnson hair products, including Afro-Sheen and Duke hair products. Along with Duke's "Wave and Curl Texturizer," which "creates a natural looking wave," and Duke's Curl Activator," a "non-greasy formula" that "allows hair to achieve a natural wave," there is Duke's "Comb-Out Oil Sheen Conditioner and Instant Spray Moisturizer," which assures "the daily upkeep of today's natural looking styles."[22]

Ebony, Black Enterprise, Emerge, and *Essence* magazines feature models sporting the look, with fades, dreads, and clean-cut Afro hair styles. In one ad for Hennessy Cognac that appears in *Emerge,* a beautiful young woman is depicted with her hair in a natural and untreated state. Her jet-black hair is combed back and is full textured. In another ad for Viagra, a middle-aged black woman who is embracing a middle-aged black man has a short Afro. Barbershops and salons that feature special haircuts, including the natural hairstyle for men and woman have become lucrative businesses. In a special feature of *Essence* titled "Celebrating Our Hair," the reader is advised: "Get to know your hair's natural state." The magazine piece has a story about a young woman by the name of Victoria who had "long, thick, heavy extensions.... Diane Baily of Tendrils House of Ujamma in Brooklyn revitalized Victoria's hair and had her looking positively diva!" After Victoria's hair was given a rest from the extensions and treated with oil and water, it was shampooed to help stimulate the scalp, treated with shea-butter moisturizer, and brushed with a soft toothbrush. Eventually, Victoria was given "naturally kinky human hair" for her new look. Black men and women who have made it in corporate America are featured in black publications with short, clean-cut afros. This is the case with Addison Barry Rand, who became the chairman and chief executive officer of Avis Rent-A-Car. He is featured in *Black Enterprise* wearing wire-framed glasses, a thick mustache, and a short neatly trimmed Afro.[23]

Despite the stress on the natural look, Sharpton continues to flaunt the "process." His hairstyle, however, should be seen as a reappropiaton and rearticulation of the black art form advanced by African Americans before the advent of Soul. Although Sharpton has noted that his hairstyle honors the famous soul singer James Brown, it is also symbolic of a rebellious youth culture having its roots in the 1940s. The "conk" was not born out of a desire to imitate whiteness. It was part of a zoot-suit culture associated with urban young Hispanic and black males who jitterbugged and used a coded language, a dialect identified with coolness, outlaw culture, decadent leisure, and vice. Young people who adopted the conk and zoot suit were challenging the mores and conventions that stressed conformity. Historian Robin Kelley comments on the zoot-suit culture:

> The conk was a refusal to look like either the dominant stereotyped image of the Southern migrant or the black bourgeoisie, whose "conks" were closer to mimicking white styles than those of the zoot suiters. Besides, to claim that black working-class males who conked their hair were merely parroting whites ignores the fact that specific stylizations created by black youth emphasized difference.... More importantly, once we contextualize the conk, considering the social practices of young hip cats, the totality of ethnic signifiers from the baggy pants to the coded language, their opposition to war, and emphasis on pleasure over waged labor, we cannot help but view the conk as part of a larger process by which black youth appropriated, transformed, and reinscribed coded oppositional meanings onto styles derived from the dominant culture.[24]

The conk style was a form of expressive culture used to symbolize resistance to those who identified hair as part of authenticated racial features. Sharpton is clearly conscious of the defiance of the conk. In his autobiography he notes that he allowed a photo of himself to be taken while he was in a salon having his hair styled. He asserts that it was a mistake and that his mentor, Jesse Jackson, reacted negatively to the photo. However, what is significant about the story is not the apology of the new Al Sharpton, who has tamed his image, but the defiance of the younger Al Sharpton. According to the activist minister, the photo was an attempt to mock white people. He was using his hair to challenge whiteness and white beauty standards. He was a black man who took what was seen as natural to whites and used it as his symbol of opposition to racism. The activist minister was turning to African-American folklore by emulating the "bad nigger." He used the process as it had been used for forty years, directly challenging conventional norms. He was openly opposing cultural hegemony and the social control of the larger society. Moreover, the pastor's hairstyle presented a style that had its roots in northern black ghettos. Kobena Mercer contends:

> In this context the conk was but one aspect of a modern style of black American life, forged in the subaltern social bloc of the northern ghettos by people who, like Malcolm Little, had migrated from southern systems of segregation only to find themselves locked into another more modern, and equally violent, order of oppression. Shut our from access to illusions of "making it," this marginalized urban formation of modern Diaspora culture sponsored a sense of style which answered back against these conditions of existence."[25]

Sharpton's hair became a symbol beyond the confines of one particular culture. The meaning was completely misunderstood by Jackson and others, who were critical of the style they identified with "legitimate" politicians and leaders with mainstream features. The Reverend Gardner C. Taylor was aware of the criticism of Sharpton's hair and his politics of representation. The "dean" of black Baptist preachers scolded many of his black bourgeois congregants, during the Tawana Brawley episode, as being "too middle class" because they judged a certain person by his hairstyle rather than by his cause or struggle.

Sharpton's opposition was aimed not just at whites, but also at middle-class blacks. His hairstyle helped revive the conk, reclaiming its diasporic roots and original oppositional position. He challenged the dominance of the commercially successful "natural" black look by flaunting his hair. His militancy made it clear that the strongest black nationalist would have trouble questioning his blackness. His look became a symbol of resistance because it was identified with Sharpton.

Despite his use of cultural symbolism and rhetoric, some of Sharpton's political activities have not been progressive. His stint as an FBI informant, supplying information on black leaders such as Brooklyn congressman Major Owens, and his endorsement of the conservative Republican Alfonse D'Amato for the Senate in 1986 demonstrated his ambivalence toward progressive politics. Moreover, his close ties with the New Alliance Party, a cultist organization led by Fred Newman, a one-time associate of the racist and self-proclaimed Marxist Lyndon LaRouche, raised serious doubts about Sharpton's understanding of progressive left politics. Although he became a cultural symbol of resistance, many of his critics claimed that his politics were marred with contradictions. They claimed that there was no clear vision and no indication of where his politics lay. He had no clear ideological bent. His politics were not grounded in Marxism, socialism, liberalism, or conservatism, but were based on whatever issue helped grab the headlines.[26]

Although Sharpton claimed that many people influenced him, including the pastor of the church he attended when he was a child, Bishop Fredrick Washington, and the eloquent Adam Clayton Powell Jr. of Abyssinian Baptist Church, one of the most important and consistent influences has been the Reverend Jesse Jackson. While a student at the Chicago Theological Seminary, Jackson took a pilgrimage to Alabama and took part in the Selma campaign. It was during that time that Jackson decided to become involved in the movement and, specifically, with the Southern Christian Leadership Conference. He volunteered his services to Martin Luther King Jr. and SCLC before officially becoming a member. Six months after the Selma campaign Jackson became the youngest member of SCLC. He was twenty-four. He was selected to head the Chicago branch of Operation Breadbasket and used a number of techniques, including boycotts, demonstrations, and negotiations, to make it one of the most successful chapters of the national organization. Jackson's success was due in large part to his knowledge of the political landscape of Chicago's ministerial community and how it operated with the political machine and the willingness ministers to oppose mayors and work with SCLC.

Because of his efforts and his ambition, Jackson later was selected to head the national Operation Breadbasket and lead several campaigns, including the boycott against the Atlantic and Pacific grocery chain. However, there were personality conflicts, and Jackson was removed from the leadership of Operation Breadbasket. He soon left SCLC to form his own organizations, People United to Save Humanity (PUSH) and the Rainbow Coalition.[27]

Like Martin Luther King Jr., Jackson was able to present himself as a conscious voice of the nation. King was able to present himself as the leading voice against several social evils. His objective was to remake America into the "beloved community" by eliminating racism, poverty and militarism. His decision to move SCLC to Chicago in 1966 demonstrated that he did not see racism as just a southern problem but as a national one. The Chicago campaign also signified that King was moving to deal with poverty. His decision to move into a Chicago housing project was a clear message of the nation's failure to address the hardships of the poor. By 1967 he had moved away from a race-specific agenda to addressing race and class in America by launching the Poor People's Campaign, attempting to empower poor people across racial lines to organize a mass movement to end poverty. King also addressed U.S. foreign policy. As early as the Montgomery bus boycott he spoke out against militarism. But it was his 1967 speech at Riverside Church in New York City in which he criticized the United States role in Vietnam that helped make King one of the leading antiwar activists in the nation.[28]

Although Jackson, too, forged an image as a conscious voice of the nation, he was no mere imitation of Martin Luther King. Jackson, unlike King and the other members of SCLC, had experience in an urban setting. While Jackson embraced King's beloved community and railed against racism and militarism, he remained focused on a broader economic agenda. This economic agenda was evident in his 1988 presidential campaign. When he announced his candidacy, Jackson declared that the issue facing the nation was no longer racial violence because it made such violence illegal. The major problem was economic violence. "When plants close on workers without notice and leave them without jobs or training for new jobs—that's economic violence. When merger maniacs make windfall profits and top management is given excessive bonuses, while workers are asked to take a wage cut, a benefit cut, and a job loss—that's economic violence. When our children are victimized with poor heath care, poor education, poor housing, poor diets, and more—that's economic violence against our children." His vision of a "New America" called for ending toxic waste dumping, defeating anti-union laws, and stopping the merger maniacs. Like King, Jackson addressed international issues, often siding with those who waged a battle for peace. He attacked Reagan's tactic of constructive engagement with the racist, apartheid regime in South Africa, the bombing of Libya, and the mining of Nicaraguan harbors. By 1988 Jackson had become the prophetic voice of the nation, transcending the image of race leader and becoming a voice for progressive causes that concerned people across racial lines.[29]

Sharpton first met Jackson in 1969. Sharpton, then a high school student, had been appointed youth director of the New York branch of Operation Breadbasket. The Reverend William A. Jones, head of the New York branch of the organization, introduced Jackson, who was then head of the national office of Operation Breadbasket, to Sharpton. Sharpton declared that soon after meeting Jackson they "became tight." Jackson served as a mentor to the young minister and became his role model. Sharpton confessed that Jackson had a strong influence on him. "Even though I dropped out of college, I was still growing intellectually. I saw Jesse Jackson reading *Love, Power and Justice* by Paul Tillich, so I went out and bought all of Tillich's books.... I was imitating my mentor, but also expanding myself as a person."[30] However, while Sharpton claimed that Jackson was his role model, it was Jackson's strategies for gaining attention and media coverage more than Jackson's vision of a New America that attracted Sharpton earlier in his political career. What was absent from the early stages of Sharpton's agenda was a clear political vision. His major focus was developing ways of bringing media attention to himself and the causes he adopted.

The New Al Sharpton

Although by 1991 Sharpton admitted that he was "impulsive" during the 1980s and ran more on emotions than political logic, he now claims that he is more serious. He argues he is working to build a progressive coalition that will address the needs of blacks and poor New Yorkers. The activist minister has noted that his change came after he was stabbed in 1991 in Bensonhurst, Brooklyn. "I was hit two inches from my heart, and I realized, all of a sudden, I could die doing the work I was doing. I began to question how I wanted to be remembered. I was getting older. I was thirty-eight. I was a husband and a father. My generation was assuming leadership in the community and I realized I had to start thinking about the generation that was coming along after mine. What were the adults and me, in particular, preparing for them? What would we leave?"[31]

Sharpton clearly used, as many do when describing a radical ideological, political, religious, or lifestyle change, the language of conversion. Like the Apostle Paul, who described his conversion from prosecutor of Christians to devout follower of Christ, or Malcolm X, who characterized his trip to Mecca as an awakening to the fact that the Nation of Islam's version of Islam was tainted with racism and was not "true" Islam, Sharpton portrays his stabbing as an act that opened his eyes. The near-death experience led to personal transformation. Like Martin Luther King, stabbed by a deranged woman and brought close to death, Sharpton used the incident to declare that he was politically born again. Thus, the stabbing, according to Sharpton, was his awakening and rebirth. He was now going to change. The incident became a means for him to reconstruct his image.

Despite what his critics say, Sharpton has been able to reconstruct a new image of himself. He and those close to him have to be given the greatest credit for reshaping his image. Wilbert Tatum, publisher of the *Amsterdam News* and loyal friend to Sharpton, presents the minister in his paper as a respected statesman. There have been a number of photographs in the newspaper of Sharpton.[32]

To help forge a new image of the responsible leader, Sharpton has changed religions, from Pentecostal to Baptist. This was not a trivial event. Although he claimed that he changed denominations for spiritual reasons, he realized that, if he wanted to extend his influence, he would have to travel in Baptist circles. Some of the most politically powerful ministers in the nation are Baptists, and Sharpton has become part of their circle. Since his conversion he has moved closer to Jesse Jackson. He now holds the position of national director of the ministers division of the Rainbow Coalition, an organization founded by Jackson. He was the leading spokesperson for the group of black New Jersey ministers who challenged campaign strategist Ed Rollins's claim that he successfully convinced them not to urge their members to vote for the Democratic candidate in the 1993 New Jersey

gubernatorial race by simply bribing them. Governor Christine Whitman
actually invited Sharpton, Jesse Jackson, and other ministers to her headquarters to discuss the matter. Sharpton is also associated with ministers of the
National Baptist Convention and the Progressive Baptist Convention, two of
the largest black organizations in America.[33]

There is little question that Sharpton has transformed his image since his
first run for the Senate. After 1992 Sharpton severed ties with Lenora Fulani
and the New Alliance Party. He attended conferences sponsored by the
Congressional Black Caucus. He appears at forums that address various
problems in the black community with such notables as Harvard University
philosophy professor Cornel West and Columbia University historian
Manning Marable. He also attended the Black Leadership Conference. And
with his new image has come growing political significance.[34]

The success of the campaign to change his image can be measured in his
electoral and political accomplishments. Since his run for the Senate in 1992,
he has received a great deal of favorable press. Both *The New York Times*
and *New York Newsday* contended that Sharpton was the responsible candidate in the Democratic senatorial primary in 1992, asserting that the minister
was the voice of reason, sticking to the issues and avoiding personal attacks.
He was endorsed by the *Amsterdam News*.[35]

His success in 1992 has made him legitimate in the eyes of many. For the
most part, he is no longer portrayed as a rabble-rouser but as an important
political leader. An article in *New York* magazine titled "What's Right with
New York?" praised the political moderation of Al Sharpton and commented
that he had grown into a statesman. In addition, *Emerge*, *The New Yorker*,
and other magazines have carried positive stories about Sharpton. During the
1992 Senate run, Cornel West wrote a glowing endorsement of Sharpton
that appeared in *The New York Daily News*. In 1993 the minister from
Brooklyn appeared on the television program *Sixty Minutes*. Host Mike
Wallace spoke of the new Al Sharpton who was moderating his views.
Sharpton also notes that journalist Dan Rather told him that he had come a
long way. In a column in *The New York Daily News* written by Dave
Saltonstall and Richard T. Pienciak and titled "Faces to Watch in 1998: Due
to Go Places," Sharpton was listed as a major challenger to Congressperson
Edolphus Towns of Brooklyn. [36]

Sharpton has had a great deal of success in reshaping his image. With the
help of the media, he has made himself more acceptable to the general public. In many ways he has become a symbol of the meaning of race and
democracy in the post–cold war United States. His success derives in part
from what historian Ben Keppel so aptly labeled the "deracialization of the
Horatio Alger Myth." That is, anyone can now move from poor person, in
Sharpton's case from rabble-rouser and out-of-control opportunist, to an
almost genteel, dependable role model who espouses basic American values.
Sharpton asserts:

That's where I differ from some, in that I will acknowledge that there are many reasons for black people to give up on life and stop trying. I had several myself, my daddy left us, we were on welfare and in the projects, the whole bit, but that was no reason for me not to try, that was no excuse just to hand white folks what they wanted, which was me on the sidelines if not in the gutter. White racism did brutalize and even distort black people, that is an unarguable historical fact. What that means is that a black person should strive harder, have a higher moral code.[37]

Sharpton argues that the struggle for equality should include not only protest but also individual initiative. In part, his appeal is for social and moral uplift. Sharpton's new approach was apparent at the funeral of a twenty-two-year-old black man gunned down by a white police officer. The officer claimed that the unarmed man, who was going to visit his mother on Christmas Day, looked like someone who had fired shots from a roof in the Carnarsie section of Brooklyn. Sharpton struck a familiar chord, denouncing the rampant police abuse of blacks and Latinos, but he also called on blacks to take the moral high ground and stop the killing in their communities.

Part of the new image package is the assertion that the "Rev." is left of center. In his run for the Senate and in his campaign for mayor, he claimed to be a progressive candidate working to build a broad-based movement that would work for the poor. There is plenty of evidence to substantiate his claim. Influenced by Jesse Jackson, Sharpton has called for full employment, adequate housing for the poor, and reform of the criminal justice system. He has attacked corporate welfare and the granting of special tax breaks. He advocates the investment of pension funds into infrastructure repair in the city. He also claims to support coalition building and now speaks to women, gay and lesbian, and labor groups. He participated in a protest led by Jim Butler, head of local 240 of AFSME, on behalf of hospital workers who had lost their jobs through budget cuts. Professor Manning Marable, an advocate of progressive coalition building, was a speaker at Sharpton's National Network Action and called for universal health care, full employment, and an end to police brutality. He also criticized the conservative politics and economic program of Louis Farrakhan. This is significant because Sharpton has been a public supporter of Farrakhan.[38]

Recently Sharpton has voiced his disapproval of narrow black nationalism, claiming its supporters are "copping out" of society. He has also asserts that he is a "Pan-Africanist" in the "Du Bois interpretation of the term."[39] The flamboyant minister still engages in class politics by attempting to appeal to the black working class. He continues to make class distinctions in black America by noting the divide between the middle class and the poor. He asserts in his autobiography that the black middle class supports the status quo and sees him as a troublemaker. According to Sharpton, middle-class blacks are terrified of him because they have made their peace with the white power structure. But Sharpton does not allow his class analysis to dominate his view on the significance of race. When it comes to determining the greatest evil for blacks, race supersedes class. "Every black person faces the same circumstances in America; I've seen the wealthiest, most famous, most successful blacks face the same circumstances as Richard Luke, a poor man from Queens. So if any black person thinks they're transcending this, they're only fooling themselves." According to Sharpton, white racism knows no class boundaries. The white middle-class suburban homeowner is just as racist as the white working-class truck driver in Howard Beach. To support his argument that race prevails over class, he cites the killing, by the police, of Phillip Pernnell, a sixteen-year-old black male living in the predominantly middle-class neighborhood of Teaneck, New Jersey. "Eddie Murphy [the wildly popular comic actor], along with many other rich and successful blacks, lived right up the road from where it happened. It could have been Eddie's kid [who was killed]." Sharpton's strategy is to go beyond class politics and build stronger support throughout the black middle class. Race remains a constant in the evolution of the Sharpton image.[40]

In an attempt to construct himself as a progressive or left of center, Sharpton has endorsed liberal candidates, making note that the race of the candidate is insignificant. For example, in the summer of 1998 his National Action Network endorsed the city public advocate Mark Green for the Senate. Green, a longtime progressive and outspoken critic of D'Amato, Pataki, and Giuliani won the endorsement after Sharpton, Geraldine Ferraro, and Charles Schumer met the organization and expressed their views on a wide range of topics. According to Sharpton, "For me, it was a matter of who has represented working-class people and poor people on vital issues. . . . I think that Green has done that better than the other two. . . ."[41]

One of Sharpton's skills is his ability to paint himself as the underdog who represents those left out of the system. By portraying himself as the voice of the people and using the collective term "we" instead of "I," he has been able to represent his success as the people's victory. According to the minister, his victories are not a case of clear self-interest, rather, they reflect the voices of the masses who challenge the establishment. At a rally shortly after the 1997 Democratic mayoral primary, when it was expected that there would be a runoff between Sharpton and Manhattan borough president Ruth Messinger, he announced to his supporters: "We will be heard in September." Playing to the enthusiastic crowd, he declared:

> They would write stories and act like we weren't even in the race. I had gotten more votes than anybody in the race. They didn't even record those numbers until after the primary. But we didn't go by what they thought of us. We went by what we thought of ourselves! They always tell us what we can't do, but we end up doing it. They always try to talk us out of winning.[42]

Although his figures were off, the activist minister was able to define his success as an empowerment of his supporters, who are alienated from city government because of cuts in social services, lack of black representation in high positions, and increased police brutality. The Rev. seems to be taking steps in a progressive direction. He adopted a strategy different from that pursued by Alton Maddox and C. Vernon Mason during the slander suit brought by Steven Pagones. While Mason and Maddox attempted to prove that the former prosecutor raped Brawley, Sharpton narrowed his defense to whether there was proof that he had deliberately lied when he accused Pagones of rape. More important, as noted, he has associated with people trying to build a progressive coalition encompassing labor, racial minorities, and feminist groups.[43]

Sharpton's greater emphasis on politics has more to do with his attempt to remain legitimate than any contemplation of his legacy. He understands that, in order for him to maintain support and gain new followers, he must deliver the goods. Merely providing people with a chance to vent their anger at rallies will lead to the early retirement of any protest leader, or at least it will house him or her in the political basement with other relics of past protests.

Despite all of Sharpton's efforts to portray himself as a moderating political force who indulges in electoral politics, it would be misleading to argue that he has given up street protest as an ineffective means to change. The call for an April 4, 1998, demonstration to protest a grand jury's decision to clear a white police officer in the shooting death of an unarmed black man on Christmas Day demonstrates how street action is used by the minister to help keep the issue of police brutality before the public. Indeed, Sharpton has skillfully connected the political climate in the city to police brutality. But the protest was not a carbon copy of past protests that he led. This one had broad appeal. It included labor leaders and religious and civil rights groups and reached out to a broad constituency. Its focus was on eradicating poverty, racism, and other forms of discrimination and aimed at the "expansion of the rights of working people to organize and bargain collectively." With little doubt, he has been emphasizing building a broader base.

The demonstrations and mass movement against police brutality growing out of the Amadou Diallo incident provide another indication of Sharpton's willingness to use street protest. In addition, the protest not only pointed to Sharpton's ability to mobilize people across racial lines but indicated that he was moving toward a more progressive political position. On February 4, 1999, four white members of the New York Police Department's street crime unit shot Guinea-born Amadou Diallo to death. The unarmed twenty-two-year-old immigrant, who had worked fourteen hours that day, had left his house to purchase something to eat when he was approached and gunned down by the officers. Soon after the shooting, Sharpton and his National Action Network organized demonstrations at several places, including One Police Plaza, demanding the arrest of the four officers involved in the shooting. The first few days of protest led to the arrest of a handful of demonstrators; however, by the middle of March two hundred people a day were being arrested. By the twelfth day of protest 820 people had been arrested, surpassing the Downstate Medical Center two-week protest in the summer of 1963, when a little more than 700 people became "jailbirds for freedom." By the fifteenth and last day of the protest the number of those arrested was 1,200, the largest number arrested in a demonstration in the history of New York City.[44]

What accounted for the huge number of arrests and daily demonstrations? Sharpton articulated the pain of people of color and their anger at what they saw as an uncaring and hostile city administration. His strategy of placing high profile figures at the front of the demonstrations lines, knowing that their arrest would generate a great deal of publicity, was successful. Newspapers covered the participation and arrests of such notable figures as Susan Sarandon, Ossie Davis and Ruby Dee, Kweisi Mfume, and Jesse Jackson. The *New York Times* contended that what Sharpton initiated "had become one of New York's most successful protest machines. The demonstrations, which sputtered to a start with twelve arrests on March 3, swelled into one of the largest and most diverse civil disobedience campaigns in recent years.[45]

But it would a mistake to argue that the success of the campaign was due to Sharpton alone. Organizations and individuals across racial and ethnic lines, who had been working to challenge the policies of the Giuilani administration, including changing the police culture, helped build the movement. The weekly meetings of Sharpton's National Action Network attracted a large and diverse audience. At one such meeting, Asian Americans, Hispanics, whites, and blacks came together to hear speeches from Bronx Democratic Congressman Jose Sarrano, who compared Sharpton to Martin Luther King Jr.; a spokesperson from an Asian-American group organized to fight police brutality; and Sharpton, who praised the multiethnic audience. He asserted that the movement was diverse because police violence against citizens touched every community.

Labor's involvement in the protest campaign was also quite evident. Dennis Rivera, president of Local 1199, the 150,000-member health-care workers' union, mobilized many of his members, convincing them that police brutality was a worker's concern. Rivera contended that union members do not live in the workshop; they live in communities and should be interested in protecting their families from police harassment. The union leader's linkage of workers' rights with civil rights convinced many to make picket signs and flyers; telephone calls rallied people to the daily demonstrations, and the union donated over $100,000 to the protest.[46]

Other labor organizations and civil rights and grassroots organizations were active in the struggle. Those participating included James Butler, president of Local 420 of AFSCME; Charles Ensley, president of Local 371, Social Workers Union; Lee Saunders of District Council 37; Jews for Racial and Economic Justice; and Gay and Lesbian activists. One participant in the demonstration, Arthur Strimling, who was invited by his rabbi to join the picket line, did so because he was outraged by the mayor's refusal to discuss the issue of police brutality with black leaders. Ministerial networking was used to draw church people to the demonstrations, as indicated by the arrest of Rev. Gary Simpson, of Concord Baptist Church in Brooklyn, and his thirty parishioners on March 24. Student groups, lawyers, and politicians stepped up to protest. Moreover, key supporters of Giuliani volunteered to be arrested. Arthur Bramwell, Kings County Republican leader, was led away in handcuffs on March 20 because he expressed his outrage and horror at the killing of Diallo. Even the mayor's closest African-American supporter, the Reverend Floyd Flake, pastor of Allen AME Church in Queens and former U.S. representative, was arrested in front of One Police Plaza. Flake accused the mayor's office of trying to "spin" its way out of the crisis instead of addressing police abuse.[47]

There are strong indications that today Sharpton possesses a clearer understanding of historical social movements. He now uses street protest, not just as means to gain attention, but as a way to help build movements and coerce political entities into conceding to the demands of the grass roots people. He contended in a television interview on January 27, 2001, that "if one studies history, those that operate in the suites are always reacting to what goes on in the streets. I think it is very naïve to feel that the suites by itself will change based on a good argument." Sharpton was arguing that those with financial and political power are not the ones who will bring about social change. Ordinary people have been responsible for social justice.

Without a doubt, he still relies on charismatic leadership model and power-broker politics. "I come out of the tradition of being a thermostat. We want to change the temperature in the suite, and you do that from the streets."[48] Nevertheless, Sharpton is gaining support, in part because he is moving toward adopting an overarching political approach that recognizes many identities struggling for justice. He has become a voice for coalition politics, and the success of the vote indicates that the potential for coalition politics exists in New York.

Contradictions Remain

Despite his new direction contradictions are still evident in Sharpton's politics, notably his strong support for the former Nation of Islam figure, the late Khalid Abdul Muhammad, and his close association with Alton Maddox, a man who has made it clear that whites and Latinos cannot be a part of any movement that involves black people. His support of those narrow nationalists raises questions about his new progressive position. Sharpton was one of many who participated in a tribute to Maddox, honoring him for "his continued work on behalf of the community." Eric Ture Muhammad, writing for The Miami Times, reported that Sharpton, representing the National Action Movement, and Alton Maddox, representing a group called the United African Movement, traveled to Princeville, North Carolina, to provide dinners for hundreds of people left homeless after a flood hit the city in September.

Where is Sharpton on the political map? He claims to be building a multiracial progressive grassroots organization, but his alliances with narrow nationalists hinder his attempt at a wider appeal. Examples of Sharpton's contradictions are his association with Khalid Abdul Muhammad and the Freedy's Fire controversies. When Muhammad was being criticized for his anti-Semitic, anti-Catholic, and homophobic diatribes, Sharpton agreed that the remarks were offensive. But he quickly pointed out the hypocrisy of the U.S. Senate in passing a resolution condemning the Nation of Islam and its leader, Louis Farrakhan, while overlooking the racist remarks made by Senator Ernest Hollings of South Carolina. This tactic does not promote coalition building or help create trust between Sharpton and those who were outraged at Khalid Abdul Muhammad's filthy language and attacks.[49]

Similarly, the Freedy's Fire incident did not move Sharpton closer to the rainbow to building a multiracial multiethnic coalition, but once again linked him with nationalists who were accused of using anti-Semitic and racist language. Morris Powells, the organizer of the protest and head of the Buy Black Steering Committee of the Mass Action Network, referred to whites as "crackers." Powells claimed at a rally in Brooklyn, "We are not gonna stand idly by and let a Jewish person come into black Harlem and methodically drive black people out of business up on 125th Street." He added, "We gonna see that this cracker suffers." Another speaker at a rally sponsored by Sharpton attacked Jews who criticized Sharpton, Farrakhan, and others: "We will boycott you and nobody loves money any more than the Jewish people." Sharpton's association with people who use racist language—and his claim during the protest that the lessee was a "white interloper"—works against his attempt to reach out to a wider audience. Although he declares that he was "not guilty of inciting violence," he does admit that he did not uphold high moral standards, allowing his organization to be manipulated by people who use hateful rhetoric. But his association and support of narrow nationalists assure that many progressives will keep their distance.[50]

Sharpton's political machine hinders his effort to reach out to those interested in progressive politics. The Brooklyn minister has built a powerful organization based in New York, consisting of politicians, the clergy, journalists, and people associated with electronic media, whose task is to help forge this new image as a political progressive and increase his political power. Wilbert Tatum, publisher of the *Amsterdam News*, and radio personalities on black-owned radio stations WLIB and WWRL are part of the Sharpton machine. Although the machine has helped raise people's consciousness and allowed them to vent their anger, it has also been used to challenge anyone who would question the "the Rev." It is not unusual to hear Sharpton, radio host Bob Laws, and others at a rally calling black leaders sellouts, "rent-a-toms" and "driving Miss Daisy Negroes." Congressman Major Owens of Brooklyn, one of the most progressive members of Congress, a longtime opponent of Sharpton, faced a barrage of these attacks because he criticized the Nation of Islam. In fact, the machine selected Eric Adams, former head of the Guardians, a black policemen's association and a close ally of Sharpton, challenged Owens in the 1994 congressional election.

Most important, although Sharpton has adopted progressive or left positions on some issues and talks about coalition building, he has not been able to articulate a clear political vision because he lacks a clear ideological position and is concerned about becoming a power broker. In his autobiography the activist minister makes it apparent that he has strong differences with leftist forces. He asserts that there "was as much, if not more racism among the liberal left as with conservatives or moderates. The left-wing whites demand the right to choose who the black heroes will be. Think of how so-called revolutionaries are created. Whites make these people poster heroes, not blacks. They don't speak for blacks because black folks were never with them."[51]

Sharpton blurs the lines between liberalism and a left alternative by lumping them together. He makes no distinction between those who want reform without any alteration of the social and economic order and those who call for a fairer distribution of resources through structural changes. In addition, he ignores the varieties of American liberalism, which ranges from those who argue for greater government intervention in the form of public social and public policy to eradicate poverty and other social ills to neoliberals who support free trade, smaller government, welfare reform, and a more therapeutic model for race relations. Moreover, by asserting that the "liberal left" does not have the interest of blacks at heart, he suggests to blacks that they should be wary of joining in a progressive coalition. This view seems to fly in the face of his professing that he is building a multiracial coalition. Turning inward, distrusting others, and emphasizing greater reliance on unfettered capitalism as the means to wealth rather than the struggle with others for resources signal that Sharpton hinders the building of coalitions with progressive forces.

His embrace of black capitalism points to a conservative tendency. He asserts in his autobiography: "The only community you go in and see everything controlled by outsiders is the black community. Everybody in the normal course of business tries to do business with his or own. We must learn to do the same." According to the minister, if blacks don't embrace the petit bourgeoisie approach advocated by Booker T. Washington a century ago, and now by a host of other black conservatives, they are reduced to being consumers rather than players in the new economy. He echoed these remarks in February 1998 at a Black History Month celebration in the McCain Auditorium, Manhattan, Kansas. "It is far more significant to me to build our own businesses and to stabilize our own community."[52]

Coupled with this rejection of a left vision is his articulation of a politics of pragmatism.

Blacks have to mature politically and realize that sometimes our interest are going to be served by Democrats, sometimes by Republicans, sometimes by independents, and sometimes by none. As the old political saw goes "No permanent friends, no permanent enemies, only permanent interests." That's how everybody else in the country plays the political game and how blacks are going to have to learn to play it.[53]

And there is little doubt that Sharpton has played the political game. In 1986 he endorsed D'Amato for the Senate and was willing, soon after the endorsement, to accept a half-million-dollar federal grant from Republican conservatives. Although the grant never materialized, it revealed Sharpton's willingness to deal with individuals opposed to expanding the role of the state in assisting the disadvantaged. Sharpton's political game-playing included his unwillingness to endorse Mario Cuomo for governor in 1994, even though his close political ally and mentor Jesse Jackson encouraged him to do so, asking Sharpton whether he would like to be responsible for helping the conservative George Pataki win. Unmoved by Jackson's appeal, Sharpton refused to support Cuomo publicly. Unlike his ally, C. Vernon Mason, who not only endorsed Pataki but also made radio ads for him, Sharpton did not publicly oppose Cuomo's bid for reelection. But the minister's reluctance to endorse the liberal Democrat and his attacks on Cuomo did not help encourage blacks to go to the polls and pull the lever for him. The *Amsterdam News* endorsed Pataki, noting in its endorsement Cuomo's "mistreatment" of Sharpton. Thus the machine operated to help defeat a liberal and elect a conservative who has carried out drastic cuts to Medicaid, education, welfare, and other social programs that aid working people.[54]

In part, Sharpton's view of "pragmatic politics" has led him to adopt insider politics. He refused to endorse Cuomo, he asserts, because the liberal governor would not have a meeting with him. He even acknowledges that his nonendorsement of Cuomo may have played a role in his defeat. What is important to the minister is not the major distinction between the liberal Democrat and the conservative Republican but who offers him a seat at the table. "After he won, Pataki invited me and twelve other ministers to breakfast in the governor's mansion in Albany on Martin Luther King's birthday. I had never been invited to the mansion by Cuomo or Hugh Carey, but Pataki invited us in, so to speak, the first month he was there." Although in his autobiography he mentions Pataki's first budget, which increased tuition at the state and city universities and included Medicaid cuts, he does not admit that an endorsement of Cuomo might have prevented those drastic cuts. Pataki's policies have been draconian. In late April 1998, the governor slashed $760 million from the state budget. Five hundred million was taken from school construction funds and half of that would have gone to New York City. This cut came after a public school in Queens was closed because bricks had fallen from its façade and after a seventeen-year-old was killed when bricks fell from a public school in Brooklyn and hit her. Pataki also cut $77.5 million in teacher aide support, $7.9 million for extra faculty at public colleges, and $5.25 million for community-based AIDS and HIV programs.

Behind Sharpton's refusal to endorse Cuomo was, not a proper assessment of Pataki and his agenda, but the suspension of Alton Maddox's law license after his horrendous behavior in the Brawley case and Cuomo's unwillingness to sit down and discuss the budget. Sharpton's declared pragmatism in the political arena and his willingness to cooperate with Republican conservatives undermines his professed agenda of helping working people.[55]

By refusing to endorse the Democratic Liberal candidate Mark Green over the billionaire Republican candidate Michael Bloomberg in the 2001 New York City mayoral race, Sharpton has demonstrated that for him power-broker politics prevails over the goal of building a broad-based progressive coalition that could impact the future of the city. Sharpton's reason for not backing Green was based on the accusation that supporters of Green ran a divisive campaign to win the Democratic primary by demonizing both his Democratic opponent, Bronx borough president Fernando Ferrer, and Sharpton. On October 4 aides to Green met with other Democratic officials in Brooklyn to discuss the distribution of racist campaign literature. The mailing would include a *New York Post* cartoon of an extremely overweight Sharpton being kissed on his rear by Ferrer and would go to Jewish voters in order to assure Green's victory in the Democratic primary. Without a doubt, Green did not show courage and fortitude by condemning this racist strategy; he showed that he was willing to win at any cost. Green's actions clearly angered blacks and Hispanics. However, Sharpton's helping Bloomberg get elected mayor might not have been in the interest of working New Yorkers. Despite allegations that Bloomberg has been indifferent to an employee who claimed she was raped by another employee of Bloomberg's, has been accused of making racist and sexist comments, and was a member of several exclusive clubs that had no black members, Wilbert Tatum's *Amsterdam News* endorsed the billionaire Republican for mayor, claiming that Bloomberg "is a decent man" and calling Green, "ruthless Mark Green, who became the Democratic nominee for mayor by stealing the primary election from Fernando Ferrer and then denying that this is what had been planned and executed by his Jewish mafia from Borough Park and other heavily populated Jewish areas in the city, especially where the Orthodox sect predominates." Sharpton refused to support Green because he had not dealt adequately with the racist attacks. The minister claimed that he had to take a position and let candidates know that many blacks and others will not support anyone who uses race to win an election. "If we don't stop it now, this will go to the governor's race next year where a black is talking about running statewide in the democratic primary. This will go into the presidential election. You cannot ask us to ignore our self-respect in the name of someone's political career." Although he claims that he was not calling on people to boycott the election, Sharpton suggested to his supporters not to support Green by declaring, "We fought also hard not to give that vote against our interest and our concerns."[56] Sharpton, who had spent years attempting to reshape his image and portray himself as a responsible statesman, was furious with Green because his onetime political ally was so desperate to win the race for mayor that he, the liberal Democratic mayoral candidate, could resort to denigrating the minister's image.

Green captured 47 percent of the vote but lost to Bloomberg, who received 51 percent. It was clear that Ferrer's tepid endorsement of Green and his refusal to campaign for him, Bronx Democratic leader Roberto Ramirez's refusal to endorse the Democrat, and the Hispanic community's anger at Green cost him the election. *The New York Times* reported that Green received 49 percent of the Hispanic vote to Bloomberg's 47 percent. Also, Bloomberg managed to obtain 25 percent of the black vote while Green only received 71. While 71 percent seems significant, it is quite low for a segment of the electorate that usually votes 80 to 90 percent for Democratic candidates. Moreover, 34 percent of Democrats crossed over and voted for the Republican candidate. These figures are quite disheartening for a progressive Democrat. There is no doubt that Giuliani's endorsement of Bloomberg helped swing the election his way and that the September 11 attack on the World Trade Center helped the Republican candidate. However, the fact is that nearly half the Hispanic voters and a quarter of the black vote went to a Republican instead of a liberal Democrat. Bloomberg's capturing a higher percentage of the black and Hispanic vote indicates the "success" of Ferrer's, Ramirez's and Sharpton's strategies.[57]

The problem with Sharpton's assessment of the mayoral election is that more than a single politician's career was at stake. Green has spent his political career fighting for women's rights, civil rights, against police brutality and racial profiling, and for consumer protection, whereas his opponent has had no experience in politics. The interest and concerns of New Yorkers are for improved public education, better policing, and better social services. The 2001 mayoral election was an opportunity for the city to move away from the Giuliani era, in which the poor of the city have suffered, police abuse and racial profiling were rampant and complaints were publicly dismissed by the mayor, and public education deteriorated. Green, who has a record of working for progressive causes, could have moved the city in a different direction by addressing these major concerns. Sharpton's refusal to endorse him helped the novice Republican billionaire whose major claim to fame has been building a media empire. Sharpton's refusal to support Green indicates it is not the larger concerns of working people that mattered but how he was personally affected. Sharpton played a similar role in Republican George Pataki's victory over Mario Cuomo. Instead of articulating a political vision that would appeal to a large segment of the New York City community, the minister showed that power-broker politics and a role as a major political player were his main priorities. Sharpton was not concerned about Green's loss and what that might mean for the future of people he claims to represent. He gave evidence of his fixation on acting as a power broker when he asserted, "I refused to help Green, and by anyone's estimation it hurt him." He went on to ponder, "But there's nothing the party can do to me. What can they do to me?" A major question that he should address is not what the party can do to him but, if he is serious about building a progressive movement in New York, what he can do to heal rifts in the party that is identified with progressive causes.

The Challenge Ahead

The inability of progressive groups and labor to mount a serious challenge to the global economy and the dismantling of the welfare state and safety-net programs have left a void and an incoherent analysis of the growing poverty and unemployment in America and elsewhere. A report by the Milton Eisenhower Foundation notes that, while the American economy did well in the 1990s, many inner-city residents were not sharing in the good times. According to the report, 40 percent of minority children attended schools where most children failed to reach basic academic levels, and there were more black males in prison than in colleges and universities. The left has been weak in America during this period of rapid privatization of public operations, the growth of multinational conglomerates, and downsizing. The gap between rich and poor has increased in New York City. The poorest one-fifth of New Yorkers earn just a little over $5,000 annually, while the average income for one district on Manhattan's Upper East Side was over $300,000. The City University of New York's Center for Urban Studies reported that the number of four-person families with four people earning between $49,000 and $98,000 decreased from 35.2 percent in 1989 to 29.2 in 1996.[58]

By 1997, 75,000 people were in the Work Experience Program (WEP). Some 35,000 of these workers have replaced thousands of regular New York City workers. While many do entry-level work, other WEP workers perform jobs once held by people who have retired or have been laid off. They are found in practically every city government department. The largest number is found in the Parks Department and in Health and Human Resources, the city agencies where the greatest number of full-time workers have been dismissed. In April 1997 it was reported that Guiliani planned to lay off 900 workers in the Health and Hospitals Corporation. Close to 300 workers were dismissed from Harlem Hospital, and Guiliani attempted to replace the fired workers, who received $20,000 a year, with WEP workers who received only their benefit payments. Although the Mayor has claimed that Harlem Hospital is underutilized, community leaders note that the city contracted out the hospital's methadone maintenance program to reduce the load.[59]

WEP workers receive stipends that are sometimes well below the minimum wage. They are denied health insurance benefits, carfare, and lunch allowances. Only a handful of workers actually find permanent employment in New York's tight job market, and WEP workers can easily be dismissed from the program and denied their stipends for missing work. If children are sick and need attention, parents in the WEP are forced to choose whether they will stay home and risk financial disaster or go to work and endanger the health of their children.

During his first term in office, Giuliani made deep budget cuts hurting the poor. By 1998, an estimated 100,000 people lost their welfare benefits, at the same time that the city slashed social services. A city advocacy group, Community Food Resource Center, reported that 400,000 New Yorkers go hungry daily. Nationally, there is a decline in the supply of food to programs that feed the desperate. A survey by the New York City Coalition Against Hunger found that 73,000 people were turned away from food emergency programs in the summer of 1997. According to the group, 60 percent of those turned away were children. Since the elimination of the national welfare program, food banks throughout the city report that they are hard pressed to feed the desperate because their numbers have dramatically increased. City Harvest, a group that collects food to feed the poor, has noted that in 1980 there were thirty soup kitchens and food pantries; in 1998, there were over 800. According to Hunger Action Network of New York State, close to a million children in the state are hungry or at risk of hunger. In their report, professors Marcia Meyers and Irwin Garfinkel, both of the Columbia University School of Social Work, claim that one-third of New Yorkers believe the economic situation has gotten worse. Seven percent declared that they go hungry quite often, and 17 percent said they could not pay their utility bills on time. Twenty-nine percent of New Yorkers live below the poverty line.[60]

Mayor Rudolph Giuliani declared during his first term in office that the city had been "too generous" to the poor. His spending cuts led to increases in class size in the public schools. Claiming that the city spends too much on health care, he attempted to sell Coney Island Hospital, Queens Hospital Center, and Elmhurst Medical Center to private interests. Although the mayor has reduced social services and has cut the overall workforce of the city he has increased the police force to 40,000, the largest in the history of New York. Governor George Pataki, with the support of the New York mayor, reduced Medicaid and Medicare benefits.[61]

New York *Village Voice* writer Wayne Barrett reported that the percentage of blacks in the city workforce dropped from 36.6 in December of 1993 to 33 percent in June of 1997. Barrett asserts that while the city's mayoral workforce declined by 17,937 positions in that period, black employment dropped a disproportionate 11,267. "Though whites account for nearly half the workforce, white employment only dropped 2,802. These figures do not include either the Health and Hospitals Corporation, where layoffs and buy-outs decimated a largely black workforce, or other non-mayoral agencies like the Board of Education." During Giuliani's reign, 12,722 people lost their jobs in the Human Resource Administration. One of the avenues for poor people to climb out of poverty has been a college education. However, in the city of New York, this avenue has been cut off. The Giuliani administration forced parents, many of them women, who were receiving Aid for Dependent Children and who were also City University students into work-fare. Because of their work schedules thousands were forced to drop out of school. Consequently, many are unable to receive training and degrees that would help them rise above menial labor.[62]

Although crime dropped drastically in the city under the Giuliani adminis-tration, complaints against police have risen. In 1994 the Civilian Complaint Review Board (CCRB) received 4,920 complaints, an increase of 37.4 per-cent over 1993. The largest number of complaints, 1,670, was for the use of excessive force. The percentage of complaints for the first half of 1995 showed an increase of 31 percent. According to Amnesty International, the New York Police Department's own statistics show an increase of 53.3 per-cent between 1993 and 1994 in the number of civilians killed in police cus-tody. The CCRB's biannual report shows that blacks and Latinos are disproportionately the victims of police brutality. Close to 76 percent of the people who filed complaints in the first half of the year in 1995 were blacks and Latinos. Over 50 percent of complaints were from African Americans, and Hispanics filed 26 percent. Over 69 percent of the complaints were against white police officers.[63]

The mayor also launched a crusade to eliminate open enrollment at the City University system. In 1969, after a protest by black and Latino students at City College demanding the university system admit more minority stu-dents, the city created open enrollment, assuring high school graduates a spot at one of the city colleges. Although problems were created by such a policy, it opened the door for many, including whites, allowing them to climb into the middle class. Now, when the system is overwhelmingly non-white, the mayor wants to end open enrollment. Critics have claimed that ending open enrollment would narrow opportunities for economic success for the poor and working class who cannot afford a private education.

In addition to accusing Giuliani of ignoring the needs of working people, his critics claimed that he contributed to racial tensions in the city. The ten-sion between blacks and Jews in the city can be traced back to the 1930s, when blacks accused landlords and storeowners, some of whom were Jewish, of overcharging for rents and commodities, and Jews saw blacks as unfairly blaming them for their troubles. In later years they noted that black anti-Semitism existed in the rhetoric of narrow nationalist groups like the Nation of Islam, and antiblack sentiment developed further over the issue of crime. Distrust increased during the 1968 teachers' strike, in which some in the black community used anti-Semitic diatribes against teachers; the United Federation of Teachers leadership responded by painting the black commu-nity as anti-Jewish. In 1991 the Crown Heights confrontation—after a driver who belonged to the Lubavicher sect ran a stoplight, and struck two chil-dren, killing one of them—led to a riot and the stabbing death of a rabbinical student named Jankel Rosenbaum. Some blamed then mayor David Dinkins for the disaster, accusing him of tying the hands of the police, and some sued him. However, a judge ruled that Dinkins and the black city police commissioner, Lee Brown, did not act with the intention of harm and that their names should be dropped from the lawsuit. Guiliani decided to issue an apology, playing to those divisive forces that accused Dinkins of participating in a pogrom. When Dinkins offered to have lunch with the mayor to work out their differences and cool racial tensions, Guiliani publicly embarrassed the former mayor by not accepting the offer. Dinkins, a man who tried to mend wounds by bringing people together, was pushed aside by Guiliani. Clearly, Guiliani's behavior was designed to foster his support among those not interested in better racial harmony and those who have a strong distrust of African Americans. But his actions only helped further polarize blacks and Jews.[64]

Deindustrialization, the rise of hypercapitalism that has forced working people into lower-wage employment with few and no benefits, and the growing conservative and neoliberal sentiment present major challenges to progressive forces. Always a significant factor in New York politics, race is also part of an interlocking system of oppression. Class, gender, and sexuality are units of this system. Progressive coalitions consisting of labor, blacks, women, Native Americans, and other historically oppressed groups can offer a good opportunity to address racial and social injustice and inequality. Coalitions are successful when they have particular marks and use a variety of tactics. As the modern civil rights movement proved, men and women working across racial and class lines are able to bring about changes in social and political policy. But, as community activist Angela Ards contends, rallies should not be the only means of addressing police issues. After a flood of protest over police brutality abates, little will have been accomplished if the mayor and city officials do not respond. According to Ards, what is needed is a protracted movement that identifies specific targets and prepares its members for a long battle to achieve its objectives.[65]

Continual dialogue among constituencies in a progressive coalition must take place, addressing not just the differences but commonality. Kobena Mercer suggests: "Alternatively, the challenge of radical pluralism demands a relational and dialogic response which brings us to a perspectival view of what antagonistic movements have in common, namely that no one has a monopoly on oppositional identity."[66]

The political situation in New York offers Sharpton an opportunity to work for significant change. He has reached out to various groups. The attempt by the American Federation of Labor and Congress of Industrial Organization's Union Summer drive, training and sending college students south to help organize workers, is a clear attempt to bridge the racial divide and improve the economic plight of poor workers. The Association of Community Organizations for Reform Now (ACORN) has also been trying to make this link. This organization of 200,000 is attempting to organize workfare workers in New York. Close to 17,000 workfare workers out of 173,000 who participated in an October 1997 election conducted by

ACORN voted for union representation. Thus, Sharpton's declaration of a more progressive politics and his desire to build a broad coalition comes at a time when there are signs of growing labor militancy. The opportunity for a strong alliance between Sharpton and labor is great. This will mean that the minister from Brooklyn must continue to pay more attention not only to civil rights but to workers' rights, including globalization, which has led to the dismantling of the welfare state, austerity methods that punish poor people, and the growing gap between rich and poor with depression of wages. He must spell out a larger political vision.[67]

CHAPTER 7

The Evolving Spiritual and Political Leadership of Louis Farrakhan

From Allah's Masculine Warrior to Ecumenical Sage

Black nationalism is not monolithic. Its range includes reformists and revolutionaries, black capitalists and cultural nationalists. Black nationalist ideologies are in opposition to cultural assimilation, and the political and economic hegemony of the dominant western societies. As scholars note, one dominant trend in black nationalism advances a broad-minded program. Proponents of this form of identity politics stress cultural pride and connect the predicament of African Americans to the problems of Africans throughout the world. These radical nationalists advocate building institutions in the black community for social, political, and economic empowerment, and they consistently challenge the dominant society's attempt to dehumanize people of African origins. They advocate racial consciousness not by denigrating other groups but by stressing the accomplishments of African people. Some nationalists have attacked patriarchy and have tried to build coalitions across race and gender lines in the struggle against economic exploitation, sexism and racism.[1]

One important form of black nationalism is grounded in religion. Advocates of this form have usually preached a messianic message, claiming a racial and moral superiority over others and predicting their resurrection and, at the same time, the damnation by God of those who are identified as their oppressors. Throughout most of its history the Nation of Islam and its leader Louis Farrakhan have been identified with this form of religious nationalism. To be sure, Farrakhan has been one of the most prominent black nationalist leaders for more than two decades. Although he has stressed black independence by advocating the development of black-owned businesses and social and cultural institutions, for most of his years as the leader of the Nation of Islam (NOI) he predicted God's retribution on those he identified as the enemy of the black masses. Moreover, as an important component of his religious black nationalism, he constructed an image of black manhood that was supported by male domination and chauvinism.

For many, Farrakhan is still seen as a hatemonger whose major mission is to demonize whites in general and Jews in particular. In fact, because of his past virulent anti-Semitic remarks, some white and black Americans are puzzled as to why so many blacks are attracted to Farrakhan. He has been able to attract, if not a large number of members to the NOI (the organization's membership is estimated at 10,000 nationwide), countless numbers of supporters. His talks on college campuses and in other venues have attracted thousands of people who admire him and, especially, his oratorical skills and message. A *Time* magazine and CNN poll in 1994 reported that the NOI leader was one of the most popular leaders among blacks. In October 1995 Farrakhan's call for black men to come to the nation's capital to atone for their transgressions attracted a crowd estimated at one million, mostly black men. Certainly, no other black leader has accomplished such a feat.[2]

But the static image of the leader of the Nation of Islam as an egotistical, maniacal hatemonger is far too simplistic. Like others discussed in this volume, Farrakhan has been consistently involved in constructing his identity as both a political and a religious leader. Without a doubt, Farrakhan relied on racism, anti-Semitism, and sexism to help construct his early image. Just as important, the fiery Black Muslim leader also relied on religion to help formulate his image as Allah's militant and masculine warrior in behalf of blacks. But religion has also been a key component used in his self-reconstruction. From the late 1970s to the very early 1990s Farrakhan depicted himself as religious-masculine warrior, doing God's bidding in behalf of dark-skinned people. Beginning in the 1990s however, he has attempted to shift his image from a masculine figure who was defending the race to the all-wise and ecumenical sage who is acting as the savior of the entire nation. Thus, he has attempted to deracialize and universalize his message and image.

God's Race Warrior

Louis Eugene Walcott (Farrakhan) was born on May 11, 1933, in the Bronx, New York. His mother was from the Caribbean island of St. Kitts, and his father, whom Louis said he never met, was from Jamaica. When he was a child, his mother relocated with him and his older brother, Alvan, to the predominantly black community of Roxbury in Boston, Massachusetts. Walcott excelled in school, and at the age of five began taking violin lessons. After years of studying and playing the violin, Louis discovered that he could actually sing and decided to seek a career as a calypso singer. Starting at sixteen, Walcott began appearing in Roxbury's nightclubs and began developing a reputation as a calypso singer. In fact, he was nicknamed "the charmer."[3]

However, in 1955, his life changed dramatically when a friend persuaded him to attend a meeting of the Nation of Islam. After hearing Elijah Muhammad speak at the event, Walcott decided to join the Nation of Islam and soon after became Louis X and an assistant and strong admirer of Malcolm X. However, when Malcolm left the organization in 1964, Farrakhan depicted Malcolm as his enemy and even wrote in the weekly organ of the NOI, *Muhammad Speaks*, that Malcolm was "worthy of death."

When Malcolm was assassinated in 1965, Farrakhan replaced him as the minister in charge of Temple Number Seven in Harlem.[4]

In 1975 Elijah Muhammad died and his son, Wallace Muhammad, became leader of the organization. In the late 1970s Farrakhan broke away from Wallace Muhammad, who changed his father's organization from an Islamic black messianic and nationalist sect to a more orthodox Islam. Farrakhan accused Wallace of transferring him from Temple Seven to a small mosque in Chicago, thereby isolating him. Farrakhan also accused Wallace (who changed his name to Warith Deen Mohammad) of abandoning the teachings of Elijah Muhammad and shortly after leaving Wallace's organization recreated the Nation of Islam emphasizing Elijah's old doctrine.

Wallace C. Fard created the Nation of Islam, first called the Allah Temple of Islam, around 1930. After his mysterious disappearance in 1934, his disciple, Elijah Muhammad, took over the leadership of the messianic black-nationalist organization. Dividing the world into good and evil forces, Elijah Muhammad claimed that personality and character were not developed or nurtured but determined by spiritual matters. Borrowing from Noble Drew Ali and his Moorish Temple, founded early in the twentieth century, the NOI leader declared that blacks were really "Asiatic" and that their natural religion was Islam. They were from the lost tribe of Shabazz and were God's chosen people. Whites were devils by nature, created six thousand years ago by Allah's enemy, Yacub. Whites were debased by nature and caused black suffering. "Today, they have filled the earth with their wickedness," Muhammad declared. Black people, or what Muhammad called the "original man" because they were the first to occupy and inherit the earth, had to endure a long period of suffering. However, Allah, proclaimed Muhammad, will soon destroy the devil race and restore the "Asiatic Blackman" to his rightful place as ruler of the earth.[5]

According to Elijah Muhammad, six thousand years ago white rule came into existence. God allowed black earthly rule to end and allowed whites to take command. Because of the evil nature of whites, blacks suffer under the dominance of the white race. Historian Claude Andrew Clegg declares that Muhammad borrowed the eschatological doctrine of the Jehovah's Witnesses, claiming that the beginning of the destruction of the world began in 1914, the start of World War I. World War I, Muhammad claimed, was the beginning of the Antichrist. It was a war against the righteous. However, Allah granted a sixty-year reprieve in order to bring Islam to the "lost tribe of Shabazz." After the end of the reprieve, God was to continue destroying the world of the "white devil." Eventually white rule was going to come to an end and black rule was going to be reestablished.[6]

Elijah Muhammad's message was meant for a black audience. Although the Prophet, as his followers called him, predicted that the end of the white race and the liberation of blacks was extremely close, it was not only whites who were facing certain death; the "so-called Negro" who refused to embrace the prophet's teaching also faced a violent end. After arguing that the destruction of white America was near, he noted that whites could actually save themselves. All they had to do was to give the "black man" freedom, justice, and equality and Allah would spare them a cruel end. Since this was highly unlikely and white racism would not be abated, whites were not part of the dialogue. There was a passive quality to Muhammad's teachings; no one could physically prepare for the end. It was simply predetermined. The fact that Elijah Muhammad first objected to Malcolm X's request to expose the Nation of Islam to a national audience in 1959 when Mike Wallace of television station CBS wanted to do a report on the NOI, demonstrated Elijah Muhammad's lack of concern for what whites thought of his organization. After the "Messenger" gave in to Malcolm's appeal and CBS broadcasted the documentary, "The Hate That Hate Produced," Muhammad expressed his unhappiness with the exposure.[7]

In his revitalization of the Elijah Muhammad version of the NOI in the late 1970s and throughout the 1980s, Farrakhan wanted his message to reach a wider audience. In stark contrast to his teacher, Farrakhan clearly sought to attract the attention of all Americans, including whites. Unlike Muhammad, Farrakhan courted white hostility because he wanted to use it to build his leadership. Farrakhan argued that such a reaction demonstrated his boldness in standing up to the enemy of blacks.

He portrayed himself not only as the defender of black manhood but also as one who has paid a tremendous price for his willingness to do so. Thus, he depicted himself as a sufferer for a cause, willing to pay the ultimate price for his people in order for them to be "free." On October 7, 1985, before a crowd estimated at twenty-five thousand, Farrakhan evoked the notion of martyrdom by claiming that he was the most persecuted black man in America and probably history. "There has not been a black man in the history of America that has been so repudiated than brother Farrakhan. I thought they did a bad job on my teacher, the Honorable Elijah Muhammad. I thought they did a bad job on Mr. Garvey [Marcus Garvey]. I thought they did a bad job on Kwame Ture [formerly Stokely Carmichael] and Martin King and Malcolm X. I thought they did a bad job on those brothers. But the stuff they do to me is a so continuously." Farrakhan declared to his audience that the governor of New York, Mario Cuomo, the mayor of New York City, Ed Koch, congressmen, and others, including "some pitiful black leaders ... have condemned me without a fair hearing."[8] By listing himself among the icons of the black freedom struggle, all of whom were persecuted by the United States government, he attempted to convince his audience that he too was a freedom fighter and a justice seeker who was suffering at the hands of the state. Therefore, he attempted to manipulate a black collective memory and sensitivity to oppression in an effort to win support among black Americans.

In an effort to extend his argument that he was a freedom fighter, Farrakhan also juxtaposed himself to contemporary black leaders and argued that, unlike him, today's black leaders are more than frightened of whites and do their bidding; he used the "traitors to the race" argument. Their action was opposed to the interest of the masses of black Americans. "I know that Mr. Dinkins [David Dinkins] has not heard one of my tapes. The black leaders, I want to say this, you are finished. Black leaders are finished if you stand with the enemy of your people and condemn your brother without giving me a hearing. Most of these leaders have my phone number. They know how to call me. They don't ask me what I said as long as white folk said he said such and such and so and so, condemn him. These silly Toms run out and do their master's bidding. I am saying brothers, brothers and sisters, the reason why a David Dinkins . . . would do that is because they don't fear us. They fear white people." He used the slave master and slave analysis when discussing contemporary black leadership to highlight his strength of character as a man. By asserting that they fear whites, he placed himself in a dissimilar political location. He, unlike the "silly Toms," could not be bought.[9] In a 1994 interview with the owner of the *Amsterdam News*, Wilbert Tatum, Farrakhan made a clear declaration of his manhood by emphasizing the inability to be controlled and bought off by Jews. "The difference with us is we're not looking to the Jew for a damn dime. They're been working since nine years to stop me from eating. But I eat and I live as good as any man . . . because they can't get a ladder to go up to heaven to cut my blessings off. And that's why when I sit down with them [I can say] I don't owe you nothing. I don't need your money. I'm a man, damn it! My leader didn't make me a punk. He made me a man!"[10] The juxtaposition of himself to other black leaders not only demonized Jews but also helped create an image of Farrakhan as the superlative figure of black manhood, God's defiant warrior.

To help his campaign of convincing followers and supporters to his cause, Farrakhan argued that his courage and determination to speak the truth had gained him the enmity of many in high positions. According to Farrakhan, the plot against him involved high officials. Implicitly, he was dangerous to them because he was telling the truth and he was the only black leader who was willing to say it. However, it is not just his life that was in danger. The vitriolic attacks on him had the objective of silencing him. But as God's valiant warrior and with the Almighty by his side, his enemies could do nothing to the NOI leader. "The mayor, governor, the president, the vice president, the Senate have called me a lot of ugly names. Now if I were a man of weaker character these kinds of names would make me feel so badly that I would not be able to appear in the public. However, it is because I know of the rightness of the truth I speak and the rightness of the cause for which I am raised up by Allah that those words only serve as fuel for the fire in me to make me fight harder. . . ." The leader of the NOI declared his willingness to wear the martyrdom label but at the same time grounded his work in religious models by declaring himself God's chosen vessel. He presented the world, as other religious black leaders have done, as divided into the camp of good and evil, and as a member of the oppressed group, God was on his side. Thus, he possessed the truth.[11]

Farrakhan portrayed himself as a person who was not only on the side of the black "masses" but one who was doing the bidding of God. He attempted to present himself as both a spokesperson for the black proletariat and as God's faithful agent. But it was not enough for the leader of the NOI to have declared himself a righteous vessel; he needed to convince his enthusiastic audience of this construction in order to help legitimize his leadership and to instill in many of the true believers a sense of self-worth. Hence, he turned to the holy book to sway his followers and admirers. But the holy book that he relied on most was not the Koran but the Bible. Farrakhan is aware of the advances Islam has made among African Americans; nevertheless, he is also conscious that Christianity is still the predominant religious form among black Americans. Therefore, his desire to reach a large audience encouraged him to rely on the Bible. He knew his audiences were familiar with the Scriptures. For this reason Farrakhan quoted and read more from the Bible than the Koran.

Charismatic religious leaders have always understood the power of rhetoric and the Bible. Martin E. Marty notes the power of the sacred text.

> The other texts that have moved people are less official but more widely and profoundly grasped. They reached the hearts of the people who heard Lincoln speak, they gave shape to the hopes and actions of the black community and the "fellow citizens" in King's time, and they still have some effect today. These are the Hebrew Scriptures and the New Testament. They cannot be the root of our "political religion"—the founders took great care to avoid that—but they have made up our "religious religion." In synagogue and church and home, most citizens have used the Bible both for salvation and for the ordering of life—voluntarily, through persuasion, not by legal establishment. On some lips the multiplicity of biblical citations, from the Hebrew prophets and from Jesus, would have been wearying. Yet American virtuosos like Lincoln and King have been so steeped in the rhetoric of the Bible that they have instinctively made it their own. Both Lincoln and King knew how to invoke prophetic biblical texts and ancient moral injunctions and join them to calls to action.[12]

Likewise, Farrakhan is steeped in the rhetoric of the Bible and makes it his own. In his speeches he turns to the Bible to justify his arguments. In a speech in Madison Square Garden on October 7, 1985, Farrakhan gave his reason for the divide between black and white America by turning to the Bible. "The Book says that this day will be great and dreadful. The day has two dispositions that are opposite each other. Then the man of God who comes in this time will manifest those two dispositions in the people. He will manifest love and manifest hate. You say he's divisive. It has to be that way.

You can't mix God and Satan. You can't mix a slave master with a slave or oppressor with the oppressed. Something has to separate them and make them see each other and we [will have to] go to war to find out who is going to rule on this earth, either God or Satan, right or wrong. This is not a play day. This is the day of war. It is not who has said it. The Scripture has said it. It is the time of war."[13] Clearly, Farrakhan did not want to take the chance and rely on his audience's knowledge of the Muslim holy book. Realizing that most African Americans are more familiar with the Bible, he quoted from it to give authenticity to his accusations. He was making a case to justify his divisive language by relying on the Bible.

One obvious trait in Farrakhan's public performance is his manipulation of the black preacher style, which emphasizes charisma and the ability to arouse an audience emotionally. This style, found among Pentecostals and Baptist clergy, was evident in his performance and was also done to win support. Accordingly, the preacher would chant instead of providing a conventional talk, starting in a low key, gradually becoming louder and working up to an emotional state.

Like some of the best charismatic preachers, Farrakhan relies heavily on the antiphonal structure, or call and response. He attempts to work his audience to a fever pitch by repetition of a phrase, the raising of his voice to a fever pitch, and constantly engaging his audience. In order to get their attention he has appropriated the technique of rhetorical questioning to assure himself that they agreed with him. In such cases the preacher will ask, "Can I get a witness?" while trying to get an emotional charge from his parishioners. Likewise, the NOI leader elicits a collective enthusiastic response from his followers and supporters by declaring after he has let off an emotional outburst, "You're not listening to me" or "You don't hear me," or by asking them "Do you hear me?" anticipating his audience's confirmation of his lecture and ability to excite them by assuring him in a loud and boisterous manner that they are hearing him and are one with him. Although a Muslim, Farrakhan's use of the Bible and the appropriation of the charismatic preacher style contribute, in part, to his popularity among blacks. He is tapping into an inherited Afro-American Christian tradition of faith. He is reaching people not just with words but through feelings. He communicates with them by making them feel. The audience eagerly participates in the sermon because they share a common experience with Farrakhan. Like preachers who participate in a religious folk culture, Farrakhan does not rely heavily on a written text. Although he has a text, to his audience it appears that he is talking spontaneously, as though the Holy Spirit had taken over him. For Farrakhan, the written text does not take priority.[14]

Farrakhan's Construction of the Jewish Menace and Black Manhood

Although Farrakhan played to the old Nation of Islam's view that whites are the natural enemies of blacks, Jews remained his primary target and came under extreme fire from the Muslim leader. Using the antiphonal structure, he asked his huge audience at Madison Square Garden who were the people who were angry with him. "Are the people angry with me the righteous? Would you say that the Jews who are angry are righteous people?" After his audience responded the way he wanted, by yelling no, Farrakhan attempted to savor the moment by asking his loyal followers, "They're not?" The audience, in an even louder response, yelled no. Not satisfied that the crowd's response was loud enough and aware that he could get his audience to demonstrate a passionate collective disgust for Jews, he told them, "I didn't hear you." The vast majority of people in attendance that night were more than willing to satisfy Farrakhan's request that they condemn Jews as unrighteous people; they cried in unison, "No!" Jovial because he seemed quite gratified with his supporters' response and he and they seemed to be on the same wavelength in their disdain for Jews, he smugly declared: "That is what I thought you said." Bringing their own misconceptions of the historical record, the crowd seemed more than eager to have gone along with Farrakhan's virulent anti-Semitic diatribe.

In what was a clear attempt to further endear himself to his followers, exploit anti-Jewish feelings among some of his followers and supporters, and manipulate tensions between blacks and Jews resulting from modern historical events, Farrakhan depicted the relationship between blacks and Jews as pure exploitation on the part of the Jews. As his biographer, Mattias Gardell, contends "Farrakhan makes no secret of his intentions to 'break up the relationship' between blacks and Jews, a relation he describes as one between exploited and exploiter, oppressed and oppressor, with roots in the slave trade." According to the NOI leader: "They never tell you that ... some of the biggest slave merchants were Jews. The owners of the slave ships were Jews. They were then masters of the channels of distribution. From that day we had a relationship. You and they. They own the house, you clean it. They buy the food, you cook it. They own the property, you rent it. They got the store, you buy from them. You got the talent, they're the agent and the manager.... It's been a master-slave relationship."[15]

The Bible also came in handy in his effort to portray Jews as the enemies of blacks. Playing on his audience's familiarity with the Bible, in particular the New Testament, Farrakhan went as far as to compare himself to Jesus. "Jesus had a controversy with the Jews, Farrakhan has a controversy with the Jews.... Jesus was hated by the Jews; Farrakhan is hated by the Jews. Jesus was scourged in the synagogues and in the temples and Farrakhan's name was ringing in the synagogues and temples of this nation as a wicked and evil man who has come against the Jewish people. What did they hate Jesus for? Was it because Jesus exposed their wicked hypocrisy? Was it because Jesus came for the poor, for the disinherited, for the despised and the rejected? The work of Jesus was the work of healing. He caused the blind to see, the deaf to hear, the dumb to speak, the lame to walk and he raised the dead to life. Was that not a good work? But look, they called a man that did a work like that a devil. Read your Bible! They called Jesus a Devil." In order to deny the charge of anti-Semitism, he attempted to convince his followers and others that his assertions are found in the Bible. "Well, if I'm anti-Semitic for talking about the transgression of Jews then burn your Bibles because the Bible from the book of Revelation all the way to Genesis talks about Jewish transgressions then nobody should read the Bible because it is an anti-Semitic book. . . . Jesus condemned them as devils in the plainest language. I say the same today. They have no respect for the truth."[16]

Using classic anti-Semitism, Farrakhan exploited the myth of the omnipotent political power of Jews in the United States. Unable to directly defeat him, they, the Jews, "use the stranglehold that they have over the government, did you hear what I say? The Jewish lobby has a stranglehold on the government." In what seemed to be irrefutable evidence to the NOI leader, Farrakhan boldly claimed that those 246 members of the House of Representatives and 46 members of the Senate were "honorary members" of the Israeli Knesset. "That is why whatever they want they get it. This is because the president himself is actually punking out to the Jewish lobby." No longer concerned about the evil monolithic white race that his teacher Elijah Muhammad warned him and his followers against, Farrakhan apparently made a distinction between Jews and non-Jews. For the NOI head, Jews were more dangerous than other whites. He warned all Americans of the Jewish menace and accused the president of "selling America right down the tube. . . ." Not only were they in control of the U.S. government but they were also guilty of "killing the prophets of God."

The leader of the NOI's anti-Semitism was strikingly similar to that of white supremacists who identify themselves as Aryans. According to the proponents of Aryanism, Jews are on one hand controlling and on the other hand "un-warriors," feminine, immoral. A proponent of Aryanism complained that Aryan children did not learn about the great conquerors and warriors and the valor of the "white race," but were instead forced to learn about the weak. "Instead of learning about the fighting spirit and valour [valor] of Achilles at Troy, they learnt about Samson and his hair. Instead of learning about and trying to emulate the great warrior deeds of an Alexander or a Caesar, they learnt about and were told to emulate the suffering of a Jew in Palestine who was reported to be the son of the Jewish god."[17]

Farrakhan's utilization of anti-Semitism was meant to portray him as the defiant leader who stood up to the true enemies of blacks. He constructed a Jewish masculinity that embraced modern notions of anti-Semitism. Using an old form of anti-Semitism, he credits Jews with being cowardly, sneaky, and very deceptive. He also utilized a more modern form of Jewish hatred by crediting Jews with dominating and controlling black bodies. He therefore constructed a Jewish masculinity in which the major characteristic was the ability to dominate others.

Farrakhan's anti-Semitism should not be seen as an irrational hatred. It was used to help construct his version of black manhood. Like his anti-Semitic notions that were based on Aryan depictions of Jews, his conception of black manhood also embraced an Aryan notion of masculinity. By "nature" and "instinct" Aryans conquer; they possess a "heroic defiance" and build civilizations and empires. Promoters of the racist concept of Aryanism also argue that the Jews have successfully plotted to destroy them and that it is up to Aryan leaders to act like warriors and rescue the race from the Jewish menace. Historian Gary Gerstle describes a similar masculinity constructed by Theodore Roosevelt. This Rooseveltian racial nationalism romanticized racial warfare because it allowed white men to prove their racial superiority over the "darker inferior" races. For Farrakhan, the struggle against what he portrayed as the Jewish menace allowed him to demonstrate what it meant to be a "righteous" black man.[18]

Declaring "I am not a prophet but I come in the footsteps of those worthies and if you rise up to try to kill me, a man that has told you the truth, then Allah promises you that he will bring to bear on this generation the blood of the righteous not just from Abel to Zechariah but from Abel all the way to the last man you killed recently. All of you will be killed outright. Now you want to kill me." As Allah's warrior, Farrakhan claimed that God protected him and that his enemies were surely doomed if they dared try to make a move against him. His religious message was mixed with a black nationalistic dogma; he played on a racial solidarity by claiming he was acting in the best interest of blacks and that if anyone opposed him they were traitors of the race.[19]

Even his criticism of Khalid Abdul Muhammad turned into an anti-Semitic rant. In 1994 Khalid Muhammad, the second highest-ranking official in the Nation of Islam, called Jews "bloodsuckers" who deserved the Holocaust. He called homosexuals "faggots" and referred to the pope as a "no good . . . cracker." In a speech at Kean College in New Jersey, the former leading spokesperson of the NOI advocated killing all white South Africans indiscriminately. "We kill the women. We kill the children. We kill the babies. We kill the blind. We kill the cripples. We kill 'em all. We kill the faggot. We kill the lesbian. We kill 'em all." Although Farrakhan denounced Muhammad's statements, he qualified his critique when he claimed that he supported the "truths" of the Kean speech. In a Savior's Day's speech he defended Khalid by accusing the Anti-Defamation League of deliberately misinterpreting him. He accused whites who had published an advertisement in *The New York Times* condemning him and Khalid of promoting white supremacy while subjugating dark people throughout the world.[20]

He disseminated the old racist myth that Jews are naturally evil in order to legitimize his leadership in Black America. To reach this goal he adroitly fabricated enemies of black America and presented himself as the preeminent defender of black manhood.[21]

The Ecumenical Sage

As noted, Farrakhan is not a static figure. Like other leaders who are in the public eye for a long period he clearly has attempted to shift his image, starting in the early 1990s. In fact, one observer of the NOI leader argues that he began moving to a more moderate position on race just before Khalid Abdul Muhammad stepped into the public arena with his divisive and racist language. Writer Salim Muwakkil contends that Farrakhan first defended Khalid because he wanted to avoid growing dissension in the ranks of his organization. He wanted to avoid a public struggle over who was going to be the black-nationalist leader. Even though he defended Khalid in the Savior's Day's Speech, he also shifted his focus and his attacks. Jews were not the central targets; instead he turned his attention to "America." He was there to speak not to just black people but to the "human family" about the danger they faced. He accused America of hypocrisy. America calls black, Native Americans, and Latinos citizens but, according to the Black Muslim leader, it treats people of color as un-Americans. By noting Native Americans and Latinos in his speech Farrakhan even moved away from the black and white divide and paid close attention to the growing diversity in America and the plight of others who are victims of racism and discrimination.[22]

But what was also noticeable was that his attack was aimed not at whites but at the "power structure." This new usage was not a euphemism for white devils or an attempt to demonize Jews but an effort to deracialize his message. The heroic defiance was still in his message. He accused the power structure of coming after him. "So the rage in your heart has caused you to be furious and uncontrollable, to blow a fuse, to boil over, to bristle, to champ at the bit, to rut, to fly off to handle, to foam at the mouth because you really want Farrakhan." With his usual bravado he declared: "Here I am. I ain't going nowhere." But after exciting the crowd, he immediately turned his attention to America's economic woes.

In his attempt to change his image from one who is seen as a hatemonger to a respected national leader, he shifted his image from Allah's masculine warrior who is more than willing to scold the enemies of blacks to a humble sage who brings a semieschatological warning to all Americans. In order to help change his image, Farrakhan turned to generic concerns that plagued most Americans. The problem of race remained central to his message, but he also concentrated on the economy and class and gender divisions. In his Savior's Day speech in 1993, the leader of the NOI said, "America is in trouble. The respect of the people for government is nearly gone. The institutions of America are beginning to crumble. The social fabric is tearing apart. The moral backbone has gone to nothing. . . ." He audaciously attempted to redefine his role by noting that he had a means to assist the country out of its economic, social, and moral quagmire. In his effort to reconstruct himself as an ecumenical leader, he declared to his audience that the country is in "need of a guide and guidance through these troubled times. . . . A guide is one who shows you the way when you don't know it." Appealing to "Muslims, Christians and Jews, agnostics, atheists and members of all religious faiths," Farrakhan employed them to gain the "true knowledge of God."

In order to remake his image Farrakhan has tried to remodel the representation of Elijah Muhammad and revise the Nation of Islam doctrine. In May 1993 Farrakhan spoke before the Capital Press Club. His talk, "Torchlight for America," was based on his new book that was going to be released later that year. He claimed that the NOI was part of the world community of Islam and that it had been misunderstood. As a Muslim, he was for peace. But as he usually does, he turned to the Bible to help explain his position. Farrakhan's use of the Bible and Jesus' words was not to prove the evil of the Jews but to paint himself as a person working for a more harmonious society. "Blessed are the peacemakers for they shall be called the children of God," the NOI leader told the group of mostly black journalists. He connected the NOI to the world community of Islam by defending Muslims and complained that their portrayal in the media as terrorists was simply based on the acts of a few fanatics. This complaint had little to do with America's white and black divide. Indeed, it was a clear attempt to internationalize the NOI and move it away from the messianic black-nationalist label.

To further distance himself from black-nationalists, Farrakhan claimed that his speech was universal, aimed at the family of humanity. His message was for blacks, whites, poor, rich, Asian, Africans, Protestants, Catholics, Jews, agnostics, and atheists. His talk was to enlighten an entire nation that was in crisis and help solve the problems of a country that was heading for destruction. Farrakhan's construction of an America that is in economic and moral decline and his claim that he has a solution to these problems is being used to persuade all Americans of his transition from black nationalist to an American leader representing the interests of all citizens. In reconstructing his image, Farrakhan is also attempting to convince a multicultural America of the universality of his message and the global appeal of Elijah Muhammad and the Nation of Islam. There was no apology for past accusations made by the leader because he did not want it to seem that he was caving in to pressure from those who have accused him of anti-Semitism and racism. He did not want to give any ammunition to his critics, within and outside the NOI, who are troubled by his move toward orthodox Islam. Instead, he presented himself and Elijah Muhammad in a deracialized way. He was simply presenting a revisionist version of the NOI without spelling it out to his audience and the general public. In a clear break with conventional NOI doctrine, with the intent of moving the NOI to a more Orthodox Islam and to make Elijah more palatable to a general audience, Farrakhan told the black journalists that Muhammad of the seventh century was the last prophet of God and that Elijah Muhammad never claimed to be a prophet. Elijah was a "messenger" to black people and a "warner" to whites. Absent was the claim that the "messenger's" role was to deliver his people from the ungodly world of the white devil, prediction of the eventual destruction of whites by Allah, and the restoration of blacks to their "rightful" positions as rulers of the earth. Instead, Farrakhan claimed that Elijah Muhammad's role was to represent all fair-minded people and to help make a "better black people and a better America." He called on America to follow Elijah Muhammad's teachings because they could help not only blacks but also America. The revisionist version of the message of Farrakhan's teacher would help America become a more harmonious society in which people would value one another regardless of race and ethnic background. The "ideas and service of the NOI guides our people and possibly the country out from its present condition toward a more peaceful and productive society in which mutual respect governs the relations between the diverse members of America."

The semieschatological message of Farrakhan was not predicting the inevitable destruction of America but was instead drenched in politically liberal cautions of the economic path that the nation's elite was taking and at the same time he was pushing a socially conservative warning of the country's moral weakening. "The root of America's sufferings is a spiritual disease." It is suffering from "basic immorality and gross vanity where greed, lust, and an inordinate self-interest to the detriment of others has become the way of life." When self-interest dominants, according to Farrakhan, then the "first casualty is truth." This conservative message, pushed by religious and more secular conservatives, has played well in a nation that is quite to the right of center.

In his deracialized message, not only are the problems Farrakhan focuses on generic ones that plague an entire nation but the culprits in America's decline are, vaguely, "leadership" and the "government." It is leadership that is the villain because it denies Americans the truth. "Without truth Americans are left paralyzed." He claimed that the denial of truth would lead people to react "destructively because their very lives are at peril's door and they know not why they are in this condition or how to save themselves.

Farrakhan's message is semieschatological because although it is loaded with predictions of doom and destruction, the obliteration is not inevitable and can be avoided if America takes the right path. This alarmist assertion on the part of Farrakhan, as noted, is to persuade them that a genuine crisis exists and that immediate action needs to be taken. Gone is the extremely fiery and angry tone, replaced by a cooler and more collected religious leader trying to convince people of his concern for the nation. He now declares that class, race, and gender divide America. "We live in one country with two realities, one rich, one poor, one black, one white, one predator, one prey, one skilled, one nonskilled. Classism, racism, and sexism are used to keep the people divided, and these evils threaten to destroy the entire country. America must deal effectively with the lines of division or face anarchy and revolution." By referring to them as evils Farrakhan couched the racial, class, and gender divisions in religious terms. However, he also used a more conspiratorial and politically radical argument by claiming that these are the means used to keep people divided. Marxists and others on the left have argued that sexism and racism are mere tools manipulated by capitalists to fragment the working class. Although Farrakhan has not made a Marxist analysis, his recognition of sexism and class divisions notes that blacks are not the only victims of subjugation. He seemed to recognize the existence of an interlocking system of oppression. This recognition is different from the earlier assertion of the NOI of the universal divisions of humanity based on essentialist views of human nature.

Farrakhan's analysis of the economic problems in the United States is a cross between radical populism on the one hand and a carbon copy of the program of the Texas billionaire and presidential candidate Ross Perot. He asserts that the American economy is in a state of grave despair, crippled by a $4 trillion debt that led to a cut in social services. But the NOI leader uses the occasion to go after the rich. He claims that the rich benefit from the debt because they are the ones who are wealthy enough to buy government securities such as savings bonds and treasury notes and collect interest. The greater the need for debt relief, the greater the need for security notes. This radical populist message includes a defense of the poor while he lashes out at the rich. According to the Muslim leader, the greatest victim of the economic crisis is blamed for it. Simply put, the rich scapegoat the poor. "The poor of this country have no real advocates." In recognition of the efforts of elected black officials and white women in power, he asserts that the Black Congressional Caucus and the few women in Congress are the closest advocates the poor have. "So if the people have no real advocates then who will become the advocate for the poor in a society that is largely poor?" The rich use the poor as scapegoats in order to avoid finding a real solution. In fact, he argues, "[I]f a person comes up with a realistic solution they are called radical." But a radical solution is what is needed, according to Farrakhan. Hence, he has tried to present himself as part of a black radical tradition, representing the underprivileged of this nation and not just African Americans. He called for action in both private and public spheres to assure that "every American has a job." He also advocated job training, a partnership between the urban poor and the business community, profit sharing, and development of black businesses. Farrakhan also joined a growing chorus of those calling for reparations by providing black Americans with federal and municipal land.[23]

Despite his self-proclaimed position as a political radical who is one of the few voices for the poor as early as 1993, he shifted his class analysis from a "radical" critique to an economic mainstream argument about debt relief; he called on the government to cut federal spending, increase taxes on the working poor and on the rich, and pay off the national debt. Like conservatives and neoliberals, Farrakhan urged the elimination of welfare. "It's not our fault that we are poor, but it becomes our responsibility to make ourselves productive." This argument is symbolic of the economic conservatism that has been a central theme of the NOI since the 1950s under the leadership of Elijah Muhammad. Muhammad stressed self-help and the black capitalist model and called on the members of the NOI to be responsible and thrifty and spend wisely. Farrakhan's and the Nation of Islam's three-year economic program is appropriated from Booker T. Washington's conservative economic agenda. It calls on black Americans to give up vices such as smoking and drinking, to curtail their visits to movie theaters, and for three years donate the money they have saved to the three-year economic program. "Even if America does not help us, with a change in our lifestyle we can begin to use the $300 billion that circulates into our community to build agribusiness, low-income housing, develop clothing manufacturing, establish banks, and create all the economic entities that our people need." Although he argues that the government should help black Americans by allowing blacks to allocate 15 percent of their taxes to the program, he remains true to Washington's vision. Like Washington, who maintained that the larger white society would recognize black self-help and eventually grant them full citizenship rights, Farrakhan argues that white America would look at blacks in a positive manner if they were doing for themselves. "It's hard to call me a nigger when I'm productive. It's hard to say we're nothing when you see us as a dignified, civilized people. We are the ones who can destroy the mentality of white supremacy and the thought in others that we are subhuman and inferior by promoting respect among black people by what we accomplish in the way of building and doing for self."[24]

Scholars writing on the NOI have noted its penchant for advocating a conservative economic model. But Farrakhan is taking his teacher's message and peeling off its racial tinge and offering it to the entire nation.[25]

When discussing education, Farrakhan also presents solutions that are indistinguishable from the evangelical wing of the American conservative movement. He notes that "true education" cultivates human beings. "But American schools have moved far from that mission and have turned to the acquisition of wealth." For Farrakhan, educators must put God first. "True and proper education starts with the knowledge of God. And yet God is taken out of the schools."[26] Sounding a more liberal message, he argues that all children across racial lines should learn about the accomplishments of people of African origin, thereby developing respect for blacks. He also advocates increasing teachers' salaries and raising educational standards. Nevertheless, he embraces some solutions that are as conservative as the solutions advocated by the Christian Right, including prayer in schools, a dress code for students, a strict code of discipline, and segregating children by sex. According to Farrakhan, "If we hope to truly develop the person, the school has to train him according to the nature that God gave him and train her according to the nature that God gave her." Although he claimed that women should be allowed to participate in all fields, he emphasized teaching women "home making skills" such as clothing making, "cooking and planning meals." Moreover, in *Torchlight for America*, women are referred to as "our women," thereby implying that black women need a male protector. It is the job of a "civilized society" to provide a woman with a "sanctuary" so she will be protected from sexual advances." While moving away from his race-essentialist arguments he maintains primitive patriarchal views. To Farrakhan men are family protectors and women need protection. According to the NOI leader, a woman's main duty is to provide domestic services.[27]

Farrakhan has further elaborated on his gender essentialist views in the Nation of Islam's weekly publication, the *Final Call.* In an article entitled "Men of This World Do Not Desire a Righteous Woman," the Muslim minister voiced some of the most traditional views on gender. He accentuated the nineteenth-century doctrine of the cult of domesticity, which emphasized the notion that the proper place for women was in the private sphere and not the public arena. In Farrakhan's view, a "virtuous woman" was the "greatest gift" a man could receive. "A man who has such a woman by his side is the most blessed of men, for her virtue is a covering for him and her virtue ensures his future." The nineteenth-century construction of the virtuous woman, according to historians, depicted women as "too" virtuous and pure to be involved in the dirty arenas of politics and business. Thus, men were less virtuous because of their activities in the public sphere. But the doctrine stressed that one of the major obligations of women was to provide worldly men with a home far removed from the pressures of business and politics. By assuring a virtuous home, men could help fight off the pressures that robbed them of their morality. Scholars have argued that a major reason for the emergence of the cult of domesticity was to remove any threat of women competing with men in the public sphere.[28]

Not only is Farrakhan enthusiastically embracing the cult of domesticity, he uses the doctrine to help promote his view of patriarchy. Elijah Muhammad, the supreme model of the patriarch, is emphasized. He is presented as the person who showed blacks the way out of their primitive condition to the path of civilization. Women are reduced to the level of children who need protection, guidance, molding. Farrakhan claimed, "His desire was to produce a very high level of civilization coming through a reformed female. He took great joy in seeing our women come from a low state or condition constantly improving themselves. He taught them about loud raucous behavior and laughter. He loved to hear the refined speech of the female. He wanted her highly educated, cultivated and refined. He taught her how to walk, sit and stand. He showed her, her mother's dressing room that she had not seen in 400 years; meaning He showed her the styles of the righteous women of the East from whom she is a descendant." In his references to Elijah Muhammad, Farrakhan selects upper case, as others do when referring to God or Jesus. Farrakhan does this in order to pay the greatest respect to the patriarch. This is a perpetual misunderstanding of the meaning of a capital letter. Nothing to do with respect, we capitalize God because he is *one* god, singular, unique. But there are no laws on usage. "The Honorable

Elijah Muhammad said that 'Seventy-five percent of His work was with the female.' Therefore, He [sic] strived mightily to make something of the Black woman. He taught her how to sew and cook, how to rear her children, how to take care of her husband, how to keep a clean home and in general He taught her how to act at home and abroad."[29]

In opposition to the virtuous woman is the depraved man, the predator who seeks to corrupt the virtuous woman. "In this world, however, the purity of a young woman's love is so overwhelming to a man that many men of this world seek and do work to destroy that purity because of our mental, moral and spiritual state.... Instead of the husband encouraging their wives to be covered and sharing her beauty only with him, there are some men who love for their women to be on display for other men to see what should only be shared with him." The article is aimed at men, instructing them on how to properly behave and treat women. "To the men who read this article, cherish a virtuous woman. To the men of the Nation of Islam, seek a female from the class that is producing such women and be good men and husbands to them."[30]

The fact that Farrakhan addresses black men indicates strongly that he portrays women as possessions whose value in life is simply determined by men. He compares women to currency, arguing that when a woman is devalued "society has caused us to live on a plane that is far beneath that which we are capable of.... In this world, the man has not given or placed a proper value on the female, and thus has caused the female to devalue her self ... for woman to accept to be displayed or kept in an inferior status is to accept the devaluation of herself by the men of this world." Farrakhan constructs women as inanimate objects who must be not only protected but also molded. In his articles the NOI leader makes it clear that women do not have value and are not in a position to construct an identity; by nature they are "virtuous." However, their fate in a society is in the hands of men. "This means that there is no limit to the depth to which we [men] have caused the woman to fall." Absent from his article is any discussion of structural inequality and the pervasive sexism of American culture. In his view, men just need to alter their attitude about women to assure her value in a society.[31]

His articles aim at the very heart of his definition of a man. The man is the leader and protector of "his" women. "Any man that will not fight for the respect and protection of the female is no man at all.... It is in the nature of a man to kill that which breaks into his family and goes after his wife and his daughter. It is also in the nature of the female.... When we as men are in a right state of mind, we will go to war with anyone or anything that devalues or destroys our families." Despite his shift away from the anti-Semitic and racial discourse, Farrakhan has not altogether forsaken the masculine construct of black men. His use of the black warrior image that would defend the race is emphasized when discussing the family.

Nevertheless, it is the sage whose mission is to save America that seems to dominate.[32]

The head of the NOI has also deracialized the lifestyle program of the NOI. In *How to Eat to Live*, Elijah Muhammad was clear on who was to blame for what he argued was the poor eating habits of African Americans. "Under this white race of people, we were not taught how to eat to live. They, the white devils, are not here to teach us, the Lost and Found members of the Aboriginal Nation, to live a long life. They were put here to cut short our lives and for the last 6000 years they have done so." To emphasize the point he reaffirmed that the "THE WHITE RACE was not made to obey the divine law. They were made to oppose it, therefore following after them and doing what they do is getting you to hell. . . . The so-called American Negro is a divine member lost from the divine circle, while the slave master, who has been his teacher, is an enemy of God, by nature."[33]

No longer are whites accused of poisoning and sabotaging the health of blacks. Instead, Farrakhan, in his speech and in his book *Torchlight for America*, has tried to reach a broad audience across racial, religious, and ethnic lines. Victimization now includes the general identity Americans. He declares that that the lifestyle of Americans is killing them. Pointing out that America spends $750 billion annually on health care, Farrakhan contends that it should rethink health care spending by focusing on preventive care. "If America seriously hopes to end its crisis in health-care, it must redirect its attention to preventive care." But instead of holding the state responsible for health care, Farrakhan contends that the government, private industry, and individuals must take on the duties by making themselves "more knowledgeable" about how to take care of the body. Despite his argument about a partnership among government, the private sector, and the American people, Farrakhan spends most of his time in the chapter entitled "Ending the Health-Care Crisis," describing the action individuals must take to take care of themselves. He advocates that Americans should turn off the television and exercise, stop overeating, taking drugs, and consuming alcohol, and cut back on medications. There is no discussion of the denial of health care services to the poor. Instead, Americans die prematurely because of what he labels their "death style."[34]

Farrakhan proclaims that stress induced by racism is partly responsible for the high rate of heart disease, cancer, and other degenerative diseases among African Americans. He also points out that blacks are four times more likely to be killed by street crime. In spite of the grim statistics that he presents in his book, he puts the burden on black Americans. "We need to understand that we have been trained in a self-destructive way of behavior and that we are caught up in a vicious cycle of death. Our lifestyle is really a death style. We all have to die. This is assured. But our time of death in most cases reflects the personal decisions of each individual. The Bible teaches that the wages of sin is death, and as long as we pursue the ways of this world, wrong over right, falsehood over truth, wealth over health, we will pay the price." Absent from this discussion is the impact of poverty and the unequal distribution of wealth and health care in the country. Instead, like his economic argument, Farrakhan relies on a self-help model for health care. "Did you know that the simple, cost-you-nothing things like prayer, proper rest, proper diet and fasting can heal whatever ails you? The Honorable Elijah Muhammad taught that 90 percent of our illnesses could be cured by just fasting." In fact, Farrakhan contends that most of the illnesses that Americans experience arise from their "rebellion against Divine Law." In what seems to be fantasy, Farrakhan declared that Elijah Muhammad taught his followers that if they lived properly they could extend their lives to "200, to 300 and 400 years." His preventive care formula consists of prayer, gaining knowledge by reading Elijah Muhammad's *How to Eat to Live*, the *Final Call,* and health care journals such as *Prevention, HealthQuest*, and *Vegetarian Times*; "eating to live" instead of eating improperly; exercising; eradicating addictions; getting proper rest; communing with nature; getting regular dental and medical checkups.[35]

What is significant about *Torchlight for America* is it reveals Farrakhan's endeavor to portray himself as a universalistic leader who has America's interest at heart. The book is a vehicle for him to try to convince Americans that he has transformed his image by moving away from the race warrior to the caring, almost patriotic guru. His Million Family March also served this purpose. While a great deal of attention has been given to the Million Man March of October 1995, the much more significant speech and event for Farrakhan was, arguably, the Million Family March, because it marked his spiritual transformation. The goal of the march, according to the NOI leader, was to save the American family. At a press conference on September 11, 2000, Farrakhan claimed that a clear sign of America's decline was the high divorce rate. "When you find that 50 percent of those who marry get divorced, [oftentimes] within the first three years of their marriage, this is not a healthy sign for the American family." He also noted the decline in voting in presidential elections as another sign of the weakening of the nation. He declared one of his the objectives was to "gather scholars, scientists of religion, social science, psychology, and penology together to craft what we believe is an agenda that is in the best interest, not only of Black, Hispanic and Native American people, but in the interest of the American people as well."

Farrakhan claimed that he hoped to attract millions of people to the march in order to use the numbers as leverage to force government to act in the best interest of Americans. He noted that America's greatest threat was not a foreign enemy but a self-destructive tendency; it was a moral decline and a government that has adopted unfriendly policies toward the American family. "Therefore, this Million Family March is not just for the Black family, though the Black family will be the cornerstone of this march/mobilization. We are appealing to the Latino family, to the Native

American family, to the Arab, Asian and White family, because each member of the American family is feeling the effect of family unfriendly public policy and family unfriendly foreign policy." Unlike the Million Man March of 1995, whose major message was the spiritual goal of "atonement" of black men, the Million Family March had a much more left-leaning political bite. The mobilization of millions, according to its organizer, could take on the sins of "Corporate America."[36]

Farrakhan's speech at the Million Family March also differed from the Million Man March in another fundamental way; it was a clear declaration of his complete transformation by indirectly repudiating his earlier divisive language that denigrated others and separated them by race. In a complete reversal of rhetoric, the Muslim minister spoke of the hate that separated "humanity" and included himself as an activist in the process of separating human beings from one another by using the pronoun *we* throughout his speech. At one point he claims, "We are destroying each other," and at another point he argued, "As I look at the children of Abraham—Muslims, Christians, and Jews—Abraham would be totally upset that we would recognize him as a father and God as a father, and then turn around and slaughter each other, as is going on even as we speak." Although he contended that white supremacy was the key culprit for the low socioeconomic position of blacks, he acknowledged that the "poison" of feeling superior and seeing others as inferior is pervasive, shared by all groups. "I respectfully say to you, my beloved brothers and sisters and members of the potential human family, that a poison exists and it starts with the thought that I am better than you because I'm black; or I am better than you because I am white; or I am better than you because I am rich; or I am better than you because I am more highly educated; I am better than you because I have something that you don't have. These are false yardsticks used by human beings to justify their ill treatment of one another." In his effort to portray himself a racial healer trying to save the human race from self-destruction, Farrakhan gave what he saw as the absolute solution for the evil scourges of racism and the attitude of superiority over other human beings. He contended that there is a "yardstick that we can say one is better than the other; it's not your race, it's not your color, it's not your creed. The thing that makes one human being better than another is our duty to God and righteous conduct.[37]

The man who spent decades trying to portray himself as a race leader went as far as to ridicule the notion of race. The Nation of Islam leader argued that one would be ludicrous to claim that a rose is superior to an orchid in a bouquet of flowers or that one color of sand is superior to another color. Appealing to logic and a religious notion of equality, he scolded the human race for putting so much value on color by declaring: "We can accept the differences in rocks, in stones, in earth, but we cannot accept the differences of color and characteristics in one another. That says that the human being is sick."[38]

While decrying the way the "human family" divided itself, he also connected all humanity to one biblical source by relying on what historian Mia Bay calls the monogenesis argument. This argument, identified with nineteenth-century black leadership, relies on the notion that all of humanity sprang from one source, God, and there are no justifiable grounds for dividing humans along racial categories. In his speech Farrakhan has rejuvenated the monogenesis argument. "If you look at the human family—now, I'm talking about black, brown, red, yellow and white—we all seem to be frozen on a subhuman level of existence.... Satan has turned us completely around where we can say, 'Ye are all dogs children of the most low Satan.'"[39]

Farrakhan assailed the adoption of symbols by people because they were used to help divide human beings from one another. "You wear your cross, I wear my crescent, so I'll be over here and you'll be over there. Wrong, wrong, wrong! That is wrong." Grounding himself in universality, he declared that he is a Christian, Jew and Muslim, Pentecostal, Jehovah's Witness, Mason and Shriner. "I'm all of that and then some, because I refuse to let things limit me as to who I really am...."

Notwithstanding his left-leaning message, Farrakhan concluded his statement by returning to a more conservative theme. "None of this should make us think that the basic responsibility for change does not rest squarely on our shoulders. So the biggest question to answer is, what are we willing to do and what price are we willing to pay to obtain freedom, justice and equality."[40]

Despite some liberal tendencies, Farrakhan remains committed to his religious conservative bent. He argues that homosexuality, premarital sex, and abortion are immoral and should be eliminated. Both his economic and social conservative leaning has gained Farrakhan the admiration of some on the political right. Robert Novak, the ultraconservative, anti–affirmative action proponent, claimed that Farrakhan was knocking at the door of the Republican Party. Novak, former Republican senator now attorney general John Ashcroft, Republican representative John Kaisch, and conservative journalist Rowland Evans all met with Farrakhan in Boca Raton, Florida. Jude Wanniski, a conservative economist and former advisor to Ronald Reagan set up the meeting. Wanniski had met with Farrakhan in December 1996 and was persuaded that the NOI leader could be convinced to adopt "Reaganomics." According to historian Manning Marable, "Wanniski later declared that Farrakhan was such a willing convert to supply-side economic theory that "he drank it in as if he had just come upon an oasis in the desert." Wanniski saw Farrakhan, the most popular black leader in the United States, as a major vehicle to lure blacks away from the Democratic Party.[41]

While the attempt at an alliance between Farrakhan and conservatives has yet to develop, Farrakhan's economic, educational, and social agenda remains couched, to a strong degree, in right-to-center dogma. But he is at best a mixed bag. Although his political leanings are conservative he has also, to a certain extent, embraced a liberal rhetoric; no matter how marginal those leftist views are to his conservative ideas, they cannot be ignored. The Nation of Islam's weekly magazine, the *Final Call* reflects the left focus of Farrakhan and his organization. Its contributing writers focus on world and national events, usually taking a left-of-center view. Articles have praised Cuba and Castro, criticized the harsh foreign and domestic policies of the United States, and criticized globalization. A good example of its left-leaning emphasis is the report of Askia Muhammad (who also works for public radio station WBAI/Pacifica in New York City) on the G-77 or "South Summit." Created in 1963 this group of developing nations met in Havana between April 12 and April 14, 2000. According to the reporter, Cuba was the ideal place to hold the G-77 meeting: "Leaders from African countries in particular, where Cuba has a history of fighting in the anti-apartheid struggle, both militarily and politically remember and respect the Cuban contribution to Africa's independence.... There are even six medical colleges that have been established on the continent to train African doctors, by Cubans, in Cuban-built facilities, with virtually all Cuban faculties doing the teaching." Other articles focus on the struggle to reform the International Monetary Fund and the World Bank, and visits of African heads of state to the United States. Hugh Price, president of the National Urban League; death-row inmate and former Black Panther Mumia Abu-Jumal; Democratic representative Cynthia McKinney; political science professor Ron Walters; rap artist Chuck D; black public intellectual Michael Eric Dyson; Russell Mokhiber, editor of the *Corporate Crime Reporter*; and Robert Weissman, editor of *Multinational Monitor*.[42]

Farrakhan's shift toward orthodox Islam has been very public. Writer Peter Noel notes in the *Village Voice* that for several years Farrakhan has moved toward orthodox Islam, journeying closer to his former nemesis, Imam Warith Deen Mohammad, the son of Elijah Muhammad, who shifted his father's Nation of Islam from a messianic black nationalist sect to a Sunni Muslim organization. On February 26, 2000, at the annual Savior's Day gathering, Warith Mohammad and Farrakhan "rekindled their relationship." According to Farrakhan, "The Imam and I will be together until death overtakes us and we will work together for the cause of Islam. We will work together for the establishment of Islam; not only among our people, but to establish Islam in the Americas." Shifting away from the NOI theology to a more universal message, Farrakhan claimed that the Prophet Muhammad was the "end of the prophets, and I know that the Qur'an is the final book that was brought to the human being to prepare us for the life of the hereafter...." This public recognition of the Prophet Muhammad as the last prophet and identification of the Koran as the final book, major tenets of orthodox Islam, meant a renunciation of Elijah Muhammad's claim that Wallace D. Fard, the founder of the NOI, was Allah and had selected him as his prophet. Farrakhan realized the danger in his pronouncement, because such a revolutionary theological shift could invite hostility, especially among some of the fundamentalists who for some time followed a strict interpretation of NOI theology. Hence, he attempted to buffer his shift away from vintage NOI doctrine as advocated by Elijah Muhammad by reassuring his followers that while he has changed he had not abandoned them. He was attempting to make a distinction by separating the changed theological position from his political position. But in reality, by moving closer to orthodox Islam, he was also changing his image as a political leader. As an orthodox Muslim, he could no longer espouse divisive rhetoric and demonize people.[43]

Farrakhan would later be more direct about both the founder of the NOI, Master Fard Muhammad and his most loyal follower, Elijah Muhammad. At the twenty-fifth annual convention of the American Muslim Society, on September 3, 2000, both men embraced. In his remarks at the convention, Farrakhan referred to Warith D. Mohammad as his "brother" and "an esteemed teacher." He then claimed that Fard is not God and that Elijah was not the last prophet but a "messenger," publicly giving notice of his transformed religious views.[44]

The orthodox Islamic Farrakhan image, like the race warrior, still emulates the black preacher. He is still a proselytizer with a major objective. Like the preacher, he wants to extend his congregation beyond its current membership, so he continues to try to convert others to his cause. But the conversion appeal goes beyond just attracting blacks; it is attempting to convert or reform the world. Like black preachers, Farrakhan has adopted the Afro-American jeremiad. His speeches, lectures, and writings consistently warn of the doom awaiting America for its treatment of nonwhites and the poor. However, his message is also one of hope—if America is willing to act in a moral fashion.

In a December 1999 press conference he claimed his objective was not to focus on his recent near-death experience with cancer but to talk about peace and an end to war and bloodshed in the world. In true jeremiad form, he warned that Jesus had "prophesied, 'And ye shall hear of wars and rumors of wars; see that ye be not troubled; for these things must come to pass, but the end is not yet. For nation shall rise against nation, and kingdom against kingdom; and there shall be famines, and pestilence and earthquakes, in various places. All these are the beginning of sorrows.'" He also noted that both the Koran and the Old Testament warned of troubled times. As evidence of troubled times, he noted that as the world entered the new millennium, there were violent conflicts in sixty nations.

His semieschatological message also had a way out of the doom. "Many prophecies of the Bible and Qur'an, however, are conditional. These prophecies do not necessarily have to be fulfilled if we are wise enough to know how to beat prophecy. However, if we do not do that which will allow us to beat prophecy, and do it in a timely manner, then, unfortunately, we will have to fulfill these horrible prophecies."[45]

Noting that prophecy is not fate, Farrakhan declared that the "cycle of violence and hatred must end." As God's ecumenical sage, he did not only address what W. E. B. Du Bois declared was the major problem of the twentieth century, the color line; instead, Farrakhan called for a halt to ethnic conflict in Africa, Eastern Europe, for an end to "national hatreds; racial hatreds; religious hatreds; gang violence in America and the senseless killings in the streets of America and the schools of America." He claimed that America, Europe, Asia, Central America, South America, the Caribbean, and the Isles of the Pacific all "need healing." According to Farrakhan, the answer to these problems is found in the Bible: "If my people, which are called by name, shall humble themselves, and pray, and seek my face, and turn from their wicked ways, then will I hear from heaven, and will forgive their sins, and will heal their land." Farrakhan's spiritual message called on "humanity" of all religious faiths to pray on December 25 for peace. Without a doubt, he has combined an ecumenical message with a religious fundamentalism, preaching a religious brotherhood and sisterhood. More important, he uses a black rhetorical tradition expressing indignation and dissatisfaction with the nation. As noted in chapter 3, this tradition has been labeled by historian David Howard-Pitney as the Afro-American jeremiad. But while scorning and predicting a terrible fate for the country because of its treatment of African Americans and the less fortunate, he offers it hope if is willing to correct its ways. According to Howard-Pitney, the Afro-jeremiad has been a major element in the black freedom struggle used by such leaders as Frederick Douglass, Ida B. Wells, W. E. B. Du Bois, Malcolm X, and Jesse Jackson. In his remaking of his image, Farrakhan has also adopted this rhetoric to advance what he sees as his ecumenical agenda. Like others, while condemning the nation and the world for its mistreatment of the less fortunate, he offers a means out of the global holocaust.[46]

What are the reasons for Farrakhan's move from the race warrior to the ecumenical sage? The minister has attributed the change to his near-death experience during treatment for prostate cancer. According to Farrakhan, the crisis caused him to reconsider his narrowly held racist views. Like the Reverend Al Sharpton and others, Farrakhan has cast his political and religious transformation in the language of conversion. But as writer Salim Muwakkil says, and as the evidence verifies, Farrakhan had begun to moderate his views before the near-death incident. One important reason is that he greatly desires to be considered a major player among black leadership. By the early 1990s Farrakhan had formed a covenant with the Congressional Black Caucus. He also participated in the Black Leadership Summit, a group that consisted of the then executive secretary of the NAACP Ben Chavis (now Benjamin Muhammad of the NOI), Professor Cornel West of Harvard University, Hugh Price of the Urban League, and Ron Daniels of the Center for Constitutional Rights. At the leadership summit Farrakhan contended that blacks, no matter their religious or political views, should unite and work for unity. The minister knows that he cannot be recognized as a major leader by constantly pushing the old NOI line.[47]

Another important reason for Farrakhan's shift is his realization of the dramatic social, economic, and political changes among African Americans. Scholar Ernest Allen has correctly noted that the old doctrine of the Nation of Islam was not as persuasive to African Americans in the late 1970s and 1980s as it was in the 1940s and 1950s. The enforcement of 1964 Civil Rights Act and the 1965 Voting Rights Act opened the doors for black political involvement and power, thus undermining the black-nationalist argument that blacks would never be a part of the American polity in the South. By the 1980s thousands of African Americans had been elected to public office in the South. In addition, there has been an increase in the black middle class, and the income among African Americans has increased. These factors coupled with war and strife on the African continent, helped deflate the view that black Americans would be "returning" to Africa. Indeed, these factors weakened the theory of territorial black nationalism, the notion of a homeland for African Americans advocated by black nationalists, and the argument for the need of a pluralistic society in which groups instead of individuals demand and receive a piece of the economic and political pie.[48]

As American urban centers experienced deindustrialization, a group of people in the urban centers who were classified by social scientists as the "underclass" emerged. This underclass consisted of people who were locked into poverty, experienced chronic unemployment, received little education, had children out of wedlock, and were socially isolated. The black middle and working classes that shared space with the very poor before deindustrialization now moved out of the inner city, leaving that space in economic ruin. Farrakhan's advocacy of the "do for self" or the Booker T. Washington approach, giving priority to economic concerns over political rights, is quite problematic because of the economic and social transformation of black communities. As Allen notes, "'For the NOI, the collapse of inner-city economic life in the 1980s revealed a twofold edge: on the one side, a growth in the numbers of disaffected African Americans who would become potential candidates for NOI recruitment; on the other, evaporating community resources that a revitalized NOI could no longer draw upon in its attempt to regain and even surpass Elijah Muhammad's former economic empire. Simply put, the time-tested entrepreneurial nationalism of former decades was no longer sufficient." In response to this changing economic reality the Nation of Islam's own security agencies solicited federal and local government contracts, thus cooperating with the forces that the organization had condemned.[49]

Another important reason for Farrakhan's transformation has been the growing number of African Americans who are converting to orthodox Islam. This increasing number isolates the Nation of Islam from the orthodox Islamic world and undermines the group's messianic black-nationalist theory. To be sure, Farrakhan, recognizing the winds of change, began to move his organization to orthodox Islam.

In his endeavor to reconstruct his image, Farrakhan faces a major quandary. Many who found his old message offensive have simply brushed him off; at the same time, the true believers who found the Nation of Islam's racist ideology appealing and loved and admired his early defiance and odious message now see him as a traitor. There is no doubt that he is responsible for the Nation of Islam's acute anti-Semitism and that he was able to attract many because of his ability to convince them that Jews were "evil" and the natural enemy of blacks and that any black person who did not embrace his message and criticize his antics was a traitor to the race. It was his NOI that anonymously published *The Secret Relationship between Blacks and Jews,* a book that falsely claims that Jews were the major backers of the international slave trade. His revival of the unorthodox theology of the Nation of Islam and its theory of Yacub, his constant bellowing about an essentialist view of racial origins, his reference to the "Honorable Elijah Muhammad" as the one who taught him about the "true nature" of whites, has earned him and the NOI the villainous label, the most hated group in America. Because of the past, few whites will remain unconvinced. Because the hurt of such horrendous remarks remains deep, some will see him locked in time as a hatemonger.

It should be noted that Farrakhan has not removed the section in the *Final Call* entitled "What the Muslims Believe." This section, adopted from an earlier Nation of Islam paper, *Muhammad Speaks,* contains the tenets of faith of the organization. The most important of the twelve articles is the last: "WE BELIEVE that ALLAH (God) appeared in the person of Master W. Fard Muhammad, July, 1930; the long-awaited 'Messiah' of Christians and the 'Mahdi' of the Muslims." Although Farrakhan has publicly disavowed this notion, the fact that it is still appears in the *Final Call* has raised concern among orthodox Muslim leaders. Abdurahaman Alamoudi, president of the American Muslim Foundation, has acknowledged Farrakhan's shift to orthodox Islam. But referring to point twelve, Alamoudi contended "that statement will not and will never be accepted by orthodox Muslims."[50]

Farrakhan has not altogether abandoned anti-Semitism. Even as he was moderating his public image, a book entitled *Controversy with the International Bankers* was published with the leader of the NOI listed as the author. It is made up of three lectures given by Farrakhan between February and April 1995. The 1996 publication examines many issues, including, the Republican takeover of Congress in 1994, destruction of the family, and the involvement of Qubilah Shabazz, the daughter of Malcolm X and Betty Shabazz, in a plot to assassinate Farrakhan. The first and the last sections deal with what the Muslim leader sees as the manipulation of world economy by "international bankers." Although he praises Jews for their accomplishments in various professional fields, he argues that not all Jews have held onto the high moral standard. He then elaborates on the Rothschild family and its control over the financial institutions of the world. Albeit he contended that the Rothschild family and "Anglo-Saxon families joined forces to control the financial institutions," he continued to point out the crimes of the Jews. Farrakhan claimed that Jews helped finance Hitler. "I mean it's hurtful that a Jew, Rothschild, loaned money to Adolph Hitler. A Jew, Rothschild. God damn it, you'd better not open your mouth to call me no anti-Semite."[51]

Farrakhan also argued that the international bankers financed the Bolsheviks and were responsible for the Russian Revolution of 1917. He even went so far as to declare that the "international bankers" helped nurture the Soviet Union.[52]

Just as disturbing and clearly a major hindrance to his effort to reconstruct his image as a ecumenical sage were his comments about the Democratic vice presidential nominee, Joseph Lieberman. On August 11, 2000, Farrakhan was at a press conference and a reporter from the *Los Angeles Focus* asked the minister whether Lieberman was a good choice. Was black America ready for a Jewish vice president? Farrakhan smartly said that it was not just a test for black Americans but for white America. He noted that he agreed with Lieberman about criticizing Hollywood, and he agreed with Bush on his pro-life position. But as though courting fate, Farrakhan questioned Lieberman's loyalty. "Mr. Lieberman, as an orthodox Jew, is also a citizen, dual citizenship, with Israel. And the state of Israel is not synonymous with the United States. And the test that he would probably have to pass is, would he be more faithful to the Constitution of the United States than to the ties that any Jewish person would have to the state of Israel. That's very real. Other people, fearing that they will be called anti-Semitic, may not raise such a point. I am not anti-Semitic, but I raise that point." Farrakhan raised the specious notion that the vice presidential nominee was also a citizen of Israel, therefore his greatest loyalty might be to another country. Despite his denial of anti-Semitism, his remarks resulted in a storm of criticism and hurt his effort to convince many of his spiritual and political conversion.[53]

Nevertheless, Farrakhan's willingness to move away from the old tenets of the NOI and his readiness to publicly embrace people he earlier cast as his enemies are steps that have been recognized by some in the Islamic world and some outside of that community as significant signs of the head of the Nation of Islam's transformation.[54] His comments on the World Trade Center attack on September 11, 2001, were evidence of his attempt at ecumenicalism. At a news conference on September 16, Farrakhan read a statement indicating his spiritual and political maturation. He expressed his willingness to embrace all groups and religions, and he thanked Allah for his guidance of the "human family" and for divine relation "through the Scriptures." He thanked God for Moses and the Torah, Jesus and the Gospel, and Muhammad and the Koran.[55]

Expressing his sorrow at the attack, Farrakhan said, "Words are inadequate to express the pain, the sadness, the anguish that has moved my spirit to come before you today to speak from my heart to your hearts, and beyond this room to the hearts of the nation in grief, anger and in mourning." Claiming to speak for the NOI and many Muslims in America and throughout the world, he declared that the Muslims were lifting their voices to "condemn this vicious and atrocious attack on the United States." In a striking departure from his usual condemnation of America and of white society, Farrakhan joined the chorus of voices that painted the New York City police and firefighters as heroes. He commended the police and firefighters "who risk their lives on a daily basis" to preserve the society from danger and crime. Although the issues of police brutality and racial profiling are major concerns, "yet it must be understood that these police and fire persons leave their homes everyday to do their duty in an ever increasing violent society never knowing whether they shall return home to their families." To augment his view of those deserving hero classification, Farrakhan depicted police officers and firefighters as those who were willing to make the ultimate sacrifice while saving human lives. "These firemen and women and these policemen and women were running toward the fierceness of the flaming fire of the World Trade Center as many were running from it. Their courage, their valor, their sense of duty caused them to run into that building not caring for their lives but for the lives of those they were intent on saving." In contrast to his 1985 speech at Madison Square Garden, in which he lashed out at Governor Mario Cuomo and Mayor Ed Koch, the Muslim sage praised Mayor Rudolph Giuliani and Governor George Pataki, as well as others, including the people who gave blood. The minister's speech was much more than a glib and patriotic communiqué. Farrakhan's purpose in giving the accolades was to notify the general public of his transformation and his move toward the mainstream.[56]

The most interesting part of Farrakhan's speech was how he ingeniously managed to criticize U.S. foreign policy without jeopardizing his new image as ecumenical leader and seeming to be anti-American. In fact, his speech went beyond bolstering his image as a universal spiritual sage; it helped promote him as a loyal American who was giving advice to save the nation. After addressing the question of how could such a tragedy take place and answering it by contending that God creates life and has a right to take it, Farrakhan used a triumphalist argument. Accordingly, he claimed that out of tragedy and despair comes hope. He argued that when a nation loses its direction, Allah raises a guide who is from the oppressed group. But aware that the nation will reject the message of the guide, God inflicts horrible acts of destruction on that nation in order to make it humble before Him. He contended that only in a state of humility "can the proud and the powerful heed the guidance of God ... Allah used this tragedy hopefully to bring a great nation to him."[57]

Although Farrakhan's speech sounded religiously fundamentalist, it should not be put in the same category as those among the religious fundamentalists who have claimed that the attack was the work of an angry God who was punishing the nation for moving away from its Christian principles. This very theme was made by the reverends Jerry Falwell and Pat Robertson soon after September 11. Falwell, the founder of the political group the Moral Majority and chancellor of Liberty University in Lynchburg, Virginia, appeared on Pat Robertson's religious program, the *700 Club*. According to Falwell, "I really believe that the Pagans, and the abortionists, and the feminists, and the gays and lesbians ... the ACLU, People for the American Way—all of them who have tried to secularize America—I point the finger in their face and say you helped this happen." The collapse of the Twin Towers was God's way of punishing a nation who rejected Him. Although Falwell later apologized for his statement, after a storm of criticism, Robertson, two-time Republican presidential candidate and the leader of the Christian Coalition, repeated Falwell's argument on the *700 Club*. He argued that pornography on the internet, the occult on television, and other "sins" are an affront to the Almighty. "We have insulted God at the highest level of our government. Then we say, 'Why does this happen?' It is happening because God Almighty is lifting His protection from us. Once that protection is gone, we are vulnerable because we are a free society." Like Falwell, Robertson depicts a vengeful God who either commits the act (Falwell) or withdraws his protection to the nation, thereby allowing it its enemies to attack it (Robertson).[58]

Although Farrakhan's speech, like Falwell's and Robertson's statements, placed the World Trade Center attack in a religious context, the NOI leader's words are drastically different. While Falwell and Robertson see September 11 as an act of righteous punishment of America for its moral lapse, Farrakhan paints it as a means of leading people to God. Farrakhan's statement, in comparison to Falwell's and Robertson's, was much more ecumenical. Falwell pointed his finger at specific groups that he saw as outside of his brand of Christianity. He did not consider that many gays and lesbians and members of the ACLU and the People for the American Way are believers in some type of faith, including Christianity. Farrakhan, on the other hand, embraced the "human family," including Jews, Christians, and Muslims. Falwell's and Robertson's comments were seen as divisive. Ralph Neas, president of the People for the American Way, accused the chancellor of Liberty University of traveling a "path of division" rather than seeking unity during this period.[59]

Farrakhan's speech is distinguishable from Falwell's and Robertson's comments in another way. He used the occasion to announce his changing attitude by expressing his admiration for America. "However, in my maturation, I know with all of America's problems, she is the greatest nation on this earth." He even went as far to declare that America has the potential of becoming the "greatest nation in history." Not only did he admire the

United States, he also declared himself a member of the American community. "So as a citizen of this nation, I do not wish to see harm come to her." So he was going to speak "out of love" for the nation. In his speech he returned to his most recent themes connected to his new image, noting the ills that are hurting the country.

Farrakhan argued that, after the attack, it was clear that there had been a dramatic change in America. "Tragedy was turned into triumph, tragedy began the spiritual awakening of a great nation and steeled its resolve to help it overcome the wickedness of those who perpetrated this assault." Hence, unlike Falwell who claimed that this was an act of a vengeful God, Farrakhan placed the blame on those who carried out the attack. He went as far as to claim that the United States was under attack and that an appropriate response was needed. But while bringing into play his patriotism, Farrakhan remained faithful to his role as Muslim leader. He noted it was wrong to say that Muslims were attacking the United States because they hated the fact the United States was a "Christian Nation" and wanted to convert it to Islam. He claimed that there are over one billion Muslims in the world and "every one of them believes in Jesus." The Koran, according to the NOI leader, refers to Jesus as the son of Mary and as the Messiah. He also noted that not only Christians but also hundreds of Muslims, along with Hindus, Buddhists, and Agnostics, were killed at the World Trade Center. "This is why it was a crime against humanity." He never spoke of God's retribution but instead said that "nineteen so-called human beings" were responsible.[60]

Farrakhan had laid the groundwork for his criticism of American foreign policy in order to prevent his critics and others from labeling him anti-American. His embedded his critique in an almost abstract observation. He noted the central role of the Israeli and Palestinian conflict. The Palestinians perceive their conditions, he said, as do many in the Arab world, as unjust. The refugee camps and the mounting death toll are the reasons why many are willing to act as suicide bombers. They care nothing about their lives or the lives of others. In fact, they want others to feel their pain. Thus, Farrakhan presented himself as one who was interpreting the mind of the terrorist. He affirmed his support of President Bush and the people of the United States and their desire to hunt down the people responsible for the attack. But he also urged that the president sit down with those who study prophecy and "religious" or "scriptural scientists," including Jews, Christians, and Muslims, because there was a danger that a war in the Middle East could turn out to be Armageddon. In fact, he claimed that if war could be avoided altogether, this peace would be the best scenario. He presented himself as a selfless religious leader whose concern was for the United States and for all of humanity.[61]

Farrakhan has always been willing to speak out against injustices carried out against people of African origins in the United States. His disengagement from the old NOI doctrine and embrace of orthodox Islam has helped him to move away from demonizing other groups. It is clear from his speeches that he has mapped out a course that will allow him to speak to what he sees as injustices to all the people. Although major problems remain with his message, clearly, the ecumenical Farrakhan can help the nation heal its long racial and ethnic problems.

CHAPTER 8

Ella Baker, Pauli Murray, and the Challenge to Male Patriarchy

Many of the figures examined in this book have used religion in some fashion when formulating ideas and ideology, interpreting political struggles, and constructing identities. From Randolph's race man to Williams's lonely Moses, Galamison's black Christian radical image, Culmer's responsible racial accommodationist, Farrakhan's race warrior and wise sage, and Sharpton's religious political progressive leader, all framed the struggle they were involved in within a religious context. Despite their emphasis on eradicating racism, they did not mount a challenge to the patriarchy so prevalent in religious cultures and pursue sexual equality. In fact, many of the religious figures in this study have advocated manhood models and the adoption of a charismatic leadership style that made no space for women in leadership.

These black intellectuals to a large degree reflected the patriarchy of religious cultures and institutions. But despite the emphasis on patriarchy, male chauvinism did not go uncontested among African Americans. In her fascinating book *Righteous Discontent: The Women's Movement in the Black Baptist Church, 1880–1920*, historian Evelyn Brooks Higginbotham argues that through everyday activity women in black Baptist churches carved out a space for themselves in the public sphere. Black women's methods, although not radical, represented evidence contrary to the dominant society's insistence that black women were inferior and incapable; for that reason the author describes these activities as "everyday forms of resistance." According to Higginbotham, women in the black Baptist churches distributed and debated news and information on both local and national levels. Through national and state conventions and their publications, National Baptist Convention women participated in a discourse on a variety of issues affecting African Americans. Just like their male counterparts, black women were struggling to be full participants in American society. Higginbotham also argues that black Baptist women created a feminist theology based on a reading of the Scriptures that challenged the notion that women were to be passive and silent in the churches. Quoting examples from noted black women, including Virginia Broughton, Mary Cook, and Lucy Wilmot Smith, Higginbotham argues that black Baptist women deserve to be classified as theologians because they articulated and acted on a theology that was in opposition to the dominance of men in the church.[1]

In her book, *If It Wasn't for the Women: Black Women's Experience and Womanist Culture in Church and Community*, sociologist and theologian Cheryl Townsend Gilkes has argued that black religious patriarchy has been limited by the persistence of black women thinkers and activists. Gilkes contends that patriarchy "has been modified by the persistent tradition of conflict that black women have maintained within black religious structures." Gilkes and others have noted a long tradition of opposition to male dominance in black religious cultures. Black women thinkers have not only challenged patriarchy but also conceived alternative models that broadened and democratized African-American and American sacred practices. Ella Baker and Pauli Murray were two very important religious intellectuals and activists of the twentieth century who offered different representations to alter the domination of men in the church.[2]

Ella Baker

Although she was not an ordained minister and never attempted to sermonize, proselytize, and convert people to Christianity or to any other religious order, Ella Baker is worth examining because she envisioned and articulated a major role for black churches and ministers in the freedom struggle. In recognition of her involvement in Afro-Christianity, Gilkes has called Baker a "traveling prophet" for the NAACP as its field director.

Ella Baker was born on December 13, 1903, in Norfolk, Virginia. Her father worked as a waiter and her mother ministered to the poor. As a child, Ella modeled herself after her mother, developing a sense of caring for the indigent and began to minister to the less fortunate. Baker recalled that her mother was religious and caring and possessed strict standards of decorum and speech. According to Baker, her mother was also a very good public speaker. Baker wanted to emulate her.[3]

Baker's grandfather was a pastor and her mother was a religious person; consequently, the church and African-American religion became an important part of her life. She joined a church when she was nine and was quite active in the church activities. Indeed, she became quite familiar with the Bible, even quoting passages of it in her correspondence. But she never grasped on to the expressive religious culture that was so prevalent among African Americans. According to her biographer, Joanne Grant:

> Throughout her life she maintained a sort of distance from the accepted role of religion in the black community. She participated but did not succumb to the general fervor. "I am always happy to think," she said, "that to some extent I was saved from the worst aspects of religiosity because my family was not emotional in its religion." This attitude carried on throughout her life. She disdained the preacherly speech, which often lacked content but had cadences, and the shouting and testifying were anathema to her. There is no doubt that Ella's approach to speechifying stemmed to a great extent from her grandfather's example. "Grandpa, who was a pastor of four churches, had an

unusual manner about him in that he did not countenance shouting. He'd stop people and tell them to be quiet and listen. Or when a young minister came to preach at his church and felt he had to act as some ministers acted, which was to put the 'rousement' over you, Grandpa would catch him by the coattails and pull them and say, 'Now you sit down and rest yourself while I sing this hymn and then get up and talk like you got some sense.'"[4]

Baker's father also was critical of ministers who spoke well but did little or nothing to help the social and material needs of black people. Probably due to her family experience, Baker selected a religion that reached God through reason rather than through experience. She was much more interested in a religion in which ministers stressed an ethical message instead of one that was aimed at provoking an emotional response. Baker also contends that her family instilled in her a sense of egalitarianism with no stress on a social hierarchy. The economically less fortunate were just as important as those with material means. "Where we lived there was no sense of social hierarchy in terms of those who have, having the right to look down upon, or to evaluate as a lesser breed, those who didn't have." Her refusal to embrace hierarchical structures as necessary components in religious and civil society would become apparent when she became involved in the civil rights movement.[5]

Baker attended Shaw University and graduated in 1927. She moved to Harlem and lived with a cousin while working at menial jobs because she was not able to find decent employment. During the Depression she became politically active, joining the Young Negroes' Cooperative League, which established stores, restaurants, and housing cooperatives for blacks throughout the country. Baker became the national director of the Young Negroes' Cooperative League. She became a member of the Women's Day Workers and Industrial League, an organization attempting to improve the plight of domestic workers. She also became active in the left-leaning American Labor Party, and by 1941 was assistant field director of the NAACP. In 1943 Walter White, national secretary of the NAACP, appointed Baker national director of branches. It is because of Baker's political activities and community involvement in the 1920s and 1930s that she became committed to the notion that the grass roots should be given the opportunity to become politically active and even take a leadership role in social protest movements. She established leadership-training conferences for local leaders. The conferences stressed skills training and consciousness raising. Participants learned to deal with several local concerns, including police brutality and other forms of racial discrimination.[6]

Although Baker worked with national leaders from the 1930s well into the 1960s, she decided to work with the less celebrated and the grass roots in order to empower them. She once stated: "I don't care how underdevelopment he is, I would be willing to say that no human relishes being set upon and beaten as if he were an animal. The natural resistance is already there." During the 1940s she traveled half the year as field secretary and director of branches for the NAACP. Her task was to build and stimulate growth of local branches of the civil rights group. Notwithstanding the top-down approach of the venerable civil rights organization, Baker carved out her own agenda, which included empowering the rank-and-file members. She worked to forge an alliance between the civil rights organization and labor unions. She also pushed the NAACP to take up the fight against anti-labor laws and for consumer goods pricing. However, she resigned from the NAACP in 1946 because she felt it was too bureaucratic and got in the way of mass organizing. Baker claimed that her resignation from the NACCP had nothing to do with her ego but she wanted to be where the people were active. Although she would later become head of the New York City branch of the NAACP, her major focus during that period was on working with parents and the Reverend Milton A. Galamison in the fight to integrate New York City schools. In 1956 Baker, a member of a grassroots organization called the Parents in Action Against Educational Discrimination, met with the Mayor Robert Wagner of New York City in an attempt to persuade the city to come up with a plan for integrating the public school system.[7]

Inspired by the Montgomery bus boycott, she traveled to Alabama to assist in the civil rights effort. Although she had not applied for the position, Bayard Rustin and Stanley Levison, associates of Martin Luther King Jr., convinced Baker to accept a position and help bring structure to the Southern Christian Leadership Conference (SCLC). Sociologist Aldon Morris points out that Baker was actually hired as the first associate director of SCLC but later became the executive director when the organization's first executive director, Reverend John Tilly, resigned. However, even before Tilly assumed his position as executive director, Baker was acting as the main administrator and had organized SCLC's central office. Baker worked on SCLC's Crusade for Citizenship project. She also persuaded King to allow Septima Clark of the Highlander School to use SCLC's space to carry on her Citizenship Education Project. The objective of the project was to train people to become involved citizens and take part in civic activity, including voting. Highlander established Citizenship schools throughout the south and Clark recruited and trained teachers for the schools. There she attempted to change the church-based organization from a ministerial organization that stressed a top-down approach to building a movement to one that would instill confidence and give power to the masses of disenfranchised and oppressed people in the South. She wanted to transform a culture that allowed ministers or leaders to have a voice but stilled the voices of ordinary people who, if given the opportunity and proper training, could lead the movement. Baker referred to this notion as "group-centered leadership." This participatory approach consisted of three principles. The first was to appeal for grassroots involvement of people throughout society in decisions that impacted their lives. The second principle was to place little reliance on hierarchy or the shift from hierarchal structure. The last principle was to call for direct action as an answer to fear, alienation, and intellectual detachment. As executive director, she also organized voter registration and citizenship-training drives.[8]

However, Baker faced entrenched sexism in the SCLC. In order for ordinary people to develop leadership skills, Baker contended, the ministers and leaders of a movement had to act as facilitators and not as prophetic voices or charismatic leaders who persuaded people to follow their every movement. One way of transforming the minister and leader to a facilitator was to de-emphasize the role of the leader and inculcate a sense of self-worth and an ability to make changes. Baker was perturbed by the ministers' refusal to make any room in SCLC for the participation of the women who were involved in the Montgomery bus boycott, although it was the women who first organized and maintained the campaign and were greatly responsible for its success. The refusal of King and the other clergy to make space for the women was blatant sexism. What also irritated Baker was the ministers' insistence on the charismatic approach and their sexist treatment of her when she asserted herself. Baker realized that the young Martin Luther King and his assistant Ralph Abernathy lacked organizational skills. She attempted to mentor them, but they rebuffed her because her efforts threatened their patriarchal status as ministers. In fact, Baker refused to back down when confronting King. In her attempt to de-emphasize the charismatic approach, she sought to limit the number of ministers who spoke at SCLC meetings. According to her biographer, Joanne Grant, King launched a defense of the approach by explaining to the executive director that once one minister excited the audience, other ministers would want to do the same. Not impressed with his explanation, Baker accused the ministers of running a "sophomoric oratorical contest" and told the young pastor that an audience responded to information with just as much enthusiasm as they reacted to "sound."[9]

Baker's attempt restrict the number of clergy speakers and limit their speeches to just a few minutes was an attempt to curtail the histrionics. Her effort was to alter the power relationship between the charismatic leader and the masses of people who had very few avenues to leadership. She understood that charisma was a means of manipulating people's behavior and getting them to act in a way determined by the charismatic leader. It also legitimized the charismatic leaders' decision-making authority and the argument that they were working in behalf of the masses instead of allowing ordinary people to make decisions. Moreover, charismatic leadership could lead to a cult of personality, in which the leader became a celebrity and was depicted as the movement.

In an interview with historian Gerda Lerner, Baker asserted:

> I have always felt it was a handicap for oppressed peoples to depend so largely upon a leader, because unfortunately in our culture, the charismatic leader usually becomes a leader because he has found a spot in the public limelight. It

usually means he has been touted through the public media, which means that the media made him and the media may undo him. There is also the danger in our culture that, because a person is called upon to give public statements and is acclaimed by the establishment, such a person gets to the point of believing that he is the movement. Such people get so involved with playing the game of being important that they exhaust themselves and their time, and they don't do the work of actually organizing people.[10]

Baker identified the movement in the 1950s and 1960s as one "carried largely by women since it came out of the church groups." Her analysis should not be interpreted as anticlerical or antichurch. She did not oppose religion or ministers, but she was in opposition to the view that all power should be placed in the hands of preachers and others who used their status to climb to formal leadership positions. As noted, she spelled out an elaborate role for churches and ministers. She argued that a major problem with the charismatic leadership model is that it puts power and authority in the hands of a few while not creating avenues for the masses to participate. Hence, this narrow approach has a tendency to foster undemocratic practices. They become "spokespeople" who do not follow democratic procedures for reaching a consensus. Her major focus was on the relationship between those in a position of formal leadership and the grass roots in a social protest movement. By redefining the role of formal leaders as facilitators and allowing the rank and file to take power, the group-centered leadership model assured that the movement would allow for the fullest participation of people and rely on a greater talent pool. It also assured that the movement would survive if a leader were incapacitated, because the social protest is reliant not on the charismatic leadership but on the people who are on the ground carrying out the daily work. These folks would be in a position to make major decisions.

Baker served as a role model, especially for the students in the Student Nonviolent Coordinating Committee (SNCC), because she was a woman in a male ministerial organization that did nothing to oppose sexism. When the ministers attempted to place her in a subordinate position, she stood up to them, reminding them that she cared little for their status and had a wealth of experience as an organizer. Hence, she practiced what she preached. What should be important in a mass movement is not someone gaining leadership through prestige and tradition but through a willingness to act.

The Reverend Wyatt T. Walker, who became the executive director of SNCC after Baker stepped down, accused her of not being diplomatic enough when dealing with the ministers. He claimed that he faced the "same difficulties" as Baker. Of course, he overlooked the fact that his maleness gave him a privilege not extended to Baker because she was a woman. He did acknowledge that as a minister he had an advantage, but only because being a minister made him more sympathetic to the thinking of his fellow clergy; implicitly, Baker's outsider status made her insensitive to this thinking. Rev. C. T. Vivian was even more blatant when assigning blame for the confrontation between SCLC and Baker. He noted that it was difficult for a woman to help organize the ministers. It was even more difficult for a woman who was not a religious person or did not give "affirmation to the church." Walker and Vivian argued that Baker, not the ministers' sexism, was the reason for the fallout.[11]

Baker had a different assessment of the responsibility for the problem between her and the ministers. "I was difficult," she once declared. "I wasn't an easy pushover. I could talk back a lot. Not only could but did. And [it was] frustrating to those that never had that kind of experience. It was strange because the men who were known to be men around town ... had never had a woman who knew how to say no under no certain terms. They didn't know what to do sometimes, especially if you talked loud." She laid the blame at the feet of ministers who just could not deal with a woman who was assertive and would not tolerate their patriarchal practices.[12]

In 1960, when Baker was still executive director of the SCLC, the sit-in movement erupted throughout the South. Beginning on February 1, four African-American students at North Carolina A & T College sat down at a Woolworth's lunch counter in Greensboro, North Carolina, challenging the code of southern segregation. When word of the activity of the four reached other students on campus, thirty students joined the four the following day and took up all of the seats at the lunch counter. As news of the protest reached other campuses, students launched sit-ins throughout North Carolina, Virginia, Tennessee, and Maryland. Before the end of February, some thirty cities had sit-in protests.[13]

Baker was excited by the sit-in demonstrations because they represented her notion of group-centered leadership and had great potential for becoming a militant mass movement that could quickly eradicate the Jim Crow system. Baker, aware that the students needed an organization for a protracted, coordinated movement, helped organize a meeting at Shaw University, in Raleigh, North Carolina, in April 1960, of students active in the sit-ins. For Baker, the students had demonstrated their leadership ability in the civil rights movement, and she was determined that they would not be controlled by Martin Luther King, who wanted to use them to create a student faction of SCLC. She also fought against the students' becoming a youth wing of CORE and the NAACP. Baker even accused the ministers of making plans to persuade the students to become part of SCLC by sending individual ministers to certain delegations and trying to convince them to join the ministerial organization. Baker went to individual students at the conference and advised the students to create their independent organization, and at the end of the meeting in Raleigh the students created the Student Nonviolent Coordinating Committee. For several years, Baker remained an advisor to SNCC and consistently emphasized that the organization should remain true to a group-centered leadership approach. SNCC launched several community-organizing projects, including the voting rights campaign in Mississippi, and nurtured leadership skills leadership skills in both women and men, including Diane Nash and Fannie Lou Hamer. To be sure, Baker has to be given credit for helping to create the most dynamic student-led civil rights organization in the history of the modern civil rights movement.[14]

Pauli Murray

Like Baker, Pauli Murray fought against racial discrimination and male chauvinism. Through her activism, writings, and sermons Murray helped alter the male leadership of the established Christian church and served as a role model for others. She dedicated her life to helping empower those denied access to power because of their race and sex. She fought in several arenas, including the legal, the political, and the religious. While Baker directly challenged a black ministerial elite and worked to empower the grass roots, Murray took on the racism and sexism of the larger society through both personal acts and organizing.

Murray was born in 1910 into a middle-class family in Baltimore, Maryland. At the age of three her world was dramatically altered when her mother died of a cerebral hemorrhage. Her father was unable to take care of her and her siblings, and she went to live with her maternal aunt Pauline in Durham, North Carolina. Her father was committed to a mental institution and was later killed by a white employee of the institution. Murray developed a racial consciousness that protected her against the segregated Durham and the harsh reality and debilitating impact of white racism in America. She described her aunts as race women. "They took pride in every achievement of 'the race' and agonized over every lynching, every black boy convicted and 'sent to the roads,' every insult to 'the race.' I would hear: 'The race is moving forward!'" Murray grew up with the NAACP's *The Crisis* in her home. As a result of her aunts' tracking the trials and tribulations and the accomplishments of "the race, Murray was instilled with a strong sense of racial pride.[15]

Because of this sense of racial pride and self-worth, Murray defied the American apartheid system by taking individualist steps such as walking instead of riding on segregated streetcars and staying away from the downtown movie theaters that relegated blacks to the Jim Crow section. In this way she avoided humiliation and inhuman treatment. Murray noted that she did come into contact with whites "whose humanity overrode their whiteness." Clearly, these contacts also helped shaped her racial consciousness. While possessing a fervent sense of racial self-respect, she did not adopt racial chauvinism or even black nationalism but instead realized that people across racial lines can be kind and compassionate.[16]

In spite of her aunt Pauline's and her own efforts to avoid incidents that would rob them of their dignity, Murray did experience racial discrimination. On occasion she was even terrified by whites. Once, when she and her aunt were in Baltimore visiting relatives, they were notified that Murray's grandfather had become ill. They had to go to back to Durham. On the way she and her aunt were forced to ride in a Jim Crow coach and had to make a connecting train in Norfolk. On their way to the train, Aunt Pauline fell, shattering her eyeglasses, some of the fragments cutting her cheek and causing her to bleed. Two white men who were sitting close by and had witnessed the event just stared and did nothing to assist the aunt. It was in Norfolk while waiting to make the connection that would take them to Durham, that Murray was terrified. "I found myself surrounded by a circle of white faces, all regarding me intently and turning to look at one another. Not a word was said, just stares, shrugs, and head scratching. I was too frightened to scream; I stood frozen with terror for one long, awful moment." In a bold move, her aunt Pauline rescued the child by calmly walking over to her, taking her hand, and telling her that they had to catch their train. When one of the men followed them onto the segregated car and began to stare at them, Murray's aunt audaciously gazed back at the intimidator. Unable to fulfill his objective of striking fear into the hearts of the black women, he relented and departed from the train.[17]

Although the man had left, Murray confessed that she and her aunt were frightened the entire ride. "The incident awakened my dread of lynching, and I was learning the danger of straying, however innocently, across a treacherous line into a hostile world."[18] But the event is also significant not only because a child was forced to experience unimagined terror at the hands of white men who attempted to assert their privilege and advantage in a racist society over black women; it is significant because she witnessed the courage and determination of a black woman who was able to protect her family. Undoubtedly, their aunt served as a role model for young Murray. Aunt Pauline displayed characteristics usually associated with men; she showed bravery and assertiveness, thus demonstrating the enormous possibilities of black womanhood.

Murray also grew up in a home where religion was a central aspect of life. She attended the Episcopal Church with her family and she read the Bible to her grandmother. Hence, religious faith became an integral part of her life.[19]

When an opportunity came to take a step opposing racism, Murray took full advantage. After she graduated from high school, she refused to attend a segregated college in the South and instead attended Hunter College in New York City. Although politically active as a student at Hunter, she would be introduced to left politics when she became a teacher under the auspices of the Remedial Reading Project of the Works Progress Administration. She came into contact with members of the Communist Party of the United States. Although she was thus exposed to Communist doctrine, she never came under its influence, mainly because she disdained the "Black Belt" theory advocated by the party in the 1930s. Murray claimed that the Black Belt theory, which emphasized self-determination for African Americans, seemed to her an advocacy of segregation. Instead, the "Lovestoneites" led by Jay Lovestone, a former communist who developed a socialist critique of Communism and the American Communist Party, influenced her.

Murray worked for the WPA's Workers Education Project teaching industrial workers who were at various educational and reading levels. She gained a greater understanding of the American labor movement. "We also had to familiarize ourselves with immediate problems of clothing workers, Pullman car porters, domestic workers, transport workers, sales clerks, the unemployed or whatever groups we were assigned to." The workers' desire to discuss current affairs persuaded Murray to take classes on the American labor movement, unionism, economics, and journalism at the Brookwood Labor College. "It was an intensive experience. One encountered in the labor movement of the late 1930s, an almost religious fervor, which would be seen two decades later in the civil rights movement and the women's movement of the early seventies. We sang labor songs, thrilled to Earl Robinson's 'Ballad for Americans,' and loudly applauded lectures given by the Reuther brothers and other visiting labor dignitaries. We threw ourselves into the Automobile Workers' General Strike in early 1937, working as volunteer organizers at the Tarrytown plant and helping to put out a local strike newspapers." She also noted that she became emotionally involved in the Spanish Civil War.[20] In 1935, Francisco Franco, a general in the Spanish army, launched a campaign to overthrow the left-leaning Republican government. He was supported by Fascist Italy and Nazi Germany; the Soviet Union supported the Loyalist government. Britain, France, and the United States maintained a policy of neutrality. The civil war became a cause célèbre among the American left. American volunteers, who called themselves the Abraham Lincoln Brigade, went to Spain to help defend it against the fascist aggression. Murray's support for the Loyalist government demonstrated her movement from merely examining the race issue to becoming interested in international struggles. Murray had become involved and shaped by early social movements that were interracial, interfaith, and community based. This experience was clear in her work and personal life. Instead of leaning toward a nationalist scheme, she embraced one that promoted interracial unity while consistently working to empower ordinary people across racial and gender lines.

As a result of her experience with the labor movement, Murray moved left politically. The study of economic oppression had broadened her view of victimization. She became aware that not only did blacks suffer in the United States but so did others. In fact, she came to the conclusion that oppression was global. Moreover, seeing oppression as global changed her; it gave her an "unequivocal understanding that equality of treatment was my birthright and not something to be earned." Global events cultivated a "new militancy" in her and made her aware of the hypocrisy of an American government that fought racism overseas but did nothing about racism at home. She also became conscious and supportive of the liberation struggles in Africa, Asia, and Latin America. But instead of seeing Communism as the answer for people struggling for liberation, Murray believed that democracy should be the ultimate objective of these movements.[21] By participating in a discourse that offered an alternative to the left view that identified freedom with state ownership of the means of production, Murray placed liberation in the realm of political expression and participation. Hence, she linked race and democracy.

Because of her growing militancy and activism Murray decided that she would attempt to break down segregation in higher education in the South by applying for admission to the University of North Carolina, Chapel Hill, in 1938 to study sociology. Murray was aware that no university in the South accepted blacks in its graduate programs and that her application would be a major challenge to the institution, for she had graduated from an outstanding college in the Northeast, making it difficult for the university to reject her on academic grounds. In fact, her action became national news. Although Eleanor Roosevelt would not give Murray her support and segregationists and black conservatives attacked her publicly, she gained support from many in the civil rights community, the black press, and academia. When UNC rejected her application on the grounds that it would violate state laws, Murray asked that the NAACP take her case. The civil rights organization had just won a Supreme Court decision in the case of Lloyd Gaines, a black college graduate who had applied to the law school at the University of Oklahoma and was rejected. The Supreme Court ruled that the state must provide Gaines with a legal education equal to the education provided to white students. But despite the NAACP's success and the national attention Murray received, the venerable civil rights group decided not to take her case because it felt that the chances of losing were greater then winning. Thurgood Marshall wrote to Murray informing her that the NAACP selected cases with care and could not go to a great expense only to lose a case. The organization contended that if it litigated the case it would lose because Murray was not a resident of North Carolina but of New York City.[22]

Murray continued to struggle for an integrated and equal society in the 1940s and 1950s. As a member of the Fellowship of Reconciliation she participated in a challenge to segregation on public transportation in March 1940. Murray and a friend of hers, Adelene McBean, were riding a bus from New York City to Durham, North Carolina. When they changed busses in Richmond, Virginia, they were forced to ride in the back. However, Murray and McBean were seated right over a wheel well of the bus and it protruded into the floor, making riding uncomfortable. As the driver drove faster and sped around turns, the two women were tossed out of their seats. McBean complained about discomfort and wanted to change their seats. Murray, who was aware of the Jim Crow practices and wanted to prevent a confrontation, asked the bus driver if he would ask two white passengers seated in the back to move to the white section and allow Murray and McBean to move to their seats. Although the bus driver refused to grant them permission to change seats, Murray and McBean decided to move two rows ahead when the seats were vacated. In spite of the fact that they remained in the Jim Crow section, the driver attempted to have the two women arrested when they refused to give up their seats to passengers who were boarding the bus. The driver had left the bus and returned with two police officers. Although the police told Murray they were only following the law, he said that they would have to move back a row. When Murray complained that the seat was broken, one of the officers instructed the bus driver to fix the seat. Although Murray and McBean eventually moved to the back of the bus, they were arrested for disorderly conduct after Murray protested that the bus driver was only asking white passengers for their names and addresses and statements about the incident. In a show of defiance Murray and McBean refused bail. The NAACP decided to take Murray and McBean's case in order to challenge the constitutionality of the state's segregation law. They lost the case when the state prosecution dropped the charge of violation of the state's segregation law and instead charged them with disturbing the peace.[23]

While a student at Howard University Law School in 1944 Murray participated in the struggle to integrate restaurants in Washington, D.C. The Howard University branch of the NAACP picketed a downtown cafeteria. When the students were denied service, they took empty trays and sat at tables, denying white costumers a place to sit. Other students demonstrated outside of the cafeteria carrying signs. Because of the students' action the company was forced to settle and open its doors to blacks. However, university authorities demanded that the NAACP branch end its protest. The students cried foul and accused the administration of hypocrisy and appealed to the board of trustees, but their campaign was over.[24]

Murray's fight for sexual equality was as passionate as her struggle for racial justice. She contended that all barriers created to stop human beings from obtaining equal opportunity kept them from reaching their full potential. However, she was not just making a libertarian argument but one that was grounded in pragmatism. Sexual discrimination, like racial bias, denied society a talent pool. "It was this time that my education in feminism took an important step forward. My discovery of the historical links between the struggles for the abolition of slavery and the rights of women gave me a new perspective that helped me balance the tensions created by the double burden of race and sex. Until now my haphazard awareness of discrimination because of gender had been submerged in an all-consuming preoccupation with racial injustice, and I tended to treat my first conscious exposure to sexism as an individual problem rather than one shared with other women. I was dismally ignorant of the history of the women's movement."[25]

While Murray was working on her doctorate at Yale University Law School, she was selected to serve on President John F. Kennedy's Commission on the Status on Women (PCSW) in 1961. According to Murray, the experience with the PCSW helped raise her awareness on the issue of gender. "I look back on this experience as an intensive consciousness raising process leading directly to my involvement in the new women's movement that surfaced a few years later." She had the opportunity to meet "like-minded women" who bonded and created an "informal feminist network" that played a significant role in pushing for women's equality. Because of her training as a lawyer, Murray wrote a memorandum that was adopted by the PCSW in 1963: "American Women: Report of the President's Commission on the Status of Women." Instead of advocating an equal rights amendment, the memo urged that sexual equality be won through litigation enforcing the Fourteenth Amendment.[26]

After the PCSW completed its work and disbanded, Murray became involved in an effort to save anti–sex discrimination legislation. When she and others from the informal network of women learned that there was an attempt by Senator Everett Dirksen to exclude the term *sex* from legislation prohibiting employment discrimination, Murray wrote a memo arguing that there are few jobs in the United States where sex is a factor. Her successful memo on the need to include sex in the bill led to sex being included in Title VII of the 1964 Civil Rights Act.[27]

Throughout her autobiography Murray elaborated on how she attempted to dismantle racial and sexual discrimination through personal efforts and accomplishments. Murray noted that in 1965 she became the first African American to receive the degree of doctor of juridical science from Yale. But the autobiographical work constantly notes a collective effort to break down barriers to equality. She called for the formation of a national ad hoc committee of women to act as a pressure group. She contended that women needed an organization similar to the NAACP. Her approach was to create an organization that could attract women across a wide political spectrum. In June 1966 Murray, Betty Friedan, and other women created the National Organization of Women.[28]

Murray's involvement in moderate approaches to winning sexual equality would give way in the 1970s to a more radical demand and put her in opposition to one of the most venerated institutions in the country, the Episcopal Church. "Inevitably, my growing feminist consciousness led me to do battle with the Episcopal Church over the submerged position of women in our denomination." As a child she realized that she could not be an acolyte but accepted this sexual exclusion without question. But as she became aware of the notable absence of women in the performance of the eucharist, she decided she would not tolerate this form of discrimination. She wrote a letter condemning the church for its official policy of excluding women from leadership positions. She adopted the language of the church by calling the institution's exclusionary policy sinful. Murray raised questions about the practice of discrimination. "If as I believe, it is a privilege to assist the priest in the solemn Eucharist, to hold the candles for the reading of the Gospel, to be the lay reader at the formal church wide 10:30 service, why is this privilege not accorded to all members without regard to sex? Suppose only white people did these things? Or only Negroes? Or only Puerto Ricans? We would see immediately that the church is guilty of grave discrimination. There is no difference between discrimination because of race and discrimination because of sex. I believe ... that if one is wrong, the other is wrong." Murray called for a frank discussion on sexism in the church with the objective of "opening every office and activity in connection with the worship services to both sexes equally, and should bars to this equality be imposed by the diocese or other church hierarchy, to take appropriate steps to request the removal of these barriers."[29] This letter was a critique of the symbols of maleness. But this seemingly moderate approach was in fact revolutionary: though Murray called for a discussion, she knew that there was no reasonable justification for sexual discrimination. The letter assumed that the church could not provide a justification for its practice; therefore, it would be forced to relinquish what was essentially no more than a male privilege grounded in religious tradition.

Murray would later learn that the Episcopal Church did not have gender-codified hurdles to a woman's gaining the position of acolyte; the exclusion of women was based on custom. In a sense, overcoming custom proved a much more difficult task than overcoming legal restrictions. There were women, whom Murray classified as "traditionalist," who publicly opposed any effort to break down gender barriers that kept women from serving as priests or acolytes or having a leading role in the hierarchy of the church. She also found an ecumenical "sisterhood," women who were of like mind in the Episcopal Church and other women who were challenging the conventional patriarchy of their religious institutions.[30]

In her autobiography Murray did not just point out her accomplishments; she also described the great personal sacrifices she made in her struggle to achieve an egalitarian society. In the 1960s she didn't think about women becoming ordained priests, but her involvement in NOW and a burgeoning women's movement raised her consciousness. As her commitment to feminism deepened, "my growing feminist consciousness led me to do battle with the Episcopal Church over submerged position of women in our denomination."[31] By the 1970s she challenged the patriarchy of the church by making a personal decision. She resigned her position as a tenured professor at Brandeis University, a position that brought her comfort and security and assured her a pension when she retired, and decided to become an Episcopal priest. This personal choice once again noted her willingness to forfeit individual gain for the collective good, and at age sixty-two, she enrolled at General Theological Seminary. As the oldest and only black woman seminarian there she encountered both racial and sexual discrimination. Because of her legal training and analytical skills, she was accused of being abrasive. Nevertheless, Murray encouraged other women not to drop out of the seminary even when the Episcopal Convention voted against the ordination of women priests. As a woman activist in the church, she joined with other women to support the effort of five women deacons who sought to be ordained as priests at St. John the Divine. When the bishop ordained men with the same qualifications and rejected the five women, Murray joined the five and other women who silently marched out of the church in protest. The women called themselves the "Church in Exile."[32]

This act was one of many protests led by women as they attempted to open the priesthood to women. One of the largest and most significant protests was the "Philadelphia Ordination" in July 1974 when over two thousand people attended the ordination of Jeannette Picard. Although the House of Bishops declared the ordination invalid, it was a moral victory because an Episcopal bishop had performed the ceremony and because a huge turnout supported the action. Because of this and other actions, the Episcopal Church in 1976 recognized the ordination of women, and on January 1, 1977, the first ordination of a woman took place. On January 8, Pauli Murray, at the age of sixty-six, became one of the first women, and the first black woman, to be ordained as a priest in the Episcopal Church.

Her personal journey to eradicate racial and sexual obstacles did not end with her ordination. She used the pulpit to continue the challenge to patriarchy and racism. In one such sermon, "Male and Female He Created Them," she contended that God created men and women in his image. In spite of the fact that they "share equally in the dominion over the earth, what has in fact happened is that sexism—the dominance of a patriarchal male-oriented society—is the oldest and most stubborn form of human oppression and has served as a model for other forms of human exploitation and alienation."[33]

Ella Baker and Pauli Murray made major intellectual contributions to the struggle for human equality. Because of their insistence that gender, along with race, take priority in the struggle for equality, they forced social protest movements, institutions, and the entire nation to place the goal of the eradication of sexual discrimination at the forefront. Through their efforts they helped raise the consciousness of men and women to the importance of gender as a civil rights issue. Just as important, they helped alter the culture of male chauvinism among America's churches. Although Baker was much more critical of a charismatic black clergy that excluded the participation of women and people at the grass roots than Murray, the latter did criticize the male-dominated leadership of the civil rights movement. She informed A. Philip Randolph, the organizer of the March on Washington, that she had been "increasingly perturbed over the blatant disparity between the major role which Negro women have played and are playing in the crucial grass-roots levels of our struggle and the minor role of leadership they have been assigned in the national policy-making decisions. It is indefensible to call a national march on Washington and send out a Call which contains the name of not a single woman leader."[34]

Scholars note that Baker and Murray fall into the category of womanist. In its simplest definition a womanist is a woman who embraces both gender and race without giving priority to one over the other. They both are central in the fight for equality.

Baker's and Murray's uphill struggle for racial and gender equality has shifted our thinking about the meaning of democracy.

Conclusion

Intellectual history in the United States usually has been described as if it were a Whites Only project. Only a handful of blacks have broken into the standard textbooks—obvious choices such as Frederick Douglass, W. E. B. Du Bois, and the rare minister such as Martin Luther King Jr. The essays gathered together in this book demonstrate that the black contribution to intellectual history has been much greater than the scholarly literature suggests. And this book is not comprehensive. It only samples that contribution. It demonstrates that there are no racial boundaries to intellectual history in the United States. Blacks have been at the center of this history, and their contributions have benefited all Americans.

This book also demonstrates that geography has not defined the black contribution. The few black religious leaders whom we read about (with the possible exception of Malcolm X) are usually from the South. This book shows that blacks throughout the United States have participated. The struggle for civil rights has not been just a southern problem. The religious intellectuals who have participated in this struggle have lived in the North and South. The struggle has been a national struggle.

But the major point of this book is that there has been an important religious content to this contribution. Intellectual history is not simply a secular project. And blacks have played a central role in that history. The role of both blacks and religion need to be better integrated into our understanding of intellectual history in the United States.

At the same time, we should not be uncritical of the role black religious leaders have played. Charismatic male clergy have made important contributions, but they are human beings and have their failings and limitations just like the rest of us. Charismatic leaders have been important, but they must be questioned and held accountable by their memberships and the broader society. We must be on the lookout for poor tactics, personal agendas, charlatans, and buffoons.

Further, a more complete history of any leader or any church would demonstrate the important role that the broader membership and community have played. No leader ever leads alone. This book has attempted to remind us of the vital role that black religious leaders have played in intellectual and political history in the United States. But social history has taught us the important leadership role that rank-and-file community members have also played in this process. A more complete history must better describe their contribution.

The two chapters that open and close this book add the important argument that religious leadership has not been restricted to male ministers. Even the contributions of a man as critical of religion and the church as A. Phillip Randolph was still strongly shaped by the black church. Although he was critical of the church, he recognized the strength of its language and the necessity of working with its ministers and membership. It demonstrates that religiously informed leadership has not been restricted to ministers. The closing chapter demonstrates that our understanding of leadership has to be broadened beyond a male model. Women such as Ella Baker and Pauli Murray have not received sufficient credit in their lifetimes for their vital leadership and service. This is still true today. Newspapers quote the comments of Jesse Jackson, Al Sharpton, and Louis Farrakhan almost every day. But how often do we hear the voices of our female leaders? And how often are they sufficiently acknowledged even within their own churches and communities? The struggle to better understand and reshape our world continues. That struggle is not only against the oppression of a broader society. It also exists within our own communities.

Black religious leaders have played a central role in shaping intellectual history in the United States. These essays are only the beginning of a better understanding of that contribution.

Notes

Notes to Introduction

1. Without a doubt, the most celebrated black intellectual of the twentieth century was W. E. B. Du Bois. There has been a plethora of works on Du Bois and his writings. In fact, one might argue that over the last ten years there has been a Du Bois industry, from David Lewis's Pulitzer Prize–winning and definitive two volumes on the life and times of Du Bois to Hazel Carbey's harsh but objective critique of Du Bois's *Souls of Black Folk* and how he mapped out a course for an exclusive black male leadership.
2. Phillip Foner, *American Socialism and Black Americans* (Westport, Conn.: Greenwood Press, 1977) is a rare exception to the academic literature on the black religious left.
3. Harold Cruse, *The Crisis of the Negro Intellectual* (New York: William Morrow & Company, 1967); Kevin Gaines, *Uplifting the Race: Race Leadership, Politics, and Culture in the Twentieth Century* (Chapel Hill, N.C.: University of North Carolina Press, 1996); W. D. Wright, *Black Intellectuals, Black Cognition, and a Black Aesthetic* (Westport, Conn.: Praeger Publishers, 1997).
4. William M. Banks, *Black Intellectuals* (New York: W. W. Norton, 1996), p. 243.
5. Ibid., pp. 247–300.
6. Cornel West, *Prophetic Fragments* (Grand Rapids, Mich.: William B. Eerdmans Publishing Company, 1988), pp. 3–12; idem., *Prophesy Deliverance: An Afro-American Revolutionary Christianity* (Philadelphia: Westminster Press, 1982), pp. 95–105.
7. Henry J. Young, *Major Black Religious Leaders Since 1940* (Nashville, Tenn.: Abingdon, 1979), p. 152.
8. Randall Burkett and Richard Newman, eds., *Black Apostles: Afro-American Clergy Confront the Twentieth Century* (Boston: G. K. Hall, 1978).
9. Mark Chapman, *Christianity on Trial: African-American Religious Thought before and after Black Power* (Maryknoll, N.Y.: Orbis Books, 1996).
10. Charles S. Johnson "The New Frontage on American Life," in Alain Locke, ed., *The New Negro: An Interpretation* (1925; reprint New York: Arno Press, 1968), pp. 285–86).
11. The most recent works on Amiri Baraka are Jerry Gafio Watts, *Amiri Baraka: The Politics and Art of a Black Intellectual* (New York: New York University Press, 1991) and Komozi Woodard, *A Nation within a Nation: Amiri Baraka (LeRoi Jones) and Black Power Politics* (Chapel Hill, N.C.: University of North Carolina Press, 1999). For Hubert Harrison see, Jeffrey B. Perry, ed., *A Hubert Harrison Reader* (Middletown, Conn.: Wesleyan University Press, 2001). Some of the best works on James are Selwyn Reginald Cudjoe and William E. Cain, eds., *C. L. R. James: His Intellectual Legacies* (Amherst, Mass.: University of Massachusetts, 1995); Martin Glaberman, ed., *C. L. R. James on Revolutionary Organization* (Jackson, Miss.: University of Mississippi Press, 1999); Ken Worcester, *C. L. R. James: A Politial Biography* (Albany, N.Y.: State University Press of New York, 1999).

12. Wright, *Black Intellectuals, Black Cognition, and a Black Aesthetic*, p. x.
13. Barry Burke and Mark K. Smith, "Antonio Gramsci," www.infed.org/thinkers/et-gram.htm

Notes to Chapter 1

1. A. Philip Randolph to Organizing Committees, Secretaries, Treasurers of the Sleeping Car Porters, July 16, 1926, box, 1, folder 8, Papers of the Brotherhood of Sleeping Car Porters at the Chicago Historical Society, hereafter BSCP Papers.
2. Jervis Anderson, *A. Philip Randolph: A Biographical Portrait* (New York: Harcourt Brace Jovanovich, 1973), p. 25.
3. Anderson, *A. Philip Randolph*, pp. 51–52.
4. Paula Pfeffer, *A. Philip Randolph, Pioneer of the Civil Rights Movement* (Baton Rouge, La.: Louisiana State University Press, 1990), pp. 11–12.
5. Ibid., pp. 23–24.
6. Benjamin Quarles, "A. Philip Randolph, Labor Leader at Large," in John Hope Franklin and August Meier, eds., *Black Leaders of the Twentieth Century* (Urbana, Ill.: University of Illinois Press, 1982), pp. 139–65.
7. Daniel Davis, *Mr. Black Labor: The Story of A. Philip Randolph, Father of the Civil Rights Movement* (New York: E. P. Dutton, 1972), pp. 4–7.
8. Susan Curtis, *A Consuming Faith: The Social Gospel and Modern American Culture* (Baltimore: Johns Hopkins University Press, 1991), pp. 2–4.
9. Ibid., pp. 5–6, 81–85.
10. Melinda Chareauvert, *Marching Together: Women of the Brotherhood of Sleeping Car Porters* (Urbana, Ill.: University of Illinois Press, 1998), p. 6; Randolph, "The New Negro, the New Crowd," *Messenger*, May–June 1919; also in Nathan Huggins, ed., *Voices of the Harlem Renaissance* (New York: Oxford University Press, 1995), pp. 18–20.
11. Randolph to Webster, Aug. 27, 1928, BSCP Papers, box 3, folder 7.
12. Ibid.
13. Hazel Carby, *Race Men* (Cambridge, Mass.: Harvard University Press, 2000); Randolph to Webster, Sept. 20, 1926, BSCP Papers, box 1, folder 10.
14. Randolph to Dear Brother and Friend, Dec. 21, 1926, BSCP Papers, box 1, folder 13.
15. Randolph to Webster, August 24, 1926, BSCP Papers, box 1, folder 9; Randolph to Webster, Feb. 28, 1927, BSCP Papers, box 1, folder 15.
16. Smith to Randolph, May 22, 1927; William H. Harris, *Keeping the Faith: A. Philip Randolph, Milton P. Webster and the Brotherhood of Sleeping Car Porters, 1925-37* (Urbana, Ill.: University of Illinois Press, 1977), pp. 121–22.
17. Harris, pp. 121–22; Flyer listing speakers (n.d.), BSCP Papers, box 3, folder 7.
18. Webster to Moore, Oct. 12, 1927, BSCP Papers, box 2, folder 8; Moore to Webster, Apr. 27, 1927, BSCP Papers, box 2, folder 2.
19. Moore to Webster, Nov. 2, 1927, BSCP Papers, box 2, folder 9; Moore to Webster, February 16, 1928, BSCP Papers, box 3, folder 2.
20. Moore to Webster, Nov. 2, 1927, BSCP Papers, box 2, folder 9; Randolph to Webster, February 19, 1928, BSCP Papers, box 2, folder 3.
21. Harris, *Keeping the Faith*, pp. 40–41.
22. Randolph to Webster, Nov. 17, 1926, BSCP Papers, box 1, folder 12.
23. Harris, *Keeping the Faith*, pp. 105–6.
24. Randolph, "Taking Strike Vote," BSCP's Bulletin, Mar. 26, 1928, BSCP Papers, box 3, folder 3.
25. Ibid.
26. Ibid.

27. Ibid.
28. Ibid.
29. Chateauvert, *Marching Together*, p. 88; "Women's Club Hears Randolph," *Flash* (n.d.), BSCP Papers, box 3, folder 9.
30. Chateauvert, *Marching Together*, pp. 30–31.
31. Randolph to Webster, Nov. 17, 1927, BSCP Papers, box 2, folder 9; Randolph to Webster, Nov. 19th, 1927, BSCP Papers, box 2, folder 9.
32. Randolph to Organizers, Secretaries, Treasurers of the Brotherhood of Sleeping Car Porters, July 16, 1926, BSCP Papers, box 1, folder 8.
33. Randolph to Webster, Nov. 19, 1927, box folder 9.
34. Randolph to Webster, Nov. 15, 1927, box 2, folder 9.
35. Randolph to Webster, Nov. 15, 1927; telegram, Randolph to Webster, May 27, 1928, BSCP Papers, box 3, folder 5.
36. David T. Beito, *From Mutual Aid to the Welfare State: Fraternal Societies and Social Services, 1890-1967* (Chapel Hill, N.C.: University of North Carolina Press, 2000), pp. 2–27.
37. Randolph to Webster, July 17, 1928, BSCP Papers, box 7, folder 7.
38. Ibid.; M.W. Frater and Claude Brodeur, "Sit Lux et Lux Fuit," June 29, 1997, http://sric-canada.org/fraternalism.html
39. Greg LeRoy, "The Founding Heart of A. Philip Randolph's Union: Milton P. Webster and Chicago's Pullman Porters Organize, 1925–1937," *Labor's Heritage*, July 1991, p. 27; Beth Tompkins Bates, "The Brotherhood," *Chicago in Modern Times*, pp. 386–87; Beth Tompkins Bates, *Pullman Porters and the Rise of Protest Politics in Black America, 1925-1945* (Chapel Hill, N.C.: The University of North Carolina Press, 2001), pp. 75–76.
40. Poster, Public Mass Meeting, Sunday, February 3, 1929, BSCP Papers, box 3, folder 9; Public Mass Meeting at Metropolitan Community Church, April 22, 1929, BSCP Papers, box 3, folder 4; flyer, Public Mass Meeting at Metropolitan Community Church, August 4, 1929, BSCP Papers, box 3, folder 1.
41. Randolph to Webster, Dec. 21, 1927, BSCP Papers, box 2, folder 8; Webster to Randolph, Jan. 4, 1928, BSCP Papers, box 3, folder; flyer.
42. Webster to Randolph, Mar. 31, 1928, BSCP Papers, 1928, box 3, folder 3.
43. Webster to Randolph, Jan. 5, 1927, BSCP Papers, box 1, folder 4.
44. LeRoy, "The Founding Heart of A. Philip Randolph's Union, p. 27: Bates, "The Brotherhood," p. 388; Webster to Randolph, Jan. 4, 1928, BSCP Papers, box 3, folder 2; Invitation to Chicago's First Labor Conference, Jan. 23, BSCP Papers, box 3, folder 1.
45. Bates, "The Brotherhood," pp. 387–88.
46. Webster to Ida B. Wells, Sept. 15, 1926, BSCP Papers, box 1, folder 10; Webster to Randolph, Sept. 16, 1926, BSCP Papers, box 1, folder 10; Webster to Randolph, Sept. 24, 1926, BSCP Papers, box 1, folder 10; Randolph to Webster, Sept. 11, 1926, BSCP Papers, box 3, folder 10.
47. Ibid., pp. 389–90; Bates, *Pullman Porters and the Rise of Protest Politics in Black America*, pp. 102–3; LeRoy, "The Founding Heart of A. Philip Randolph's Union," p. 27.
48. Randolph to Webster, Jan. 8, 1927, BSCP Papers, box 1, folder 14; Webster to Randolph, Dec. 17, 1927, BSCP Papers, box 2, folder 10.
49. LeRoy, "The Founding Heart," p. 37.
50. D. W. Johnson to John Fitzpatrick, President of the Chicago Federation of Teachers, Jan. 25, 1928, BSCP Papers, box 3, folder 1; Program, Lincoln Community Men's Club Presents the Brotherhood of Sleeping Car Porters, Jan. 29, 1928, BSCP Papers, box 3, folder 1.

51. Sixth Negro Labor Conference, Feb. 5, 6, 7, 1928, BSCP Papers, box 3, folder 2.
52. Address of Hon. William Green, President, American Federation of Labor, at Mass Meeting Held under the auspices of the Pullman Porters Organization Affiliated with the AF of L, Abyssinian Baptist Church, New York, June 30 1929, BSCP Papers, box 3, folder 10.
53. New York Leading Negro Ministers Endorse Pullman Porters Union (n.d), BSCP Papers, box 2, folder 2.
54. Flyer, Sixth Negro Labor Conference, February 5, 6, 7, 1928; E. J. Bradley to Webster, Apr. 13, 1927, BSCP Papers, box 2, folder 2.
55. Congregational Education Society Records, 1816–1956, www.14beacon.org
56. Ibid.; Webster to Randolph, Mar. 5, 1928, BSCP Papers, box 3, folder 2.
57. Randolph to Webster, Mar. 7, 1928, BSCP Papers, box 3, folder 3.
58. Randolph to Chaffee, Mar. 29, 1923, box 5, Randolph, A. Philip, folder; Chaffee to Randolph, Dec. 5, 1927, BSCP Papers, box 13, Randolph, A. Philip, folder, Special Collections, Syracuse University.
59. Randolph to Webster, Sept. 28, 1928, BSCP Papers, box 3, folder 3.
60. Information Service, Feb. 9, 1929, published by the Department of Research and Education of the Federal Council of Churches of Christ in America. A copy of this edition is found in the BSCP Papers, box 3, folder 9.
61. Ibid.
62. Robert Lee Sutherland, "An Analysis of Negro Churches in Chicago" (Ph.D. dissertation, University of Chicago, 1930), pp. 55–59; Benjamin Elijah Mays and Joseph William Nicholson, *The Negro's Church* (New York: Russell & Russell, 1933), p. 312.
63. St. Clair Drake and Horace R. Cayton, *Black Metropolis: A Study of Negro Life in a Northern City* (Chicago: University of Chicago Press, 1993), pp. 611–21.
64. Webster to Randolph, Mar. 26, 1927, and Randolph to Webster, Mar. 28, 1927, BSCP Papers, box 2, folder 1; Randolph to Webster, Aug. 23, 1923, BSCP Papers, box 3, folder 7.
65. Randolph to Webster, Sept. 27, 1926, BSCP Papers, box 1, folder 10.
66. Kevin Damato, "Language & Consciousness," www.wpunj.edu/cohss/philosophy/course/nietnet/speak.htm
67. Randolph to Webster, Aug. 25, 1926, BSCP Papers, box 1, folder 9; Randolph to Organizing Committees, Secretaries, Treasurers of the Sleeping Car Porters, July 16, 1926, BSCP Papers, box 1, folder 8.
68. Randolph to Webster, Mar. (?), 1928; Civilla wrote the words to the song in 1905 and her husband composed the music in 1905. "God Will Take Care of You," http://www.cyberhymnal.org/htm/g/w/gwiltake.htm
69. Randolph letter to the membership, Feb. 15, 1927, BSCP box 1, folder 15.
70. Randolph to Webster, Apr. 23, 1927, BSCP Papers, box 2, folder 2.
71. Randolph to "Dear Friend and Brother," Feb. 15, 1927, BSCP Papers, box 1, folder 15.
72. Randolph to Webster, July 5, 1927, BSCP Papers, box 2, folder 5.
73. Randolph to Webster, May 5, 1927, BSCP Papers, box 2, folder 3.
74. Randolph to Webster May 4, 1928, BSCP Papers, box 3, folder 5; Randolph to Webster, Sept. 10, 1928, BSCP Papers, box 2, folder 8.

Notes to Chapter 2

1. Gerald Horne, "Myth and the Making of Malcolm X," *American Historical Review* 98, no. 2 (April 1993), pp. 442–43.
2. Thomas J. Sugrue, *The Origins of the Urban Crisis: Race and Inequality in Postwar Detroit* (Princeton, N.J.: Princeton University Press, 1996), p. 7.

3. Manning Marable, *Race, Reform and Rebellion: The Second Reconstruction in Black America, 1945–1990* (Jackson, Miss.: University Press of Mississippi, 1991), pp. 27–28; idem., *How Capitalism Underdeveloped Black America* (Boston: South End Press, 1983), pp. 204–6.
4. Harold Cruse, *The Crisis of the Negro Intellectual* (New York: Quill, 1984), pp. 147–70, 180–89, 220–24, 267–307.
5. Clarence Taylor, *The Black Churches of Brooklyn* (New York: Columbia University Press, 1994), p. 118.
6. Ibid., pp. 116–18.
7. Ibid., p. 119.
8. Kevin Gaines, *Uplifting the Race: Black Leadership, Politics, and Culture in the Twentieth Century* (Chapel Hill, N.C.: University of North Carolina Press, 1996), pp. 19–46; Glenda Elizabeth Gilmore, *Gender and Jim Crow: Women and the Politics of White Supremacy in North Carolina, 1996–1920* (Chapel Hill, N.C.: University of North Carolina Press, 1996), pp. 147–75; Evelyn Brooks Higgenbotham, *Righteous Discontent: The Women's Movement in the Black Baptist Church, 1880–1920* (Cambridge, Mass.: Harvard University Press, 1993), pp. 188–229.
9. Protestant Council of the City of New York, *Protestant Directory of Metropolitan New York, 1950–1952*.
10. Taylor, *Black Churches of Brooklyn*, pp. 133–35.
11. *Amsterdam News*, Aug. 22, 1953.
12. Andrew Michael Manes, *Southern Civil Religions in Conflict: Black and White Baptists and Civil Rights* (Athens, Ga.: University of Georgia Press, 1987), p. 53; Taylor, *Black Churches of Brooklyn*, p. 119.
13. Author interview with Milton Galamison, Oct. 12, 1987; oral history interview, Moorland-Spingarn Research Center, Howard University; Clarence Taylor, *Knocking at Our Own Door: Milton A. Galamison and the Struggle to Integrate New York City Schools* (New York: Columbia University Press, 1997), pp. 37, 68–72.
14. Author interview with Gardner C. Taylor, Aug. 1, 1988; Taylor, *Black Churches of Brooklyn*, pp. 139–63. Although Galamison participated in the protest and was one of the ministers who signed the agreement with Rockefeller, he would state that it was a betrayal of the protesters, Author interview with Milton Galamison, Oct. 21, 1987.
15. *Amsterdam News*, Feb. 29, 1936; Taylor, *Black Churches of Brooklyn*, pp. 122–23; *Amsterdam News*, Dec. 21, 1931; *New York Age*, Dec. 2, 1943.
16. *Amsterdam News*, Apr. 29, 1944; Taylor, *Black Churches of Brooklyn*, pp. 125–27.
17. Taylor, *Black Churches of Brooklyn*, pp. 123–24.
18. Taylor, *Knocking at Our Own Door*, pp. 26–37; Taylor, *Black Churches of Brooklyn*, p. 128.
19. Taylor, *Knocking at Our Own Door*, pp. 55–65.
20. Ibid, pp., 116–207; Lisa Yvette Waller, "Holding Back the Dawn: Milton A. Galamison and the Fight for School Integration in New York City, a Northern Civil Rights Struggle, 1948–1968" (Ph.D. dissertation, Duke University, 1998), pp. 344–494.
21. *Amsterdam News*, Feb. 29, 1936; Harold Connolly, *A Ghetto Grows in Brooklyn* (New York: New York University Press, 1977), p. 93.
22. Taylor, *Knocking at Our Own Door*, pp. 35–46.
23. Ibid., pp. 35–38.
24. Taylor, *Black Churches of Brooklyn*, pp. 125–26; E. David Cronon, *Black Moses:*

The Story of Marcus Garvey and the Universal Negro Improvement Association (Madison, Wis.: University of Wisconsin Press, 1969), pp. 178–82.

25. David Howard-Pitney, *The Afro-American Jeremiad: Appeals for Social Justice in America* (Philadelphia: Temple University Press, 1990), pp. 5–56.
26. Grant Wacker, *Heaven Below: Early Pentecostals and American Culture* (Cambridge, Mass.: Harvard University Press, 2001), pp. 5–17, 217–26; Taylor, *Black Churches of Brooklyn*, pp. 53–65.
27. Gary Marx, *Protest and* Prejudice (New York: Harper and Row, 1969); Hans A. Baer and Merrill Singer, *African-American Religion in the Twentieth Century: Varieties of Protest and Accommodation* (Knoxville, Tenn.: University of Tennessee Press, 1992), pp. 171–78; C. Eric Lincoln and Lawrence Mamiya, *The Black Church in the African-American Experience* (Durham, N.C.: Duke University Press, 1990), pp. 78–91, 221–27.
28. Author interview with Ulysses L. and Louise Corbett, Brooklyn, Apr. 20, 1990; author interview with Samuel Gibson, Brooklyn, May 8, 1990.
29. Taylor, *Black Churches of Brooklyn*, pp. 56–57.

Notes to Chapter 3

1. Smallwood Williams, "Against U.S. Filibuster Tactics," in *Significant Sermons* (Washington, D.C.: Bible Way Church, 1971), pp. 110–11.
2. Other black Pentecostals who were politically active are Bishop Frederick D. Washington, pastor of Washington Temple Church of God in Christ in Brooklyn, and Bishop Frank Clemons, pastor of the First Church of God in Christ in Brooklyn. See Clarence Taylor, *Black Churches of Brooklyn* (New York: Columbia University Press, 1994).
3. William H. Becker, "The Black Church: Manhood and Mission," in Timothy E. Fulop and Albert J. Raboteau, *African-American Religion: Interpretive Essays in History and Culture* (New York: Routledge, 1997), pp. 180–81.
4. For works on gender and African-American history, see Darlene Clark Hine and Earnestine Jenkins, *A Question of Manhood: A Reader in Black Men's History and Masculinity* (Bloomington, Ind.: Indiana University Press, 1999); Gail Bederman, *Manliness and Civilization: A Cultural History of Gender and Race in the United States, 1880–1917* (Chicago: University of Chicago Press, 1996); Hazel V. Carby, *Race Men* (Cambridge, Mass.: Harvard University Press, 1998).
5. Smallwood Williams, *This Is My Story: A Significant Life Struggle* (Washington, D.C.: William Willoughby Publishers, 1981), pp. 39–47; Sherry Sherrod DuPree, *Biographical Dictionary of African-Americans Holiness-Pentecostals, 1880–1990* (Washington, D.C.: Middle Atlantic Regional Press, 1989), 162–63.
6. Ibid., pp. 49–50; Pauline Marie Rosenau, *Post-Modernism and the Social Sciences: Insights, Inroads, and Intrusions* (Princeton, N.J.: Princeton University Press, 1992), p. 6.
7. Ibid.
8. Ibid., pp. 41–42.
9. Ibid., pp. 43–45.
10. Williams, *This Is My Story*, pp. 48–50, 70.
11. Ibid., pp. 49–52; Taylor, *Black Churches of Brooklyn*, pp. 39–42; Williams, *This Is My Story*, p. 23; Williams, *Significant Sermons*, pp. 26–27.
12. Williams, *This Is My Story*, pp. 60–61.
13. Howard Thurman, *Jesus and the Disinherited* (Nashville, Tenn.: Abingdon, 1949), p. 2; see Charles H. Long, "Assessment and New Departures for a Study of Black Religion in the United States," in Gayraud Wilmore, ed., *African-American Religious Studies: An Interdisciplinary Anthology* (Durham, N.C.: Duke University

Press, 1995), pp. 33–47; Walter Earl Fluker and Catherine Tumber, eds., *A Strange Freedom: The Best of Howard Thurman on Religious Experience and Public Life* (Boston: Beacon Press, 1998), pp. 131–47.

14. Mark Chapman, *Christianity on Trial: African-American Religious Thought before and after Black Power*, pp. 22–23; Fluker and Tumber, *A Strange Freedom*, pp. 211–19.
15. Ibid., pp. 52–53.
16. Williams, *This Is My Story*, pp. 53–54.
17. Ibid., pp. 53–54.
18. Ibid., pp. 59–64.
19. Ibid., pp. 65–72; Sherry DuPree, *Biographical Dictionary of African-American Holiness-Pentecostals*, pp. 162–63.
20.
21. James Henretta, David Brody, and Lynn Dummenil, *America: A Concise History*, vol. 2 (Boston: St. Martin's, 1999), pp. 689–90.
22. Ibid.
23. Williams, *Significant Sermons*, pp. 112–13.
24. Williams, *This Is My Story*, pp. 172–73.
25. Ibid., pp. 88–89; John 10:10, King James Bible.
26. Ibid., pp. 90–91.
27. Aihwa Ong, "Cultural Citizenship as Subject Making: Immigrants Negotiate Racial Boundaries in the United States," in Rodolfo Torres, Louis Miron, and Jonathan Xavier Inda, eds., *Race, Identity and Citizenship, a Reader* (Malden, Mass.: Blackwell, 1999), pp. 263–64.
28. Renato Rosaldo, "Cultural Citizenship, Inequality, and Multiculturalism," in Rodolfo D. Torres, Louis F. Miron, and Jonathan Xavier Inda, eds., *Race, Identity and Citizenship, a Reader* (Malden, Mass.: Blackwell, 1999), pp. 254–55.
29. Williams, *Significant Sermons*, pp. 112–14.
30. Williams, *Significant Sermons*, pp. 145–52.
31. Stanley Elkins, *Slavery: A Problem in American Institutional and Intellectual Life* (Chicago: University of Chicago Press, 1966).
32. Clarence Taylor, "Work for Democracy: Annie Stein and the Campaign for Civil Rights in Washington D.C.," manuscript.
33. Williams, *Significant Sermons*, pp. 54–56.
34. Ibid.
35. Ibid., pp. 58–64.
36. Lawrence Levine, *Black Culture and Black Consciousness* (New York: Oxford University Press, 1977), pp. 155–57; Hans Baer and Merrill Singer, *African-American Religion in the Twentieth Century: Varieties of Protest and Accommodation* (Knoxville, Tenn.: University of Tennessee Press, 1992), pp. 162–63, 166–72.
37. Bill Ashcroft, Gareth Griffiths, Helen Tiffin, *The Post-Colonial Studies Reader* (London: Routledge, 1995), p. 321.
38. Audio Tape Sermons (not titled), Jan. 1, 1990, Jan. 2, 1990, Jan. 3, 1990.
39. Ibid.
40. Williams, *Significant Sermons*, p. 62.
41. Williams, *This Is My Story*, p. 97.
42. Ibid., pp. 97–98.
43. Ibid.
44. Ibid., pp. 98–103.
45. Ibid., pp. 106–8.
46. Ibid., pp. 108–14.

47. Ibid., pp. 98–99.
48. Taylor, *Knocking at Our Own Door: Milton A. Galamison and the Struggle to Integrate New York City Schools* (New York: Columbia University Press, 1997), p. 45.
49. Richard Wright, *Black Boy* (New York: Harper & Row, 1996), pp. 174–76.
50. Gail Bederman, *Manliness and Civilization: A Cultural History of Gender and Race in the United States, 1880–1917* (Chicago: University of Chicago Press, 1996), pp. 7–31.
51. Elaine May, *Homeward Bound* (New York: Basic Books, 1988), pp. 93–98, 146.
52. Hazel V. Carby, *Race Men* (Cambridge, Mass.: Harvard University Press, 1998), pp. 21–22.
53. Photo insert in Williams's *This Is My Story*.
54. Williams, *This Is My Story*, p. 189.
55. Ibid., pp. 169–84.
56. Ibid., pp. 88–96.
57. *Washington Post* interview with Julius Hobson, July 3, 1972.
58. Smallwood Williams, "Bishop Rebuts Hobson's Story," *The Washington Post*, July 3, 1972.
59. Kobena Mercer, *Welcome to the Jungle: New Positions in Black Cultural Studies* (New York: Routledge, 1994), p. 136.
60. Miles Davis and Quincy Troupe, *Miles: The Autobiography of Miles Davis* (New York: Simon and Schuster, 1989), pp. 26–27.
61. Ibid. pp. 96–97.
62. Ibid. p. 183.
63. Ibid. p. 203.
64. Ibid. pp. 21–26.
65. Ibid., pp. 228, 366–77.
66. Ibid. p. 148.
67. James Cone, "The Theology of Martin Luther King, Jr.," *Union Seminary Quarterly Review* 40, no. 4 (1986), pp. 21–22.

Notes to Chapter 4

1. *Florida Historical Quarterly* 76, no. 1 (Summer 1997), p. 61; *Tequesta*, no. 48 (1988), pp. 158–59; Marvin Dunn, *Black Miami in the Twentieth Century* (Gainesville, Fla.: University Press of Florida, 1997), pp. 177–81, 194, 183, 191–93, 215, 218, 220–23, 228.
2. Peta Stephenson, "The Social Construction of Whiteness: 'Race' and White Privilege in the Class Room," http://www.ssn.flinders.edu.au/soci/SCW/stephenson.html
3. Raymond Mohl, "Shadows in the Sunshine: Race and Ethnicity in Miami," *Tequesta*, no. 49 (1989), pp. 68–69; Paul S. George, *Florida Historical Quarterly* 56, no. 4 (April 1978), pp. 433–39; Paul S. George and Thomas K. Petersen, *Tequesta*, no. 48 (1988), pp. 54–55; Paul S. George, "Policing Miami's Black Community, 1896–1930," in *Florida Historical Quarterly* 57 no. 4 (1979).
4. Paul S. George, "Colored Town, Miami's Black Community, 1896–1930," Florida Historical Quarterly 56, no. 4 (April 1978), pp. 438–40.
5. Dunn, *Black Miami*, p. 70; George, "Colored Town," pp. 440–41.
6. *Miami Times*, June 6, 1953.
7. The Cwest Club Calendar for the Year, 1941, The Black Archives, Miami, Florida.
8. Dunn, *Black Miami*, pp. 177–79.
9. Ibid., p. 179.
10. File on St. Agnes, Black Archives.

11. Pepper to Lovick P. Williams, February 11, 1944. Folder 16, box 14 Sect/31A Clark Pepper Papers, Florida State University.
12. John Egerton, *Speak Now Against the Day: The Generation before the Civil Rights Movement in the South* (Chapel Hill, N.C.: University of North Carolina Press, 1945), pp. 9–10, 29.
13. George, "Colored Town," p. 445.
14. David Colburn, "Rosewood and America in the Twentieth Century," *Florida Historical Quarterly* 76, no. 2 (Fall 1997), p. 3; Dunn, *Black Miami*, pp. 117–24; George, "Colored Town," p. 445; Eric Tscheschlok, "'So Goes the Negro'": Race and Labor in Miami, 1940–1963," *Florida Historical Quarterly* 76, no. 1 (Summer 1997), pp. 52–53.
15. Sidney Poitier, *This Life* (New York: Knopf, 1980), p. 41.
16. Ibid., pp. 42–43.
17. Dunn, *Black Miami*, pp. 133–36; Eric Tscheschlok, "'So Goes the Negro,'" pp. 60–61.
18. Weil R. McMillen, *Dark Journey: Black Mississippi in the Age of Jim Crow* (Chicago: University of Illinois Press, 1990), p. 285.
19. Culmer, "Black and White," Black Archives.
20. Culmer to Quigg, May 30, 1938, John Culmer Family Papers, Black Archives; *Miami Daily News*, June 10, 1938.
21. John E. Culmer, "Keeping the Record Straight" in "Black and White," John Culmer Family Papers, Black Archives.
22. Ibid.; Dunn, *Black Miami*, pp.194–97.
23. Ibid.
24. Interdenominational Ministers' Alliance letter Mar. 15, 1938 in John Culmer Family Papers, Black Archives.
25. Culmer to Earl Brown, managing editor of *The Amsterdam News*, Aug. 18, 1938, John Culmer Family Papers, Black Archives.
26. Culmer to Stephen Munulty, Jan 14, 1947, in John Culmer Family Papers.
27. Address delivered by Rev. John E. Culmer over Station WKAT, Miami, Jan. 12, 1941, Black Archives.

Notes to Chapter 5

1. *Florida Historical Quarterly* 76, no. 1 (Summer 1997), p. 61; *Tequesta*, no. 48 (198), pp. 158–59; Marvin Dunn, *Black Miami in the Twentieth Century* (Gainesville, Fla.: University Press of Florida, 1997), pp. 177–81, 194, 183, 191–93, 215, 218, 220–23, 228). There are master's theses that focus on the struggle the NAACP had with the Florida Legislative Investigation Committee; for example, see, Kisha King Williams, "The Civil Rights Movement in Miami" (master's thesis, Florida International University, 1999), Bonnie Stark, "McCarthyism in Miami: Charley Johns and the Florida Legislative Investigation Committee, July1956 to July 1965" (master's thesis, University of Florida, 1985).
2. Carita Swanson Vonk, *Theodore R. Gibson: Priest, Prophet and Politician* (Miami, Fla.: Little River Press, 1997), p. 15.
3. Ibid., pp. 16–18.
4. *Miami Times*, June 11, 1949, Sept. 23, 1950; Ben Green, *Before His Time: The Untold Story of Harry T. Moore, America's First Civil Rights Martyr* (New York: Free Press, 1999), pp. 24–37, 57–64.
5. *Miami Times*, Jan. 14, 1950.
6. Moore, *Before His Time*, pp. 44–108, 164–90, 252; Robert W. Saunders Sr., *Bridging The Gap: Continuing the Florida NAACP Legacy of Harry T. Moore* (Tampa, Fla.: University of Tampa Press, 2000), p. 119.

7. *Miami Times*, Apr. 1, 1950.
8. *Miami Times*, Apr. 7, 1951.
9. J. N. Byrd and J. A. Roberts to William W. Wolfarth; W. A. Morris to O. Henderson, *Miami Times*, Feb. 3, 1951.
10. *Miami Times*, Mar. 18, 1950.
11. Press Release, "NAACP to Protest Discrimination in Local Builders Union," (n.d., 1963), Branch Files 1956–65. Part III: C 23, NAACP Papers, Library of Congress.
12. Special Report by W. C. Patton, "The Campaign in the Miami Area," Branch Files, 1956–1965, Part III, C 23, NAACP Papers; *Miami Times*, July 2, 1949, Jan. 14, 1950, Feb. 24, 1951, May 13, 1950, Apr. 29, 1950, Apr. 4, 1951.
13. Gloster Current to Theodore Gibson, Jan. 30, 1957, Branch Files, NAACP Papers.
14. Copies of the resolutions are found in the Florida Legislative Investigation Committee brief presented to the Supreme Court of Florida; Juan T. Williams, *Thurgood Marshall: American Revolutionary* (New York: Times Books, 1998), pp. 255–57.
15. Lucille Black to Theodore Gibson, Mar. 14, 1958, Branch Files, 1956–65, III: c23.
16. Gary Gerstle, *American Crucible: Race and Nation in the Twentieth Century* (Princeton, N.J.: Princeton University Press, 2001), pp. 4–7, 246–47.
17. Mary Dudziak, *Cold War Civil Rights: Race and the Image of American Democracy* (Princeton. N.J.: Princeton University Press, 2001), pp. 37–46.
18. Gary Gerstle, *American Crucible*, pp. 249–251, Mary Dudziak, *Cold War Civil Rights*, 79–104.
19. *Eyes on the Prize* (film), episode 2, "Fighting Back."
20. Theodore Gibson to the editor of *Look* magazine, May 21, 1958. Branch files 1956065, Container No. 5 III: c23.
21. Aldon Morris, *The Origins of the Civil Rights Movement: Black Communities Organizing for Change* (New York: Free Press, 1984), pp. 30–33.
22. Thomas Borstelmann, *The Cold War and the Color Line* (Cambridge, Mass.: Harvard University Press, 2001), pp. 65, 108; Carol Polgrove, *Divided Minds: Intellectuals and the Civil Rights Movement* (New York: Norton, 2001), pp. 74–75.
23. Gerstle, *American Crucible*, p. 263.
24. Saunders, *Bridging the Gap*, p. 159; Confidential State of Florida Legislative Committee Progress Report," January 1957, Florida State Archives; Bonnie Stark, "McCarthyism in Florida: Charley Johns and the Florida Legislative Investigation Committee, July 1956 to July 1965" (master's thesis, University of Florida, 1985), pp. 21–35.
25. Report of the Florida Legislative Investigation Committee, Florida State Archives, Department of State, Series 1486, Carton 1, pp. 1–2.
26. Ibid., pp. 4–7.
27. Ibid., pp. 9–10.
28. Stark, "McCarthyism in Florida," pp. 35–37.
29. Stark, "McCarthyism in Florida," pp. 38–39; Kisha King Williams, "The Civil Rights Movement in Miami, 1930–1965" (master's thesis, Florida International University, 1999), pp. 62–64.
30. Transcript of Testimony before Florida Legislative Investigation Committee, February 9, 1961, pp. 247–48. A copy of the transcript is found at the Dade County Record Center.
31. "Statement to Be Made by Father Gibson before the FLIC."
32. Ibid.
33. Ibid.

34. *Gibson v. Florida Legislative Investigation Committee*, 372 U.W. 539 (1963); NAACP Press Release, Sept. 29, 1961, Branch Files 1956–65, Part III: c23 NAACP Papers.
35. Brief of Appellee in *Theodore Gibson, Ruth Perry, Vernell Albury and Grattan E. Graves, Jr. (Appellants) v. Florida Legislative Investigation Committee (Appellee) before the Supreme Court of Florida*, pp. 2–3.
36. Ibid., pp. 10–15.
37. Ibid., pp. 16–21.
38. "Communism and the NAACP," published by Georgia Commission of Education (n.d), Box AB-007, folder-33544-b.
39. Florida Legislative Investigation Committee (Appellee) before the Supreme Court of Florida, pp. 21–25.
40. Williams, "The Civil Rights Movement in Miami," p. 167.
41. Supreme Court Case, Gibson v. Florida Legislative Investigation Committee, case 372US539.
42. Ibid.
43. Godfrey Hodgson, *America in Our Time* (New York: Vintage Books, 1976), pp. 72–90.
44. Ibid.; Eric Foner, *The Story of American Freedom* (New York: Norton, 1998), p. 258. For the FLIC's investigation of homosexuals, see Bonnie Stark, "McCarthyism in Florida."

Notes to Chapter 6

1. Jim Sleeper, *The Closest of Strangers: Liberalism and the Politics of Race in New York* (New York: Norton, 1990), pp. 28–31.
2. Ibid, pp. 31–36.
3. Ibid., pp. 34–36.
4. Jim Sleeper, *Liberal Racism: How Fixating on Race Subverts the American Dream* (New York: Penguin Books, 1991), pp. 29–23.
5. Sleeper, *Closest of Strangers*, pp. 134–36.
6. Christopher Lasch, *The Revolt of the Elites and the Betrayal of Democracy* (New York: Norton, 1995), pp. 129–40.
7. David Horowitz, *Hating Whitey and Other Progressive Causes* (Dallas, Tex.: Spence Publishing Company, 1999), p. 6; *The Bob Grant Radio Show*, televised on C-Span, November 14, 1999.
8. Boston Public Radio, "The Connection," Mar. 2, 2000; Derrick Z. Jackson, "Sharpton: New Packaging, Same Guy," *Miami Herald*, Feb. 9, 2000.
9. "E. R. Sharp, "The Rev. Al Throws Pundits for a Loss," *New York Daily News*, Sept. 12, 1997; *Amsterdam News*, Aug. 7, 1997, Aug. 14, 1997, Jack White, "Big Al's Finest Hour," *Time*, Mar. 6, 2000, p. 28.
10. Jonathan Birnbaum and Clarence Taylor, eds. *Civil Rights Since 1787: A Reader on the Black Struggle* (New York: New York University Press, 2000), p. 758.
11. National Coalition for the Homeless, "Employment and Homelessness," Fact sheet number 4 (1998); www.nationalhomeless.org, "The New Poverty: A Generation of Homeless Families," Fact sheet number 2 (1992); Jack Newfield and Wayne Barrett, *City for Sale: Ed Koch and the Betrayal of New York* (New York: Harper and Row, 1988), pp. 156–57; Sleeper, *Closest of Strangers*, pp. 112–13).
12. Herbert D. Daughtry Sr., *No Monopoly on Suffering: Blacks and Jews in Crown Heights and Elsewhere* (Trenton: Africa World Press, 1997), pp. 59–61; Al Sharpton and Anthony Walton, *"Go Tell Pharaoh": The Autobiography of the*

Reverend Al Sharpton (New York: Doubleday, 1996), pp. 162–63); Leonard Buder, "Police Kill Woman Being Evicted; Officers Say She Wielded a Knife," *New York Times*, Oct. 30, 1984; Selwyn Raab, "Police and Victim's Daughter Clash on Shooting," *New York Times*, Nov. 2, 1984; "Ward Defends Police Actions in Bronx Death," *New York Times*, Nov. 3, 1984.

13. Daughtry, *No Monopoly on Suffering*, p. 82; Newfield and Barrett, *City for Sale*, p. 137; Edward I. Koch, *Mayor: An Autobiography* (New York: Simon & Schuster, 1984), pp. 209–14.

14. *Salon* interview with Al Sharpton, *Salon Magazine*, com\weeks\sharpton.2html

15. Sharpton, *Go and Tell Pharaoh*, pp. 115–16. Recently, there have been new works on the civil rights struggle in New York City, including Adina Back, "Up South in New York: The 1950s School Desegregation Struggles" (Ph.D. diss., New York University, 1997); Lisa Y. Waller, "Holding Back the Dawn: Milton A. Galamison and the Fight for School Integration in New York City, A Northern Civil Rights Struggle" (Ph.D. diss., Duke University, 1996).

16. Ibid., pp. 118–19.

17. Ibid., p. 134.

18. E. R. Ship, "The Rev. Al Throws Pundits for a Loss" *New York Daily News*, Sept. 12, 1997; Herb Boyd, "Town Hall Meeting Questions Attacks on Don King," *Amsterdam News*, Feb. 26, 1998.

19. Lynn Yaeger, "Al Sharpton's Fashion Journey: The Reverends's New Clothes," http://www.villagevoice.com/issues/0102/yaeger.shtml, January 10, 2001.

20. Ibid.

21. William Van Deburg, *New Day in Babylon: The Black Power Movement and American Culture, 1965–1975* (Chicago: University of Chicago Press, 1992), p. 201.

22. *Ebony* 52, no. 5 (March, 1998).

23. Ibid., p. 5; *Emerge* 11, no. 3 (December/January 2000); *Emerge* 10, no. 10 (September 1999); *Essence* 30, no. 9 (January 2000); *Black Enterprise* 30, no. 6 (January 2000).

24. Robin D. G. Kelley, *Black Rebels: Culture, Politics, and the Black Working Class* (New York: Free Press, 1994), pp. 167–68; Mauricio Mazon, *The Zoot-Suit Riots: The Psychology of Symbolic Annihilation* (Austin, Tex.: University of Texas Press, 1984), pp. 7–9.

25. Kobena Mercer, *Welcome to the Jungle: New Positions in Black Cultural Studies* (New York: Routledge, 1994), p. 118.

26. Clarence Taylor, *Black Churches of Brooklyn* (New York: Columbia University Press, 1994), pp. 231–33; *Village Voice*.

27. Marshall Frady, *Jesse: The Life and Pigrimage of Jesse Jackson* (New York: Random House, 1996), pp. 189–202.

28. For biographies of King, see David Garrow, *Bearing the Cross: Martin Luther King Jr., and the Southern Christian Leadership Conference* (New York: William Morrow, 1986); Taylor Branch, *Parting the Waters: America in the King Years, 1954–63* (New York: Touchstone Books, 1989); and David Levering Lewis, *King, A Biography* (Champaigne, Ill.: University of Illinois Press, 1978).

29. Jesse L. Jackson, "A Chance to Serve," *Black Scholar*, March/April 1988, pp. 17–21.

30. Sharpton, *Go and Tell Pharaoh*, pp. 64–65.

31. Ibid., pp. 175–90.

32. William Tatum, "For Sharpton, a Party at Ruth's Place," *Amsterdam News*, Aug. 14, 1997; Samgba Browne, "Sharptons Renew Wedding Vows," *Amsterdam News*, Feb. 26, 1998.

33. Sharpton, *Go and Tell Pharaoh*, pp. 141; "Ed Rollins Meets the Press," *Columbia Journalism Review*, January/February, 1994; *New York Times*, Nov. 13, 1993.
34. Herb Boyd, "Scholar Calls for Unity without Uniformity" *Amsterdam News*, Feb. 5–11, 1998.
35. Allison Mitchell, "Sharpton's Headache: To Get Out the Vote," *New York Times*, Sept. 9, 1992; *New York Newsday*, Sept. 8, 1992; Clarence Taylor, *Black Churches of Brooklyn*, p. 229.
36. Sharpton, *Go and Tell Pharaoh*, pp. 226–28, 253–54; Dave Saltonstall and Richard T. Pienciak, "Faces to Watch in 1998: Due to Go Places," *New York Daily News*, Jan. 4, 1998.
37. Ben Keppel, *The Work of Democracy: Ralph Bunche, Kenneth B. Clark, Lorraine Hansberry, and the Cultural Politics of Race* (Cambridge, Mass.: Harvard University Press, 1995), pp. 7–23; Sharpton, *Go and Tell Pharaoh*, pp. 188–89.
38. "Hospital Cuts," Apr. 24, 1998, .
39. Sharpton, *Go and Tell Pharaoh*, pp. 216–17, 246–47.
40. Ibid., pp. 166–69.
41. April Dicomo, "National Action Network Endorses Green for U.S. Senate," *New York Amsterdam News*, May 28–June 3, 1998.
42. Lula Strickland, "Sharpton Ties Up Vote in the NY Primary," *Black World Today*, Dec. 14, 1997, www.tbt.com\articles\usa63.htm
43. Nekesa Mumbi Moody, "Sharpton Says He Had No Obligation to Investigate Brawley's Rape Claims," http://www.jrnl.com/news/98/feb/jrn855120298.html
44. Taylor, *Black Churches of Brooklyn*, pp. 139–63; *New York Times*, Mar. 27, 1999.
45. Cathy Burke, "More Diallo-Slay Rage—Protest Hit Wall St. As Rudy Takes Heat in D.C.," *New York Post*, Mar. 4, 1999; Rachel S. Swarns, "The Diallo Shooting: Unlikely Protesters: Diallo Case Draws Diverse Group," *New York Times*, Mar. 27, 1999.
46. David Lefer, "Rivera's Star Rising: Local 1199 Chief Is Emerging as Rights Leader," *New York Daily News*, Apr. 18, 1999.
47. Boo Liff, "GOP Leader Joins Diallo Protest Push," *New York Daily News*, Mar. 25, 1999; Floyd Flake, "From Protest to Prosperity," *New York Post*, Apr. 12, 1999.
48. Transcript, *Like It Is Show*, no. 1230, Jan. 27, 2001.
49. Eric Ture Muhammad, "Maddox and Sharpton Lead Delegation in North Carolina," *Miami Times*, Dec. 9, 1999; *Amsterdam News*, Mar. 5–11, 1998.
50. The *New York Jewish Post* provided a transcript of a WWRL broadcast of a rally sponsored by Sharpton, Sept. 19, 1995; Sharpton, *Go and Tell Pharaoh*, p. 268.
51. Sharpton, *Go and Tell Pharaoh*, p. 54.
52. Ibid., p. 265; Kansas State University *Collegian*, Feb. 4, 1998; http://collegian.ksu.edu
53. Sharpton, *Go and Tell Pharaoh*, p. 244.
54. Ibid., pp. 255–56; Wayne Barrett, "Sharpton Flaps his Wings, But the Real Question Is Can Ruth Fly?" *Village Voice*, Dec. 14, 1997.
55. Ibid., p. 256; Corky Siemaszko "Gov. Axes Budget 760 M," *New York Daily News*, Apr. 28, 1998; Fredric U. Dicker, "Pataki Slashes $1.6B from State Budget Plan, *New York Post*, Apr. 28, 1998.
56. Wayne Barrett, "Bloomberg's Sexual Blind Spot," *Village Voice*, Nov. 6, 2001, pp. 21–22; Wilbert Tatum, "Bloomberg for Mayor," *Amsterdam News*, Oct. 25–31, 2001; Al Sharpton interview on New York One, "Road to Gracie Mansion," Nov. 5, 2001; Maki Becker and Derek Rose, "Sharpton Won't Back Green," *New York Daily News*, Nov. 6, 2001.

57. Adam Nagourney, "Conquered Party Bitterly Divided across the City," *New York Times*, Nov. 8, 2001, pp. A1, D4.

58. Michael A. Fletcher, "Prophecy on Race Relations Comes True," *Washington Post*, Mar. 1, 1998; Thomas L. McMahon, Larian Angelo, and John Mollenkopf, Hollow in the Middle: The Rise and Fall of New York City's Middle Class, City University of New York's Center for Urban Studies, Dec. 1997, www.council.nyc.us/finance/middleclass.htm

59. Juan Gonzalez, "Sacrificing Workers to Rudy's Workfare," *New York Daily News*, Apr. 21, 1998. The Giuliani Administration announced that it was withdrawing 1,400 WEP workers assigned to Harlem and other city hospitals after Jim Butler and Local 420 took the case to the state Supreme Court in an attempt to stop the layoff of over 900 nurses aides and other hospital workers. David L. Lewis, "1,400 WEP Jobs Yanked at Hospitals," *Daily News*, Apr. 28, 1998.

60. New York City Coalition Against Hunger web page; Hunger Action Network of New York State web page; City Harvest, www.city harvest.org; James Ridgeway, "Feeding Desperate People," *Village Voice*, Dec. 16, 1997; Irwin Garfinkel and Marcia K. Meyers, "A Tale of Many Cities," New York City Social Indicators Survey Center, 1977.

61. David Seifman "Rudy Wants 1,600 More Cops, for Starters" *New York Post*, Jan. 2, 1998.

62. Wayne Barrett, "Rudy's Milky Way: An Administration 'Of, For, and By White People' Has No Time or Room for Blacks" *Village Voice*, Feb. 14, 1999.

63. Amnesty International "Statistics on Complaints, www.voyager.com\amnesty\ai-2.9html

64. Jonathan Kaufman, *Broken Alliance: The Turbulent Times between Blacks and Jews in America* (New York: Scribner's, 1988); Peter Noel, "Crown Heights: The Full Monty," *Village Voice*, Apr. 6, 1998; Wayne Barrett, "The Cape Man of Crown Heights," *Village Voice*, Apr. 6, 1998; Herb Boyd, "New York City Mayor Apologizes to Hasidim but Ignores Black Victim," *Black World Today*, Apr. 6, 1998.

65. Angela Ards, "When Cops Are Killers," *Nation*, Mar. 8, 1999.

66. Kobena Mercer, *Out of the Jungle*, p. 290.

67. The link between blacks and labor has become a vital issue in New York and elsewhere. Manning Marable notes: "The most important factor in rebuilding the black freedom movement lies in the linkage of distinct yet overlapping constituencies within the African-American community. Two critical groups here are the low wage workers and welfare recipients.... Both groups are manipulated against each other to protect the interests of employers who want to keep labor cost low. The only long-term solution to this dilemma is to bring poor people into the organized labor movement." Manning Marable, "Labor Organizing and the Black Poor," *Black World Today*, Nov. 10, 1997; "ACORN Campaigns," July 1997; William Greider, "Saving the Global Economy," *Nation*, Dec. 15, 1997, p. 116.

Notes to Chapter 7

1. William L. Van DeBurg, *New Day in Babylon* (Chicago: University of Chicago Press, 1993), pp. 297–98; Manning Marable, "On Malcolm X: His Message and Meaning" *Open Magazine* Pamphlet Series No. 22 (Westfield, N.J., 1992), pp. 5–6.

2. Clarence Taylor, "How Should Black Leadership Respond to Farrakhan's Attempt to Legitimize His Leadership in Black America," in Felton O. Best, ed., *Black Religious Leaders from the Slave Community to the Million Man March: Flames of Fire* (Lewiston, N.Y.: Edwin Mellen Press, 1998), p. 212.

3. Mattias Gardell, *In the Name of Elijah Muhammad: Louis Farrakhan and the Nation of Islam* (Durham N.C.: Duke University Press, 1996), pp. 119–20; Arthur J. Magida, *Prophet of Rage: The Life of Louis Farrakhan and His Nation* (New York: Basic Books, 1996), pp. 16–30.

4. Gardell, *In the Name of Elijah Muhammad*, pp. 120–21.

5. Ibid., pp. 122–23; Elijah Muhammad, *Message to the Blackman in America* (Chicago, Final Call, n.d.), pp. 20, 100–12.

6. Elijah Muhammad, *Message to the Blackman in America*, pp. 153–55, 267.

7. Ibid., 293–94; Claude Andrew Clegg III, *An Original Man: The Life and Times of Elijah Muhammad* (New York: St. Martin's Press, 1997), pp. 125–27.

8. Tape, Farrakhan's Speech at Madison Square Garden, Oct. 7, 1985; "Like It Is with Gil Noble"; Farrakhan's speech in Madison Square Garden, Radio Islam http://abbc.com/historical/Farrakhan.htm

9. Ibid.

10. Wilbert Tatum, Interview with Min. Louis Farrakhan, *Amsterdam News*, January 8, 1994.

11. Speech at Madison Square Garden, Oct. 7, 1985. Aired on "Gil Noble's Like It Is" Oct. 1985.

12. Martin E. Marty, "Martin Luther King: The Preacher as Virtuoso," www.religion-online.org/cgi-bin/relsearched.dil/shoearticle?item_id=839

13. Ibid.

14. Bruce A. Rosenberg," The Black Preacher," www. Arts.mis.us/crossroads/narrative/church/na_text.html

15. Gardell, *In the Name of Elijah Muhammad*, p. 260.

16. Speech at Madison Square Garden, Oct. 7, 1985.

17. David Myatt, "Aryan Culture," David Myatt Online Resource www.davidmyatt.f2s.com/articles.htm

18. Ibid.; Gary Gerstle, *American Crucible: Race and Nation in the Twentieth Century* (Princeton, N.J.: Princeton University Press, 2001), p. 16.

19. Speech at Madison Square Garden, Oct. 7, 1985.

20. *New York Times*, Jan. 16, 1994.

21. Louis Farrakhan, "Torchlight for America," Capitol Press Club, May 1993.

22. Salim Muwaffil, "We Are Family: Louis Farrakhan Has Big Plans," *InTheseTimes.com*, Nov. 27, 2000, www.inthesetimes.com

23. Ibid., pp. 77–91.

24. Ibid., pp. 84–87.

25. Ibid., p. 91.

26. Louis Farrakhan, *Torchlight for America*, pp. 47–48.

27. Ibid., pp. 49–64.

28. Farrakhan, "Men of This World Do Not Desire a Righteous Woman," *Final Call*, Sept. 9–14, 2000.

29. Ibid.

30. Ibid.

31. Farrakhan, "Heaven Lies at the Foot of Mother," *Final Call*, Sept. 4, 2000.

32. Ibid.

33. Elijah Muhammad, *How to Eat to Live* (Atlanta, Ga.: Messenger Elijah Muhammad Propagation Society, 1972), pp. 7, 191; E. U. Essien-Udon, *Black Nationalism: A Search for an Identity in American* (New York: Dell, 1962), pp. 48–49.

34. Farrakhan, *Torchlight for America*, pp. 123–48.

35. Ibid., 127–37.

36. Farrakhan, "The Need for a Million Family March," *Final Call*, Oct. 10, 2000.

37. Excerpt from Farrakhan's Speech at the Million Family March, *Final Call*, Oct. 31, 2000.
38. Ibid.
39. Ibid.
40. Ibid.
41. Manning Marable, "Strange Bedfellows: Louis Farrakhan and the White Conservatives," *Along the Color Line*, Apr. 29, 1997.
42. Hugh Price, "Can America Reclaim Souls Left on Ice?" *Final Call*, Aug. 8, 2001; Mumia Abu-Jamal, Carlo's Way," *Final Call*, Sept. 4, 2001; Cynthia McKinney, "America Must Reverse Legacy of Shame," *Final Call*, Sept. 4, 9001; Ron Walters, "Is Bush Racism Conference Copout a Smoke Screen?" *Final Call*, posted Sept. 6, 2001; Chuck D, "Eyes on Hip Hop," *Final Call*, Aug. 8, 2001.
43. Toure Muhammad and Askia Muhammad, "'We Are a Family': Min. Farrakhan and Imam Mohammed Unite," *Final Call*, Mar. 3, 2000; "Talk of the Nation," National Public Radio, Mar. 9, 2000.
44. "Muslim American Society Marks 25th Anniversary," *Final Call*, Sept. 9–14, 2000.
45. "Minister Farrakhan Offers a Prayer for Peace: For the New Century and Millennium," *Final Call On-Line Edition*, Dec. 22, 1999.
46. Ibid.
47. Salim Muwakkil, "Every Rose Has Its Thorn: Louis Farrakhan's New Tune Is Making Many African-Americans Anxious," In These Times.Com, Dec. 25, 2000; Clarence Taylor, "The Millennial Concept and the Evolution of Leadership in Black Pentecostalism and the Nation of Islam," in Charles B. Strozier and Michael Flynn, *The Year 2000: Essays on the End* (New York: New York University Press, 1997), pp. 226–27.
48. Ernest Allen, "Louis Farrakhan and the Continuing Evolution of the Nation of Islam," in Amy Alexander, ed., *The Farrakhan Factor: African-American Writers on Leadership, Nationhood, and Minister Louis Farrakhan* (New York: Grove Press, 1998), pp. 75–76.
49. Ibid., pp. 77–78.
50. Transcript, "Talk of the Nation," National Public Radio, Mar. 9, 2000.
51. Louis Farrakhan, *Controversy with the International Bankers* (London: Hakiki Publishing, 1996), pp. 38, 105–9.
52. Ibid. pp. 111–12.
53. "Excerpt of Farrakhan's August 11, 2000, Press Conference, Lieberman: A Test for White America," *Final Call*, posted Aug. 17, 2000.
54. Salim Muwakkil, "Every Rose Has Its Thorn."
55. Farrakhan's Speech and Press Conference, Sept. 16, 2001, *Final Call*, Online, Sept. 16, 2001.
56. Ibid.
57. Ibid.
58. www.adl.org/terrorism-america/saying_091401.asp-28k, and tom.paine.com/opinion/2001/09/21/1.htm/-22k
59. www.religioustolerance.org
60. Farrakhan's speech and Press Conference, Sept. 16, 2001.
61. Ibid.

Notes to Chapter 8

1. Evelyn Brooks Higginbotham, *Righteous Discontent: The Women's Movement in the Black Baptist Church, 1880–1920* (Cambridge, Mass.: Harvard University Press, 1993), pp. 7–18, 120–49.
2. Cheryl Townsend Gilkes, *If It Wasn't for the Women: Black Women's Experience*

and Womanist Culture in Church and Community (Maryknoll, N.Y.: Orbis Books, 2001), pp. 108–9.

3. Joanne Grant, *Ella Baker, Freedom Bound* (New York: Wiley, 1998), pp. 12–18.
4. Ibid., pp. 18–20; Charles M. Payne, *I've Got the Light of Freedom: The Organizing Tradition and the Mississippi Freedom Struggle* (Berkeley: University of California Press, 1995), p.80.
5. Payne, *I've Got the Light of Freedom*, p. 80.
6. Grant, pp. *Ella Baker*, pp. 30–44; Payne, *I've Got the Light of Freedom*, pp. 89–90.
7. Grant, pp. 45–61, 63–79; Clarence Taylor, *Knocking at Our Door: Milton A. Galamison and the Struggle to Integrate New York City Schools* (New York: Columbia University Press, 1997), p. 76; Payne, *I've Got the Light of Freedom*, pp. 91–92.
8. *Fundi: The Story of Ella Baker*, film produced by Joanne Grant, 1981; Vicki Crawford, Jacqueline A. Rouse, and Barbara Woods, eds., *Women in the Civil Rights Movement: Trailblazers and Torchbearers, 1841–1965* (Bloomington, Ind.: Indiana University Press, 1993), pp. 51–68; Aldon Morris, *The Origins of the Civil Rights Movement: Black Communities Organizing for Change* (New York: Free Press, 1984), pp. 102–3; Grant, *Ella Baker: Freedom Bound*, pp. 100–104. Highlander was founded during the Depression in Tennessee and became a school for the poor, workers, and farmers. By the 1950s, it became a meeting place for civil rights activists. The school's philosophy was that oppressed people had sufficient knowledge to alleviate their oppression. Through workshops, students at Highlander developed leadership skills that would allow them to return to their local communities and train others. One project that came out of Highlander was the Citizenship Education Project (see Payne, *I've Got the Light of Freedom*, pp. 71–77).
9. Grant, *Ella Baker, Freedom Bound*, pp. 112–13.
10. Ella Baker, "Women and Community Leadership," in Gerda Lerner, *Black Women in White America: A Documentary History* (New York: Pantheon, 1972), pp. 346–52.
11. *Fundi.*
12. Ibid.
13. Clayborne Carson, *In Struggle: SNCC and the Black Awakening of the 1960s* (Cambridge, Mass.: Harvard University Press, 1995), pp. 9–11.
14. Grant, *Ella Baker*; Carson, *In Struggle*, pp. 19–24; Carson, "Student Nonviolent Coordinating Committee"; Darlene Clark Hine, Elsa Barkley Brown and Rosalyn Terborg-Penn, eds., *Black Women in America: An Historical Encyclopedia* (Bloomington, Ind.: Indiana University Press, 1993), pp. 1122–23.
15. Pauli Murray, *Pauli Murray: The Autobiography of a Black Activist, Feminist, Lawyer, Priest, and Poet* (Knoxville, Tenn.: University of Tennessee Press, 1997), pp. 1–30.
16. Ibid., pp. 32–34.
17. Ibid., pp. 37–38.
18. Ibid., p. 39.
19. Ibid., p. 20.
20. Ibid., pp. 104–7.
21. Ibid., p. 107.
22. Ibid., pp. 108–26.
23. Ibid., pp. 137–48; Belinda Robnett, *How Long How Long: African-American Women in the Struggle for Civil Rights* (New York: Oxford University Press, 1997), p. 55.

24. Murray, *Pauli Murray*, pp. 220–31.
25. Ibid., pp. 214–15.
26. Ibid., pp. 339–52.
27. Ibid., pp. 356–58.
28. Ibid., pp. 359–68.
29. Ibid., pp. 369–71.
30. Ibid. p. 372.
31. Ibid. p. 369.
32. Ibid., pp. 426–30.
33. Sermon reprinted in Bettye Collier Thomas, *Daughters of Thunder: Black Women Preachers and Their Sermons, 1850–1979* (San Francisco: Jossey-Bass, 1998), pp. 234–38.
34. "Anna Murray," www.spartacus.schoolnet.co.uk/USAmurrayA.htm

Bibliography

Alexander, Amy, ed. *The Farrakhan Factor: African-American Writers on Leadership, Nationhood, and Minister Louis Farrakhan.* New York: Grove Press, 1998.

Anderson, Jervis. *A. Philip Randolph: A Biographical Portrait.* New York: Harcourt Brace Jovanovich, 1972.

Baer, Hans, and Merrell Singer. *African-American Religion in the Twentieth Century: Varieties of Protest and Accommodation.* Knoxville, Tenn.: University of Tennessee Press, 1992.

Banks, William. *Black Intellectuals.* New York: W. W. Norton, 1996.

Bates, Beth Tompkins. *Pullman Porters and the Rise of Protest Politics in Black America, 1925–1945.* Chapel Hill, N.C.: University of North Carolina Press, 2001.

Bederman, Gail. *Manliness and Civilization: A Cultural History of Gender and Race in the United States, 1880–1917.* Chicago: University of Chicago Press, 1996.

Beito, David T. *From Mutual Aid to the Welfare State: Fraternal Societies and Social Services, 1890–1967.* Chapel Hill, N.C.: University of North Carolina Press, 2000.

Best, Felton. *Black Religious Leaders from the Slave Community to the Million-Man March.* Lewiston, N.Y.: Mellen Press, 1998.

Burkett, Randall, and Richard Newman, eds. *Black Apostles: Afro-American Clergy Confront the Twentieth Century.* Boston: G. K. Hall, 1978.

Carby, Hazel. *Race Men.* Cambridge, Mass.: Harvard University Press, 1998.

Chapman, Mark. *Christianity on Trial: African-American Religious Thought before and after Black Power.* Maryknoll, N.Y.: Orbis Books, 1996.

Chareauvert, Melinda. *Marching Together: Women of the Brotherhood of Sleeping Car Porters.* Urbana, Ill.: University of Illinois Press, 1998.

Clegg, Claude Andrew. *An Original Man: The Life and Times of Elijah Muhammad.* New York: St. Martin's Press, 1997.

Crawford, Vicki, Jacqueline A. Rouse, and Barbara Wood, eds. *Women in the Civil Rights Movement: Trailblazers and Torchbearers.* Bloomington, Ind.: Indiana University Press, 1993.

Cruse, Harold. *The Crisis of the Negro Intellectual.* New York: William Morrow, 1967.

Curtis, Susan. *A Consuming Faith: The Social Gospel and Modern American Culture.* Baltimore: Johns Hopkins University Press, 1991.

Daughtry, Herbert. *No Monopoly on Suffering: Blacks and Jews in Crown Heights and Elsewhere.* Trenton, N.J.: Africana World Press, 1997.

Davis, Daniel. *Mr. Black Labor: The Story of A. Philip Randolph, Father of the Civil Rights Movement.* New York: E. P. Dutton, 1972.

Davis, Miles, and Quincy Troupe. *Miles: An Autobiography.* New York: 1990.

Dodson, Jualynne. *Engendering Church.* New York: Rowman and Littlefield, 2001.

Dudziak, Mary. *Cold War Civil Rights: Race and the Image of American Democracy.* Princeton, N.J.: Princeton University Press, 2001.

Dunn, Marvin. *Black Miami in the Twentieth Century.* Gainesville, Fla.: University Press of Florida, 1997.

DuPree, Sherry Sherrod. *Biographical Dictionary of African-American Holiness-Pentecostals, 1880–1990.* Washington, D.C.: Middle Atlantic Regional Press, 1989.

Farrakhan, Louis. *Controversy with the International Bankers*. London: Hakiki Publishers, 1996.

———. *Torchlight for America*. Chicago: FCN Publishing, 1993.

Fluker, Walter Earl, and Catherine Tumber, eds. *A Strange Freedom: The Best of Howard Thurman on Religious Experience and Public Life*. Boston: Beacon Press, 1999.

Foner, Eric. *The Story of American Freedom*. New York: W. W. Norton, 1998.

Franklin, John Hope, and August Meier, eds. *Black Leaders of the Twentieth Century*. Urbana, Ill.: University of Illinois Press, 1982.

Fulop, Timothy E., and Albert J. Raboteau, eds. *African-American Religion: Interpretive Essays in History and Culture*. New York: Routledge, 1997.

Gaines, Kevin. *Uplifting the Race: Black Leadership and Political Culture in the Twentieth Century*. Chapel Hill, N.C.: University of North Carolina Press, 1996.

Gardell, Mattias. *In the Name of Elijah Muhammad: Louis Farrakhan and the Nation of Islam*. Durham, N.C.: Duke University Press, 1996.

Gerstle, Gary. *American Crucible: Race and Nation in the Twentieth Century*. Princeton, N.J.: Princeton University Press, 2001.

Gilmore, Glenda Elizabeth. *Gender and Jim Crow: Women and the Politics of White Supremacy in North Carolina, 1896–1920*. Chapel Hill, N.C.: University of North Carolina Press, 1996.

Grant, Joanne. *Ella Baker, Freedom Bound*. New York: Wiley, 1998.

Green, Ben. *Before His Time: The Untold Story of Harry T. Moore, America's First Civil Rights' Martyr*. New York: Free Press, 1999.

Harris, William. *Keeping the Faith: A. Phillip Randolph, Milton P. Webster, and the Brotherhood of Sleeping Car Porters, 1925–37*. Urbana, Ill.: University of Illinois Press, 1991.

Higginbotham, Evelyn Brooks. *Righteous Discontent: The Women's Movement in the Black Baptist Church, 1880–1920*. Cambridge, Mass.: Harvard University Press, 1993.

Hine, Darlene, and Ernestine Jenkins, eds. *A Question of Manhood: A Reader in Black Men's History and Masculinity*. Bloomington, Ind.: Indiana University Press, 1999.

Horowitz, David. *Hating Whitey and Other Progressive Causes*. Dallas. Tex.: Spence Publishing, 1999.

James, Joy, and Lewis Gordon. *Transcending the Talented Tenth: Race Leaders and American Intellectuals*. New York: Routledge, 1996.

Kelley, Robin D. G. *Black Rebels: Culture, Politics and the Black Working Class*. New York: The Free Press, 1994.

Keppel, Ben. *The Working of Democracy: Ralph Brunch, Kenneth B. Clark, Lorraine Hansberry, and the Cultural Politics of Race*. Cambridge, Mass.: Harvard University Press, 1995.

Koch, Ed. *Ed Koch: An Autobiography*. New York: Simon and Schuster, 1984.

Lasch, Christopher. *The Revolt of the Elite and the Betrayal of Democracy*. New York: W. W. Norton, 1995.

Lincoln, C. Eric, and Lawrence Mamiya. *The Black Church in the African-American Experience*. Durham, N.C.: Duke University Press, 1990.

Levine, Lawrence. *Black Culture and Black Consciousness*. New York: Oxford University Press, 1977.

Locke, Alain, ed. *The New Negro: An Interpretation*. New York: Atheneum, 1992.

Magida, Arthur J. *Prophet of Rage: A Life of Louis Farrakhan and His Nation*. New York: Basic Books, 1996.

Manes, Andrew Michael. *Southern Civil Religions in Conflict: Black and White Baptists and Civil Rights*. Athens, Ga.: University of Georgia Press, 1987.

Marable, Manning. *Race, Reform and Rebellion: The Second Reconstruction in Black America, 1945–1990*. Jackson, Miss.: University Press of Mississippi, 1991.

May, Elaine. *Homeward Bound*. New York: Basic Books, 1988.

Mazon, Mauricio. *The Zoot-Suit Riots: The Psychology of Symbolic Annihilation*. Austin: University of Texas Press, 1984.

Mercer, Kobena. *Welcome to the Jungle: New Positions in Black Cultural Studies*. New York: Routledge, 1994.

Muhammad, Elijah. *How to Eat to Live*. Atlanta, Ga.: Secretarius Publishers, 1997.

———. *Message to the Blackman in America*. Chicago: The Final Call Inc., 1997

Murray, Pauli. *Pauli Murray: The Autobiography of a Black Activist, Feminist, Lawyer, Priest, and Poet*. Knoxville, Tenn.: University of Tennessee Press, 1997.

Newfield, Jack, and Wayne Barrett. *City for Sale: Ed Koch and the Betrayal of New York*. New York: Harper Trade, 1988.

Pfeffer, Paula. *A. Philip Randolph: Pioneer of the Civil Rights Movement*. Baton Rouge, La.: Louisiana State University Press, 1990.

Pitney, David Howard. *The Afro-American Jeremiad: Appeals for Social Justice in America*. Philadelphia: Temple University Press, 1990.

Poitier, Sidney. *This Life*. New York: Knopf, 1980.

Rodolfo, Torres, Louis Miran, and Jonathan Xavier. *Race, Identity, and Citizenship, A Reader*. Malden, Mass.: Blackwell, 1999.

Rosenau, Pauline Marie. *Post-Modernism and Social Science, Insights, Inroads, and Intrusion*. Princeton, N.J.: Princeton University Press, 1992.

Seraile, William. *Fire in His Heart!: Bishop Benjamin Tucker Tanner and the AME Church*. Knoxville, Tenn.: University of Tennessee Press, 1999.

Sharpton, Al. *Go and Tell Pharaoh: The Autobiography of Al Sharpton*. New York: Bantam Doubleday Dell, 1996.

Sleeper, Jim. *The Closest of Strangers: Liberalism and the Politics of Race in New York*. New York: W. W. Norton, 1990.

Strozier Charles, and Michael Flynn, eds. *The Year 2000: Essays on the End*. New York: New York University Press, 1997.

Sugrue, Thomas, J. *The Origins of the Urban Crisis*. Princeton, N.J.: Princeton University Press, 1996.

Taylor, Clarence. *The Black Churches of Brooklyn*. New York: Columbia University Press, 1994.

———. *Knocking at Our Own Door: Milton A. Galamison and the Struggle to Integrate New York City Schools*. New York: Columbia University Press, 1997.

Thomas, Bettye Collier. *Daughters of Thunder: Black Women Preachers and Their Sermons, 1850–1979*. San Francisco: Jossey-Bass, 1998.

Van DeBurg, William. *New Day in Babylon: The Black Power Movement and American Culture, 1965–1975*. Chicago: University of Chicago Press, 1992.

Washington, Joseph R. *Rulers of Reality and Ruled Races: The Struggle of Black Ministers to Bring Afro-Americans to Full Citizenship in America*. Lewiston, N.Y.: Edwin Mellen Press, 1990.

West, Cornel. *Prophesy Deliverance. An Afro-American Revolutionary Christianity*. Grand Rapids, Mich.: Eerdmans, 1988.

———. *Prophetic Fragments*: Philadelphia: Westminster, 1982.

Williams, Juan. *Thurgood Marshall: American Revolutionary*. New York: Times Books, 1998.

Williams, Smallwood. *This Is My Story: A Significant Life Struggle.* Washington, D.C.: William Willoughby Publishers, 1970.

Wilmore, Gayraud. *African-American Religious Studies: An Interdisciplinary Anthology.* Durham, N.C.: Duke University Press, 1989.

Wright, W. D. *Black Intellectuals, Black Cognition, and a Black Aesthetic.* New York: Praeger, 1998.

Young, Henry J. *Major Black Religious Leaders Since 1940.* Nashville, Tenn.: Abingdon Press, 1979.

Index

Abernathy, Ralph, 185
Abraham Lincoln Brigade, 190
Abyssinian Baptist Church, New York, 28
accommodationism, 9, 78–79, 83–93, 98
Adams, Eric, 140–41
Adelphian Club, 82
African Methodist Episcopal Church (AME), 24–25, 28, 31, 32, 41
African Orthodox Church, 45, 83–84
Afro-Insurance Company, 82
Afro-Protective League, 43
AFSME local 240, 135, 138
A.K.A. Sorority, 82–83
Alamoudi, Abdurahaman, 175
Alcantara, Theophilus J., 42–43, 45
Ali, Noble Drew, 152
ambassadorship for the race, 39–42
ambivalence on liberation of black church, 36–38
American Communist Party, 43–44
American Federation of Labor, 28, 99, 148–49
American Jewish Committee, 101
American Labor Party, 43, 182
American Muslim Foundation, 175
American Muslim Society, 172–73
Amos 'n' Andy, 68–69
Amsterdam News, 38–39, 90–91, 133, 140, 142, 143, 154
Anderson, Jervis, 11–12
Anglican Church, 45
anti-Communism, 37–38, 41–47, 62, 70, 91, 94–117
Anti-Defamation League, 159
anti-Semitism, 61, 124, 140, 147, 150–51, 154–64, 170, 175–76

Apollo Theater, 120
Aryanism, 158–59
Association of Community Organizations for Reform Now (ACORN), 148–49
Austin, Junius C., 25–27
Azusa Movement, 53

Baker, Ella Jo: 1, 10
  and NAACP, 182–84, 187
  and SCLC, 184–88
  and SNCC, 186–88
Banks, William, 2–3
Baptist churches, 28, 31, 32, 38–47, 133, 181–82
Baraka, Amiri, 5
Becker, William H., 50
Bedford-Stuyvestant Health Council, 41
Bethel AME Church, Chicago, 24
Bevel, Jim, 125
Bible Way Church of Our Lord Jesus Christ World Wide, Inc., 8–9, 48–49, 54, 56–78
Black, Lucille, 103
Black Apostles: Afro-American Clergy Confront the Twentieth Century (Newman/Burkett), 3–4
Black Boy (Wright), 69
Black Intellectuals (Banks), 2–3
Black Intellectuals, Black Cognition, and a Black Aesthetic (Wright), 2
Black Leadership Summit, 173–74
Black Miami in the Twentieth Century (Dunn), 79, 94
Bloomberg, Michael, 143–45
Blyden, Wilmont, 3

Bonus March, the, 57–58
bourgeois culture, black, 69–70, 78–95, 99
Bradley, Bill, 120
Bradley, E. J., 28–29
Bramwell, Arthur, 139
Brawley, Tawana, 120, 126–27, 130, 137, 143
Bridging the Gap (Saunders), 94
Briggs, Cyril, 5
Brooklyn, religious leaders in, 8–9, 37–47, 119, 124–25
Brotherhood of Sleeping Car Porters (BSCP), 7–8, 11, 14–36
Brown, Earl, 90–91
Brown, George Thomas, 38–39
Brown, James, 127, 129
Brown, Lee, 148
Brown v. Board of Education of Topeka, 68, 101–102
Bumpurs, Eleanor, 123–24
Burdine's Department Store, 85–86
Burkett, Randall, 2–3
Burton, Charles Wesley, 25–26
Bush, George W., 176, 179
Butler, James (Jim), 135, 138
Byrd, J. N., 99

Carby, Hazel, 71
Carey, A. J., 24
Carey, Luther O., 82
Carrington, William Orlando, 38–39
Cashmere, John, 38–39
Chafee, Edmund, 29
Chapman, Mark, 2, 4
Chavis, Ben, 173
Chicago, religious leaders in, 24–32
Christ Episcopal Church, Coconut Grove, 96
Christian Right, 164–65, 170, 178–79
Christianity on Trial: African-American Religious Thought Before and After Black Power (Chapman), 4
Church of God in Christ, 31
Church of Our Lord Jesus Christ of the Apostolic Faith (COOLJC), 51–52, 54, 56
Churches of Christ, Federal Council of, 29–30
Citizens Protective League, 84

citizenship:
  and anti-Communism, 94–117
  cultural, 59–60
Citizenship Education Project, 184
Civic League of Colored Town, 82
Civil Rights Act of 1964, 193
civil rights movement:
  reluctance of black churches in, 36
  religious leaders in, 72–73, 79–117
  school integration in, 44, 66–68, 97, 101–102, 184, 191–92
  women in, 182–97
Clark, Septima, 184
class divisions, 30–32, 46–47, 70–71, 99, 127, 135–36
Clinton, Bill, 123
Closest of Strangers (Sleeper), 118–21
clothing:
  patrician, 70–71
  in politics, 127–30
Cleage, Albert, 4
clubs, women's, 82–83
cold war, the:
  in Brooklyn, 8–9, 37–47
  and gender, 70
  loyalty of black Americans in, 94–117
Coleman, John, 38, 39
Collins, LeRoy, 105
Colored Town community, Miami, 80–83, 86–87
Commission on the Status of Women (PCSW), 192–93
Communist Party U.S., 113–15, 189
Concord Baptist Church, Brooklyn, 38–42
Cone, James, 3–4, 78
Congregational Educational Society, 29
Congress of Industrial Organizations (CIO), 84–86, 116, 148–49
Congress of Racial Equality (CORE), 73–74, 125, 187
Congressional Black Caucus, 134, 163, 173
Consolidated Parents Group, 66–67
consumer market, black, 128–30
Controversy with the International Bankers (Farrakhan), 175–76
conversion, language of, 133, 173
Cook, William, 24–27
cool jazz image, 75–77

Cooper, Anna, 4
Corbett, U. L., 47
Cornerstone Baptist Church, Brooklyn, 38, 40
Cousins, S. A., 100
Crisis, The, 188
Crisis of the Negro Intellectual (Cruse), 2
Crown Heights confrontation, 147–48
Cruse, Harold, 2
Cuban Revolution, 44, 45, 103
Culmer, John: 9
  accomodationist politics of, 83–93
  as negotiator, 78–79
"culture of poverty," 123
Cuomo, Mario, 142–43, 153, 177
Curtis, Susan, 14–15
Cwest Club, 83

Dade County Women Civic
    Improvement Association, 82–83
D'Amato, Alfonse, 130, 136, 142
Dames, S. G., 82
Daniels, Ron, 173
Daughtry, Herbert, 124
David Walker's Appeal, 21
Davis, Daniel, 13
Davis, Miles, 75–77
Davis, Ossie, 138
Day of Outrage demonstrations, 125–26
D.C. Coalition of Conscience, 72
Debs, Eugene, 42–43
Dee, Ruby, 138
Deep Is Hunger (Thurman), 55–56
Dellums, C. L., 18
Delta Sigma Theta, 82–83
Democratic Leadership Committee, 123
Democratic Party, 43, 107, 123, 126
denominations:
  "mainline," 49
  predominantly white, 45
Dent, Boise, 39
Depression, the, 57–58
Dewey, Thomas, 39
Diallo, Amadou, 121, 137–39
diaspora, African-American, 61
Dinkins, David, 121, 147–48, 154
Dixon, J. E., 103
double consciousness, 58–59
Douglass, Frederick, 69, 196

Downstate Medical Center demonstrations, 41–42
D'Souza, Dinesh, 119
Du Bois, W. E. B.: 2–5, 8, 196
  on clothing, 71
  and Randolph, 11–12
  Sharpton and, 135
  suppression of, 37
  and Williams, 58–59
Duke, David, 120
Duke hair products, 128
Dunn, Marvin, 79, 94

Eckstine, Billy, 76
Elkins, Stanley, 62
Emerge magazine, 128–29
Ensley, Charles, 138
Episcopal Church, 79–96, 193–95

faith healing, 46
Falwell, Jerry, 178
Fard, Wallace C., 152, 172–73
Farrakhan, Louis: 1, 9–10, 197
  anti-Semitism of, 150–51, 154–64, 170, 175–76
  and Bible, 155–58, 172–73
  early life, 151–53
  and Elijah Muhammad, 151–53, 164–68, 172–73, 175
  image change of, 160–80
  and Islam, orthodox, 171–76, 179–80
  and Malcolm, 151–53
  as nationalist, 150–51
  self-portrayal of, 153–56
  and Sharpton, 135, 140
FBI, 102, 130
Fellowship of Reconciliation, 191
feminism, 70, 193–97
Ferrar, Fernando, 143–45
Final Call, 165, 172, 175
First AME Zion Church, Brooklyn, 38–40
Flake, Floyd, 139
Flash, the, 21–22
Florida Association for Constitutional Government, 108
Florida Legislative Investigation Committee (FLIC), 94, 106–17
Ford, Arnold J., 3
Fort-Whitman, Lovett, 25

Fraizer, Franklin, 4
Freedy's fire incident, 140
Fulani, Lenora, 134

G–77 Meeting, Havana 2000, 172
Gaines, Kevin, 2
Galamison, Milton A., 9, 41, 42, 44–45,
    62, 101–102, 125, 184
gambling, 82, 98–99
Gandhi, Mahatma, 55, 68
Garvey, Marcus, 45, 54, 83–85
gender:
    in churches, 75, 181–82, 193–95
    and cold war, 70
    and intellectual role, 65–78
    and liberalism, 8
    literature on, 4
    and NAACP, 182–84, 187
    and NOI, 162–67
    and Pentecostalism, 49–50, 65, 75
    and race, 14–15
    in SCLC, 185–88
    in unions, 20–22
Gerstle, Gary, 103–104, 107
Gibson, Samuel, 47
Gibson, Theodore: 1, 9
    anti-Communism of, 94–95, 101–17
    vs. Culmer, 94–95, 106–107
    early life, 95–96
    and NAACP, 96–101
    and Supreme Court, 114–17
Gibson v. FLIC, 113–17
Gilkes, Cheryl Townsend, 182
Gilroy, Paul, 61
Giuliani, Rudolph, 121, 138–39, 144–48,
    177
"God Will Take Care of You" (Martin),
    33
Good Citizenship Sunday
"Good Will Racial Meeting," Miami, 98,
    101
"Good News," Gospel as, 33
Gore, Al, 120
Graham, Edward T., 99, 100
Grant, Joanne, 182–83
Greater Bethel AME Church, Miami,
    100–101
Greater Miami Right to Work
    Committee, 99
Green, Mark, 136, 143–45

Green, William C., 28
Guardian, Boston, 43
Guardians, the, 141

hair styles, 128–30
Hamer, Fannie Lou, 188
Hancock, Gordon Blaine, 3
Harlem Hospital, 145–46
Harlem Renaissance, 2, 4
Harrison, Hubert, 5, 42
Harten, Thomas, 42–43, 45
Harvey, Marchita, 47
Hawes, Mark R., 108, 112–15
Haynes, George Edmund, 3
Haywood, Garfiled T., 53
Health and Hospitals Corporation, New
    York, 145–46
Henderson, O.D., 98–99
Herrell, Cliff, 110
Higginbotham, Evelyn Brooks, 181–82
Higgs, H. H., 85
Hitler, 62–63
Hobson, Julius, 73–74
Hodgson, Godfrey, 116
Holy Spirit, 51
homosexuality, 70, 75, 117
Hoover, Herbert, 57–58
Hoover, J. Edgar, 102, 111
Horowitz, David, 120
How to Eat to Live (Muhammad),
    167–68
Howard Beach incident, 124–25, 136
HUAC, 113
Hughes, Langston, 2, 4
Hurston, Zora Neale, 2 , 4
hypermasculinity, 75–77

If It Wasn't for the Women (Gilkes), 182
individualist approach, 72–73
Industrial Reporter, 82
intellectuals, black:
    and gender, 65–78
    literature on, 2–5
    "organic," 6
    and religion, 3–10, 48–49, 196
Interdenominational Ministers' Alliance,
    Miami, 88, 90, 100–101
Interstate Commerce Commission, U.S.,
    20, 22
Islam, orthodox, 171–76, 179–80

Jackson, Derrick Z., 120–21
Jackson, Jesse, 3, 121, 125, 130–35, 138, 142, 197
Jackson, Joseph H., 36
James, C. L. R., 5
Jehovah's Witnesses, 152
jeremiad form, 172–73
Jesus and the Disinherited (Thurman), 55
Jewish-black relations, 61–63, 101, 124, 140, 143–45, 147–48, 150–51, 154–64, 170
Jewish diaspora, 61
Johns, Charley, 108
Johnson, Charles S., 4–5
Johnson, David, 26
Johnson, James Weldon, 2
Johnson, Mordecai, 55, 68
Johnson, Thedford, 100
Johnson hair products, 128
Jones, Quincy, 77

Kelley, Robin, 129
Kennedy, John F., 192
King, Don, 127
King, Martin Luther Jr.: 1, 3, 68, 196
    and Baker, 184–85
    church opponents of, 36
    and Jackson, 131–32
    and Sharpton, 133
Kingsley, Harold M., 26–27
Koch, Ed, 122–24, 153, 177
Ku Klux Klan, 29, 84–85, 89–90, 97, 108, 120

Labor Relations Committee, Negro Service Council, 99
labor unions, 11–36, 85–86, 99–100, 116, 135, 138, 148–49
Ladies' Auxiliary, BSCP, 21–22
LaRouche, Lyndon, 131
Lasch, Christopher, 119–21
Laws, Bob, 140
Lawson, Robert, 51–52, 56
leadership:
    accomodationist, 78–79, 83–93, 98
    charismatic, 1–2, 118–49, 185–86, 196
    by community members, 196
    female, 182–97
    God-chosen, 50–56, 72–73

group-centered, 184–88, 196
male, 1–2, 65–78, 196–97, 162–67
militant, 94–95, 98–99, 118–80
and power broker, 140–49
religious, 1–10
as representation, 79–95
left, black:
    in cold war, 37–47
    and Pentecostalism, 48–74
    pre-war, 189–90
Levison, Stanley, 184
liberalism, Afro-Christian: 8–9, 84
    in Brooklyn, 38–42
    and cold war, 116–17
    and Pentecostalism, 48–74
Lieberman, Joseph, 176
Lincoln Memorial Congregational Church, 26–28
Little Rock Nine, 102, 104
Local 1199, 138–39
Locke, Alain, 4, 16
Logan, Rayford, 4
Lovestone, Jay, 189
Lowery, Benjamin, 39, 41–42
loyalty of black Americans in cold war, 94–117
lynching, 18, 43, 85, 96, 189

MacArthur, Douglas, 58
Maddox, Alton, 137, 139–40, 143
maids' role in Porters' union, 20–22
Major Black Religious Leaders Since 1940 (Young), 3–4
Malcolm X, 1, 52, 54, 126, 133, 175, 196
manhood, language and politics of, 14–24, 50, 65–78, 124–26, 154, 166–67
Marable, Manning, 37–38, 134, 135
Marshall, Thurgood, 102–103, 191
Martin, Civilla D., 33
Marty, Martin E., 155
Marxism, 44–45, 163
Mason, C. Vernon, 137
Mason, Charles Harrison, 53
Masonic Oath, 23–24
Masters of Deceit (Hoover), 111
Matthews, J. B., 113–14
Mays, Benjamin E., 4, 31, 55
McBean, Adelene, 191

McCarthyism, 37, 41, 108–109
McGuire, George Alexander, 45, 83–84
Mediation Board, U.S., 20
Mercer, Kobena, 74–75, 130
Messenger, the, 12, 16–18, 25
Messinger, Ruth, 121, 136
Metropolitan Community Center,
    Chicago, 24–26
Mfume, Kwesi, 127, 138
Miami, religious leaders in, 9, 78–117
Miami Herald, 87
Mickens, L. C., 100–101
Miller, Arthur, 123–24
Miller, George Frazier, 42–45, 62
Million Family March, 168–70
Million Man March, 10, 168
Mississippi Democratic Freedom Party,
    126
Mohammad, Warith Deen, 152, 171–72
Montgomery Bus Boycott, 184, 185
Moore, Harriette, 97–98
Moore, Harry T., 96–97
Moore, Morris "Dad," 18–19
Moorish Temple, the, 152
Morris, W. A., 98–99
Moses figure, 68, 72–73, 89–90
Mount Olivette Baptist Church, Miami,
    100–101
*Mr. Black Labor: The Story of A. Phillip
    Randolph, Father of the Civil Rights
    Movement* (Davis), 13
Muhammad, Elijah, 3–4, 151–53,
    164–68, 175
Muhammad, Khalid Abdul, 139–40,
    159–61
Muhammad, Wallace. *See,* Mohammad,
    Warith Deen
Muhammad Speaks, 151–53
Murray, Pauli: 1, 10, 182
    early life, 188–89
    ordination of, 193–95
    and Randolph, 195
    and Supreme Court, 191–92
    and WPA, 189–90

NAACP:
    and anti-Communism, 94, 102–17
    and Baker, 182–84, 187
    in Brooklyn, 40, 41, 44; in Florida,
    94–117

and Murray, 191–92
    and Randolph, 19, 22
    and voting rights, 97–98
NAACP v. Alabama, 113
Nash, Diane, 188
Nation of Islam, 9–10, 133, 140–41,
    147–48, 150–80
National Action Network, 121, 127,
    135–36, 140–41
National Baptist Convention, 32,
    181–82
National Organization of Women,
    193–94
nationalism:
    black, 9–10, 45, 103–104, 107–108,
    135–36, 139–41, 150–80
    white, 159
Nazis, 61–63
Negro Citizens League, 90
Negro Labor Congress, 25–26, 28
*Negro Spiritual Speaks of Life and Death,
    The* (Thurman), 55–56
Negro Uplift Association of Dade
    County, 82
Negro's Church, The (Mays/ Nicholson),
    31
New Alliance Party, 130–31, 134
New Deal liberalism, 38–40, 58–61,
    89–90–91, 115–16, 189–90
"New Negro," 4, 16
New Protestantism, 14–15, 17, 19, 21
New York:
    mid-century religious leaders in,
    28
    school integration in, 44, 101–102
    Sharpton in, 118–49
New York Daily News, 119–21, 134
New York Newsday, 134
New York Times, 134
Newman, Fred, 131
Newman, Richard, 2–3
Niagara Movement, 21
Niceo-Constantinopolitan Creed, 45
Nicholson, Joseph W., 31
Non-Pareil Study Club, 82–83
nonviolence, 55, 68
Novack, Robert, 170

Operation Breadbasket, 131–32
oral tradition, 49, 63–65, 125–26

Origins of the Urban Crisis (Sugrue), 37–38
Owen, Chandler, 12, 17, 42
Owens, Major, 130, 140

Pagones, Steven, 137
Pan-Africanism, 135
Parents in Action Against Educational Discrimination, 184
Parents Workshop for Equality in New York City Schools, 44, 101–102
Pataki, George, 142–45, 177
patriarchy, 10, 49–50, 54, 70, 76, 181–97
Pentecostal Assemblies of the World, 53
Pentecostalism, black: 3, 8–9
  in Brooklyn, 38, 46–47
  and liberalism, 48–78
  and public intellectual role, 48–49
  and Randolph, 30–32
  and Sharpton, 133
People United to Save Humanity (PUSH), 131
People's Community Church, Chicago, 24–26
Pepper, Claude, 84
Pernell, Phillip, 136
Perot, Ross, 163
Perry, Ruth, 110
Pfeffer, Paula, 12
Plasterers, Masons, and Bricklayers International Union, 100
Poitier, Sydney, 85–86
police brutality, 43, 82, 86, 90, 96–98, 121, 123–24, 135–39, 147
poll tax, 84
Poor People's Campaign, 131–32
Powell, Adam Clayton, Sr., 28
Powell, Adam Clayton, Jr., 9, 131
Powells, Morris, 140
power broker role, 140–49
Prairie View Law School, 97
preaching:
  antiphonal structure in, 157
  cultural meaning of, 63–65
  and folk tradition, 49, 127
  jeremiad in, 172–73
  and power, 185–86
Price, Hugh, 173
Progressive Voters League (PVL), 97

Prophesy Deliverance: An Afro-American Revolutionary Christianity (West), 3
Prophetic Fragments (West), 3
public intellectual role, 48–49
Pullman Company, 7, 15–24, 27, 33

Quarles, Benjamin, 12
Quigg, H. Leslie, 86, 88

"race hustler" label, 118–22
"race man" role, 14, 16–19, 75, 77–78
Race, Reform, and Rebellion (Marable), 37–38
radicalism, black Christian: 8–9
  in Brooklyn, 38, 42–45
  Farrakhan and, 155–58
  Sharpton and, 118–49
  in unionism, 32–36, 99-100, 135-38
Rainbow Coalition, 131–33
Ramirez, Roberto, 144
Rand, Addison Barry, 129
Randolph, A. Philip: 1, 7–8
  atheism of, 11
  and clergy, 11–13, 24–32
  early struggle, 15–24
  impact of religion on, 32–36, 196-97
  literature on, 11–15, 32
  Murray on, 195
  as preacher's son, 12, 13
  and Socialist Party, 42
Rangel, Charles, 124
Rather, Dan, 134
Ray, Gloria, 102
Ray, Sandy F, 38–42
red baiting, 40–41
religion, black:
  ambivalence on liberation, 36–38
  folk tradition in, 45, 49, 127
  and intellectuals, 1–10
  and leadership, 196-97
  and political struggle, 6, 127
reparations, 163
Republican Party, 39–40, 43, 57–58, 170
Righteous Discontent: The Women's Movement in the Black Baptist Church, 1880–1920 (Higginbotham), 181–82
Rivera, Dennis, 138
Roberts, J. A., 99
Roberts, Terrence, 104–105

Robertson, Pat, 178–79
Robeson, Paul, 4, 8
Robinson, Sugar Ray, 76
Rockefeller, Nelson, 39, 41–42
Rollins, Ed, 133–34
Roosevelt, Franklin Delano, 43, 58–61
Roosevelt, Theodore, 159
Rosenbaum, Jankel, 147–48
"rowdiness," working class, 82, 88
Rustin, Bayard, 184

700 Club, the, 178
Saint Agnes Church, Miami, 83–84,
    88
Saint Augustine Protestant Episcopal
    Church, 42–43
Sarandon, Susan, 138
Saunders, Lee, 138
Saunders, Robert W., 94, 97–98, 100
school integration, 44, 66–68, 97,
    101–102, 184, 191–92
Schuyler, George, 25
Scott, Albert L., 27
Scottsboro Nine, 43
Secret Relationship between Blacks and
    Jews, The (Anonymous), 175
segregation, 44, 52, 65–68, 79–117,
    181–88
Seymour, William J., 3
Shabazz, Betty, 175
Shabazz, Qubilah, 175
Sharpton, Al: 1, 9–10, 197
    and Brawley, 120, 126–27, 130, 137,
        143
    contradictions in, 139–45
    critics of, 118–22, 126–27
    and FBI, 130
    and Jackson, 121, 125, 130–35, 138,
        142
    as power broker, 140–49
    reconstruction of image, 121–22,
        133–39
    rise of, 122–33
    stabbing of, 133
    style of, 127–30
    supporters of, 126–27
Ship, E. R., 126–27
shout, the, 64
Simpson, Gary, 139
Simpson, R. B. (Schoolboy), 90

sit-in movement, 187
slave narratives, 69
Slavery: A Problem in American
    Institutional and Intellectual Life
    (Elkins), 62
Sleeper, Jim, 118–21
Smith, Bennie, 18
Smith, Ezekiel, 96
Smith, Karl, 53
Smith Act, 43, 113
Smolikoff, Charlie, 85–86
" 'So Goes the Negro': Race and Labor
    in Miami, 1940–63" (Tschechlok),
    94
social gospel, 14–15, 40
Socialist Party, 42–43
Society for the Promotion of Collegiate
    and Theological Education, 29
Solomon, Sam, 89–90
Souls of Black Folk, The (Du Bois), 12,
    71
Southern Christian Leadership
    Conference (SCLC), 131–32,
    184–88
Southland Singers, 101
Soviet propaganda on race, 104, 107
Spanish Civil War, 190
speaking in tongues, 46, 51, 53
"Spiritual Significance of the Supreme
    Court" (Williams), 68
Stark, Abe, 39
Stein, Annie, 44, 62
stereotypes, 68–69, 71–72
Stewart, Michael, 123–24
Strimling, Arthur, 138–39
Student Nonviolent Coordinating
    Committee (SNCC), 186–88
style:
    in masculinity, 75–77
    in politics, 128–30
Sugrue, Thomas J., 37–38
Supreme Court, U.S., 94, 97, 117–17,
    191–92
Sweatt v. Painter, 97

Tatum, Wilbert, 133, 140, 143, 154
Taylor, Frances, 77
Taylor, Gardner C., 38–42, 130
Terrell, Mary Church, 4
terror, racial, 85, 97

Theodore R. Gibson: Priest, Prophet, and Politician (Vonk), 95–96
This Is My Story (Williams), 50–53
Thomas, Bowden, 84
Thomas, L. E., 81
Thurman, Howard, 3, 55–56, 61
Thurman, Wallace, 2
Tillich, Paul, 132
Tilly, John, 184
Torchlight for America (Farrakhan), 164–65, 167–68
Townes, Edolphus, 134
Trotter, William Monroe, 43
Trump, Donald, 123
Tschechlok, Eric, 94
Turk, Harold, 98–99
Tyson, Cicely, 77

United Africa Movement, 139–40
Universal Negro Improvement Association, 85
Uplifting the Race: Black Leadership, Politics, and Culture in the Twentieth Century (Gaines), 2
Urban League, 19, 40

Victorian virtues, middle class and, 69–70, 88–89, 99
violence, misogynist, 75–77
Vivian, C. T., 187
Vonk, Carita Swanson, 95–96
voting rights, 84–93, 97–98, 184

Wagner, Robert, 41, 184
Walker, Wyatt T., 186–87
Wallace, Mike, 134, 153
Wallach, Benno M., 101
Wanniski, Jude, 170
warrior role, 154–56, 158–59, 173
Washington, Booker T., 2, 92, 164, 174
Washington, Frederick, 131
Washington, D.C., restaurant integration, 72–73, 192
Webster, Milton P., 16, 18, 25–27, 29–30, 32–35
West, Cornel, 2–3, 71, 134, 173
"white devils," 152–53, 167, 175
white elites:
  accommodation with, 9, 78–79, 83–93, 98
  alliance with, 38–39, 53–54
  challenge to, 11–36, 74
  defiance of, 126–27, 118–49
  demands on, 94–95, 98–99
  negotiation with, 78–79, 95
white skin privilege, 52, 110
Whitman, Christine, 134
"Will to Segregation, The" (Thurman), 55
Williams, L. K., 32
Williams, Smallwood: 1, 8–9
  autobiography of, 50–53, 68
  and Bible Way Church, 54, 56–78
  family of, 71–72
  and Hobson, 73–74
  as patriarch, 49–50, 54
  as public intellectual, 48–49
  on race, 52–54
  sermons of, 63–65
  and Thurman, 55–56
Williams, Smallwood Jr., 71
Williams, Verna, 71
Williams, Wendell, 65–68, 71
Williams, Yvonne, 71
Wilson, William Julius, 123
Wing, John D., 91–92
Wolfarth, William, 98–99
womanist views, 4
women, ordination of, 51, 54, 193–95
Women's Day Workers and Industrial League, 183
Women's Suffrage Movement, 43
Woodson, G. Carter, 4
Work Experience Program, New York, 145–46
Works Progress Administration (WPA), 189–90
World War II, 62–63
World Trade Center attack, 144, 175–79
Wright, Richard, 69
Wright, William D., 2

Young, Henry J. Jr., 2–3
Young Negroes Cooperative League, 183

Zion Baptist Church, Brooklyn, 38, 40
zoot suit culture, 129–30